S0-AQJ-830

that wild fellow John Neal

John Neal around 1823

From a portrait attributed to Sarah Miriam Peale
Collection of Mrs. Sherwood Picking
Photo Frick Art Reference Library

Benjamin Lease

that wild fellow John Neal

and the American Literary Revolution

The University of Chicago Press
Chicago and London

920
ID 341L
159006

The University of Chicago Press, Chicago 60637
The University of Chicago Press, Ltd., London
© 1972 by The University of Chicago
All rights reserved. Published 1972
Printed in the United States of America
International Standard Book Number: 0–226–46969–7
Library of Congress Catalog Card Number: 72–81630

For Mariam

How slowly our literature grows up!
Most of our writers of promise have come to
untimely ends. There was
that wild fellow, John Neal,
who almost
turned my boyish brain with his romances;
he surely has long been dead,
else he never could keep himself so quiet.

HAWTHORNE, 1845

Contents

CONTENTS

Illustrations

ix

Acknowledgments

"No figure in American literature more startling than John Neal," observed Fred Lewis Pattee in 1937. Almost as startling is the fact that this fascinating, once influential figure has been so little noticed; this is the first book about him. My work on it has been greatly facilitated by a grant from the Penrose Fund of the American Philosophical Society and the generous cooperation of Northeastern Illinois University. The great Portland fire of 1866 destroyed most of Neal's papers, but copies of William Blackwood's letters to him have been preserved in the firm's letterbooks at 45 George Street, Edinburgh; the firm's incoming letters were turned over to the National Library of Scotland during World War II, among them the numerous letters of "Carter Holmes." The Pierpont Morgan Library is the repository of Neal's voluminous correspondence with John Pierpont. The Houghton Library of Harvard University holds several Neal letterbooks and scrapbooks that survived the fire; they were placed on deposit at the library by the late Sherwood Picking, Neal's great-grandson. For their gracious and unfailing assistance, I am deeply indebted to G. D. Blackwood, present head of the House of Blackwood; James S. Ritchie, of the National Library of Scotland; Herbert Cahoon, of The Pierpont Morgan Library; Rodney G. Dennis III, Carolyn Jakeman, and Marte Shaw, of The Houghton Library.

To the other libraries that granted permission to reproduce manuscripts and rare printings, I am also grateful: Yale University Library; The Clifton Waller Barrett Library of the University of Virginia Library; The British Museum; Library of Congress; The New York Public Library; The Historical Society of Pennsylvania; University of Pennsylvania Library; Maryland Historical Society; Maine Historical Society; New England Deposit Library; Brown University Library; Portland Public Library; University of Illinois Library; University of Chicago Library; and The Newberry Library, which provided a base of operations for my research.

Eugenia L. Southard of the Portland Public Library responded to my many requests patiently and resourcefully. Joseph Wolf of the Newberry Library helped me sort out and resolve some of the genealogical problems. Mrs. Dorothy L. White of the Northeastern Illinois University Library provided valuable assistance in tracking down elusive volumes. Mrs. Henry W. Howell, Jr., of the Frick Art Reference Library helped me locate the portraits of John Neal and John Pierpont that enrich this book; their owners, Mrs. Sherwood Picking, The Pierpont Morgan Library, and the Union League Club of New York, kindly granted permission to reproduce them. William Allan's portrait of William Blackwood is reproduced by permission of his great-great-grandson, G. D. Blackwood.

I wish also to thank others who answered questions and provided help along the way: George W. Corner, Benjamin T. Spencer, David Daiches, Howard P. Vincent, Duke Frederick, Peter J. King, James F. Beard, Edgar Johnson, Mrs. Thomas O. Mabbott, Mrs. John Neal Hodges, Mrs. Sherwood Picking, and the late Irving T. Richards. The personal interest and encouragement of Napier Wilt, Lawrence W. Towner, Nelson F. Adkins, Herbert Cahoon, and Hans-Joachim Lang have put me permanently in their debt. For his wise counsel and unfailing support, I am deeply grateful to Walter Blair.

This book is dedicated to my wife, Mariam Dubovik Lease, as a small token of my greatest debt.

I
a quaker
broken loose

1 A Wide Field of Observation

shipwrecked, when I was a child. . . .

WANDERING RECOLLECTIONS

When he was just two years old, he experienced his first hailstorm. On a bright summer afternoon a violent storm suddenly erupted, and down clattered a great cascade. Little John hastened to gather a treasure of white beads into a wooden dish and hide it away in a safe place. Alas, when he returned to his treasure, he found nothing but a little dirty water. "It was in vain they told me my hailstones had melted; I did not believe them, and could not," Neal wrote seventy-one years later. "If I may trust my memory," he adds, "the loss of my kitten-yoke and little steers [kittens], and the loss of my seed pearl, were the sorest of my trials, up to the age of twelve." [1]

His greatest loss took place before he had a memory to trust. John Neal and his twin sister Rachel were born in Falmouth, now Portland, in what was then known as the District of Maine, on August 23, 1793. Less than a month later their father, a Quaker schoolmaster, died of a contagious fever contracted while watching over the sick during an epidemic; he was in his thirtieth year. That is what the schoolmaster's Quaker friends told his son many years later. His mother's version was different: "she claimed that the fatal fever was brought on by a severe cold taken at the door

1. John Neal, *Wandering Recollections of a Somewhat Busy Life: An Autobiography* (Boston, 1869), p. 37.

3

when a stranger called on him and refused to enter." A portentous event had preceded this mysterious visit. While sitting before the fire awaiting her husband's return, she had reached for a stick of wood to add to the dwindling flames. A disembodied hand had appeared—"a long slender hand like thy father's"—and placed the stick where it belonged. She knew the hand to be a warning but never told her husband for fear of troubling him. Among the numerous relatives of Rachel Neal, the belief later took hold that the spectral hand had been that of her father, Daniel Hall, who had died suddenly five years before in the prime of health of an infected hand: "Mortification set in: the ablest physicians were sent for, but nothing could be done; and he walked the floor day and night till he died." [2]

It was among the portents and visions of a tightly knit Quaker community that John Neal grew up. Though the quarrelsome boy soon rebelled against the nonviolent creed of the Quakers, their superstitions and legends stirred his imagination to the end of his days. Rachel Neal's grandfather, father of the unfortunate Daniel Hall, was the redoubtable and prolific Hate Evil (or Hatevil) Hall who died in 1797 at the age of ninety, "leaving four hundred and seventy-five descendants." [3] John's paternal grandfather, James Neal, was a Quaker preacher, "a godly man" but also "a great favorite with the young and merry-hearted, and full of quiet humor." The oldest and youngest of his sons, Stephen and James, inherited something of their father's drollery. But the second son, John, seems to have had little disposition for joking. He may have been "overshadowed, from early age, by the angel of death," Neal suggests about the father he never knew.[4]

The sudden death of her husband was a terrible but not a shattering blow to the young mother of infant twins—widowed

2. Ibid., pp. 17–18.

3. William Willis, *The History of Portland, from 1632 to 1864* (Portland, 1865), p. 812. Neal, with a characteristic flourish, refers to "My grandfather, on my mother's side—Daniel Hall, one of ten thousand descendants of Hatevil Hall" (*Wandering Recollections*, p. 18).

4. *Wandering Recollections*, p. 13.

scarcely more than a year after her wedding day. Rachel Neal was made of sturdy stuff. She lost little time in setting up a school of her own where her young scholars learned reading, writing, spelling, and arithmetic.[5] And she supplemented her meager income by taking in boarders. Her plight was eased somewhat by the presence of numerous relatives ready to lend a hand—and by the Quakers. But self-reliance was the watchword, and young John learned all too thoroughly the lessons of genteel poverty in Maine.

The Portland into which John Neal was born was a new town, a part of Falmouth known as The Neck until it achieved civic independence on July 4, 1786. It had only recently been rebuilt after being burned to the ground by Captain Henry Mowatt in retaliation for its "unpardonable rebellion" in 1775. The rebuilding had proceeded slowly, but a rapid expansion at the close of the war brought the number of dwelling places in 1793, the year of John's birth, to "three hundred and thirty-four, being one hundred and four more than there were before the town was burnt." Five of these were of brick.[6]

The new, expanding town was still isolated and remote—a frontier village at the edge of a great wilderness to the west and north, still teeming with lore about Indian wars and massacres. Its inhabitants were a people accustomed to danger and unaccustomed to political restraint. A commissioner's report to the King in 1665 had complained that the townspeople "for the most part are fishermen, and never had any government among them; most of them are such as have fled from other places to avoid justice. Some here are of the opinion that as many men share in a woman as they do in a boat, and some have done so."[7] A century later the descendants of these troublesome fishermen had let the town burn rather than surrender their arms to Captain Mowatt. Their

5. Neal to Elizabeth Oakes Smith, August 21, 1856, Yale University Library. Neal's letter is a seventeen-page autobiography written at the request of Mrs. Oakes Smith (hereafter cited as MS. Autobiography).

6. Willis, *The History of Portland*, pp. 580, 551–52; also William Goold, *Portland in the Past* (Portland, 1886), pp. 337–53.

7. Willis, *The History of Portland*, p. 142, n. 2.

rebellious spirit was displayed on a gayer occasion in 1793, when some of the townspeople simultaneously celebrated Washington's birthday and the French Revolution with a jolly party at "Citizen Motley's." Thirteen toasts were given—for example, to the French and "their victorious struggle for liberty"; to "The enlightener of the world, Thomas Paine"; to "Brave Irishmen" in their fight for freedom—"at each of which a cannon was discharged, under the direction of Citizen Weeks of the artillery company, followed by three cordial cheers." [8]

There were others, equally if not more representative of Portland, who thought Thomas Paine an abomination. One of these was the Reverend Thomas Smith, first ordained minister in the town after its resettlement, whose death in 1795 ended a ministry of sixty-eight years. When he had assumed his charge in 1727, Falmouth had been a wretched collection of hovels and "the meeting-house upon which the people had exhausted their means, sightless windows, without seats or pulpit, a mere shell." At his funeral a speaker proclaimed that "The wilderness where he pitched his tent, is now the place of vineyards and gardens." Another testified to Parson Smith's service to the Revolution: "In the late war, which our unnatural enemies made upon us, he deeply commiserated the case of his oppressed and bleeding country; and most affectionate and persevering were his supplications to heaven for her deliverance." Puritanism did not die with Parson Smith despite the dilution of Calvinist doctrine that followed his death. And it did not die among the Quakers—a small but active and persistent sect in Falmouth, one that "greatly disturbed the pious feelings of our staid ancestors, who were shocked at any attempts to be more *puritan* than they were themselves." [9]

Young Neal's Quaker upbringing seemed to him at times

8. As reported in the *Eastern Argus* (Portland) for February 1793; quoted in Goold, *Portland in the Past*, pp. 401–2.

9. Willis, *The History of Portland*, pp. 360–61; also his "Memoir of the Rev. Thomas Smith," in *Journals of the Rev. Thomas Smith and the Rev. Samuel Deane* (Portland, 1849), pp. 31, 34, 94, n. 1.

the central fact of his existence, though he very early rebelled against its central tenet. When he attended the Portland public school, the larger boys bullied him and the smaller ones settled for trailing behind sounding the mocking refrain "Quaker Neal." One day a small boy walked up to him and, "without a word of warning or explanation," struck him in the face. A man who witnessed the incident laughed and asked John whether he was not ashamed of himself for letting a little fellow strike him without returning a blow. All his life he had been taught to do as he would be done by and to return evil with good. "That settled the question with me for life," he wrote many years later. The nine-year-old boy made a promise to himself that night "to bear these outrages, no longer, and to take my own part against all the world, Quaker or no Quaker." [10]

And so he did, though the fatherless boy was striking back as much against his own fear and insecurity as against real indignities: "The world had used me unkindly; and, I was sure, would crush me if it could. Beside, I knew . . . that I was a coward at heart; and it appeared to me that everybody else knew it. . . . Therefore, did I quarrel with *everybody*." [11] Quarrelling became as unavoidable and inevitable as breathing. Late in life he warned his seventeen-year-old son about the dangers of being bullied into a duel if he did not begin early "to set a guard upon [his] temper and impulses." He confessed to his son, "I myself have so long and so frequently suffered by this unworthy—this wretched and pitiful want of self command, that I am doubly anxious about you." [12]

Toward other aspects of Quaker doctrine young Neal was almost equally rebellious. He witnessed testimonies of faith in the meetinghouse that were moving and impressive; and how could he question the sincerity of his grandfather, his mother, the relatives

10. *Wandering Recollections*, p. 67.

11. John Neal, *Errata, or the Works of Will. Adams*, 2 vols. (New York, 1823), 1:152.

12. Neal to his son James, June 6, 1848, The Clifton Waller Barrett Library of the University of Virginia Library.

and family friends who surrounded him? Nonetheless he found "most of their preaching very tiresome, religion itself a terrible bugbear, and the promptings of the Holy Spirit anything but desirable." In his young manhood he had "no more notion of religion, than of the black art" and retained his Quaker affiliation only to escape military service.[13] A formal break with the Friends followed a street brawl with an Irishman. The judge sympathized with Neal for the provocation that precipitated the fight but fined him ten dollars and costs for assault and battery. A visiting Quaker delegation, "finding me obstinate in my notions about non-resistance . . . yielded to my request, and consented to disown me." [14]

Though he found Quaker preaching and doctrine tiresome, the Bible was from earliest childhood a source of endless fascination. When he was six or seven, Rachel Neal bribed her son with a fifty cent piece to read it through: "It was a tough job; and I thought I earned the money, long before I had plowed through the Pentateuch," but was "delighted beyond measure with the warlike achievements of Moses and Joshua, and with the stories about Samson and Gideon and Saul, and the witch of Endor, and was quite carried away with the tremendous visions of the Apocalypse." [15] Preaching was a bore, religion a bugbear, and the Holy Spirit did not call to him. But the passionate poetry and storytelling of the Bible excited the boy as a deluge of hailstones had transported the infant toddler.

The Portland of John Neal's early childhood was beautiful and prosperous. The town straddled a peninsula jutting out into the blue waters of Casco Bay, "studded with 'islands that were [a decade later] the Hesperides' of Longfellow's boyish dreams, and dotted with the incoming and outgoing craft in the channel." [16]

13. *Errata*, 1:230–31.

14. Neal's unorthodox views on the divinity of Christ, and his authorship of a play also contributed to the final break. See *Errata*, 1:294–96; *Wandering Recollections*, pp. 81–82.

15. *Wandering Recollections*, p. 89.

16. George Thornton Edwards, *The Youthful Haunts of Longfellow* (Portland, 1907), pp. 3–4.

Inland to the west were meadows, streams, forests—and the White Hills of New Hampshire looming out of the clouds ten miles away.

Neal was to celebrate this land and seascape in the years to come, but his vividest early memories were of hunger and cold and grinding poverty. When he was seven, young John was sent to a Quaker boarding school in nearby Windham "where they starved and froze me for two long winters, and where I learned, to the best of my knowledge and belief, just nothing at all." He recalls watching three large boys squabbling like famished wolves over a salted fish skin, while he stood by with a watering mouth. "The misery and weariness of spirit; the poverty and famine of the very heart, that I endured *there*," he wrote twenty years later, "make me, even at this moment, in my warm study, with a bright fire at my side, feel as if I had been shipwrecked, when I was a child, upon some desert island." [17]

In the Portland public schools he fared little better. The floggings and other humiliations he was subjected to by one of his teachers so rankled the boy that years later, as a young man revisiting Portland, he could barely restrain himself on encountering this schoolmaster, now an elderly man. He passed him by with a terrible effort, for "I knew that, if I once laid my hand upon his collar—there would be no mortal help for him." The next morning, "when I got up, I was stiff, and sore, all over—even to the roots of my hair; as if I had taken a violent cold." [18]

At the age of twelve it was time for him to make his own way. He was ready for the world of business, where—he quickly learned—the curriculum consisted of one subject: sharp practice. His first job was in the retail establishment of Munroe and Tuttle, where he "was soon able to cheat, lie, and steal with the best of our trade." He was the youngest employee and—with his blue eyes, yellow hair, and Quaker bobtail coat—the most innocent

17. The quoted passages are from *Wandering Recollections*, p. 28, and *Errata*, 1:98. No records of the school have survived, but Neal's attendance was "probably about the year 1800, or a little before" (Zora Klain, *Educational Activities of New England Quakers: A Source Book* [Philadelphia, 1928], p. 159).

18. *Errata*, 1:62.

looking. The year was 1805 and the country was being deluged with counterfeit money; young John's assignment was to recirculate bad bills. The victim was usually a backwoodsman or woman. If the customer returned to complain, Neal was instructed to exchange the bill instantly but with a put-upon air that left the victim in a state of guilty confusion and gratitude. Another policy of the firm "was always to show the poorest first, thereby enhancing by comparison; to keep the windows and doorway so dark, partly by hanging shawls and other showy goods both inside and out, and partly by painting the back windows, that people were often astonished at their bargains, after they had got back to their own houses; not only the quality, but the very color of their purchases, undergoing a change for the worse." There were many other tricks of the trade, and the eager young clerk learned them all.[19]

Two years later the firm failed. The Neal family had suffered poverty during a prosperous period in Portland's development. Now Jefferson's nonintercourse policy and the embargo which followed suspended shipping and paralyzed business. Grass literally grew upon the wharves of Portland.[20] It was a difficult and desperate time for young John. Eventually he was able to secure another position as clerk, this time in the store of Benjamin Willis, where, at a wage of forty dollars a year, with board and washing, he learned a few new tricks—"for example, how to convert a hogshead of old Jamaica or Santa Cruz, into a hogshead and a half, . . . by rolling it back and forth between the store and a town-pump that stood just in front of the old city-hall; and how to give Spanish brandy the flavor of cognac, by charging it with burnt sugar." But these ingenious practices could not save the Willis establishment from going under. He was once more cut adrift.[21]

19. "Yankee Notions," *London Magazine*, n.s. 4 (1826):443–44; *Errata*, 1:71–72; *Wandering Recollections*, p. 125.

20. Edward H. Elwell, *Portland and Vicinity* (Portland, 1876), pp. 14–15.

21. *Wandering Recollections*, pp. 127–29.

Attracted by the prospect of travel, adventure, and quick profits, Neal joined a wandering adventurer named Rockwell who taught New England villagers eager for self-improvement a sure-fire penmanship course in twelve lessons for five dollars. For a time young Neal practised his new profession in Brunswick. There he had a class of Bowdoin College students and townspeople, "some of whom had never had a pen in their hands." The Rockwell Method was classic in its simplicity: "in the course of these twelve lessons a person was made to write more *lines* and *pages*, than he usually did in a whole year; and this too under the eye of the master, with the best of pens, the best of ink, and his paper so ruled, that, for his life, he could not go wrong." Neal and Rockwell soon fell out, and the young disciple ventured out on his own, adding India ink portrait sketching and lessons in water-colors to his repertoire. He had always had a passion for drawing and painting, and what he lacked in talent and training he made up for in shrewdness and audacity—at three dollars a sitting:

> You know how *sore* people are, when they cannot *guess* for whom a picture has been taken; and how delighted they are, when they happen to guess right. I took advantage of this. I always painted profiles; and if there were a big nose, or a wen, or a wart, or a long chin, *that* was enough for me—if not I was fain to content myself with a cocked hat, or a pair of spectacles—the likeness of which, I could not miss; and all the world could see, at a glance. . . . I knew that no blundering of mine, could ever destroy a likeness, once acknowledged: and therefore, I went on, working as fearlessly with my India ink, as if I were blacking a pair of boots.[22]

By practising upon the good nature of Hallowell, Augusta, Waterville, and Norridgwock "after a fashion the inhabitants will never forget, or forgive," the young confidence man soon amassed the substantial sum of two hundred dollars. Weary of the itinerant life and drawn to the great city to the south, he answered an

22. Ibid., pp. 38–39, 108; John Neal, *Randolph: A Novel*, 2 vols. ([Philadelphia], 1823), 2:82–84.

advertisement in a Boston paper and started anew in the drygoods establishment of Mr. Murphy.

When the War of 1812 constricted sources of supply and provided tempting opportunities for quick profits, Neal opened his own shop as a wholesale jobber. For a time he ranged back and forth from Boston to Baltimore selling smuggled goods in one place and bills of exchange in another. These activities eventually brought him into a business partnership with John Pierpont and the latter's brother-in-law, Joseph Lord. At the close of the war the partners opened a branch store in Baltimore, followed soon after—as speculative fever boomed their enterprise—by two other openings. "It looked for a few weeks as if the principle of perpetual motion, or at least of the chain store, had been discovered and put into triumphant practise." [23] But the store in Charleston, South Carolina, proved a disaster, and a postwar recession burst the bubble. "Nobody wanted to buy, unless from hand to mouth; and everybody wanted to sell." In 1816 "the firm blew up." [24]

John Pierpont had turned to business after struggling unsuccessfully to support himself and his family in the practice of law. When they met in the winter of 1814, he was in his thirtieth year, eight years older than Neal. A Yale graduate and a poet, rather frail in health at the time, Pierpont was extremely different in background, temperament, and constitution from the robust, aggressive, self-educated Neal. But the two men were linked by strong emotional ties and, except for a three-year rupture in their relationship a decade later, remained fast friends for more than half a century—until Pierpont's death in 1866.

Now they were adrift in Baltimore, no prospect before them,

23. John T. Winterich, "Savanarola of Hollis Street," *Colophon*, Part 20 (1935), n.p. There is no evidence that Pierpont knew about Neal's smuggling activities.

24. For Neal's business ventures in this period see *Wandering Recollections*, pp. 132–33, 137–59; John Neal, "John Pierpont," *Atlantic Monthly* 18 (1866):657–59; James Brooks, "Letters from the East—John Neal," no. 2, *New-York Mirror* 11 (1833–34):77.

"destitute and helpless—Pierpont wholly unfitted for business
. . . and I desperate enough for anything short of the highway."
Neal sensed, however, that he had salvaged something of importance from his disastrous adventures in the world of business.
His horizon had expanded, "had opened a wide field of observation." And now he had a close friend to consult with, "much as
. . . shipwrecked mariners might be supposed to do, upon a rock
in mid-ocean." The friends consulted, and both soon found themselves embarked on new careers.[25]

25. *Wandering Recollections*, pp. 148, 160.

2 Law and Literature

We cannot learn to swim upon a table.
We must go among the breakers.

WANDERING RECOLLECTIONS

Neal resolved to study law and qualify for the Baltimore bar, then already noted for its eminent practitioners and its exclusiveness. It was a thoroughly impractical decision, for he was penniless, with no means of support; he was lacking in any kind of formal education; and his course of study would be at least four years, culminating in a rigorous examination.[1] But he seemed to thrive most when confronted by an impossible challenge, one that offered the chance of confounding his friends: "with languages, literature, law, and poetry, the mere spirit of contradiction—the desire to do what my best friends believed me incapable of— has done more for me than any and all other influences which have been brought to bear upon my character." [2] On occasion this spirit of contradiction was a compulsive, destructive force that might better be labeled perverseness.

As for his lack of formal education, he liked to repeat: "We cannot learn to swim upon a table. We must go among the breakers." He believed that "The best-educated man is, after all, more self-educated than he is anything else." While acknowledging the advantages of a college education, he felt keenly—and apparently not defensively—that it had its disadvantages too. The

1. *Wandering Recollections*, pp. 163.
2. Ibid., p. 47.

14

college man, he observed, grows to a mold and tends to adopt the views of his teachers—not invariably, but "so generally, that, if you know where a man has been educated, you know what his views and opinions are upon a great variety of subjects—in literature, in philosophy, in languages, and sometimes in politics and religion." [3] (Emerson says it more succinctly: "A man must consider what a blindman's buff is this game of conformity. If I know your sect I anticipate your argument.") When he began his law studies at the age of twenty-four, Neal could think only of the wasted years. Later he came to the belief that schooling was a small part of education and that he had learned more about human nature behind the counter than at any other period of his life. As for failure, "we *may* learn more by running our heads against a stone-wall, than by missing it." [4]

Pierpont also emerged from the ruins with resilience. He was a poet turned lawyer who then left law for the world of business. His experience had been far more traumatic than that of his partners: for a brief, terrible time he had been jailed for debt.[5] Now he felt the call to the ministry. To earn funds for study at the Harvard Divinity School, he sent his wife and children to live with her family in Connecticut, pawned the family silver, and "took a chamber in North Howard-Street where he remained till he brought forth the 'Airs of Palestine,'" an eight-hundred-line tribute in verse to sacred music. It was a huge success, and the sale of its copyright enabled him to move from Baltimore to Boston and to undertake the study of Hebrew in preparation for entering Harvard.[6]

Pierpont's literary success emboldened Neal to try his hand.

3. Ibid., p. 104.
4. Ibid., p. 169.
5. John Earle Uhler, "The Delphian Club," *Maryland Historical Magazine* 20 (1925):314; *Wandering Recollections*, pp. 161–62. Juliet, third child of John and Mary Lord Pierpont, born July 30, 1816, in the midst of the anguish and turmoil of the business collapse of Pierpont, Lord, and Neal, was destined to become the mother of J. Pierpont Morgan.
6. MS. Autobiography; *Wandering Recollections*, pp. 160–61.

In the midst of childhood misery he had found pleasure in reading and in telling stories to his schoolfellows. Bible stories had fired his imagination, and when he had encountered the *Arabian Nights* in the garret, he had disappeared for a whole day until his mother found him "behind a trunk, so deeply engaged in the book before me, that I had not even heard her step, nor the voices below; nor had I eaten a mouthful during the day." Soon after, thanks to an acquaintanceship with a boy who kept shop for a bookseller, young Neal gobbled up the contents of a large circulating library. The books he vividly remembered sixty years later were Charles Brockden Brown's *Wieland, Edgar Huntly,* and *Ormond*; William Godwin's *Caleb Williams*; the standard classics by Cervantes, Swift, Fielding, and Smollett; and, among his continuing favorites, *Paul and Virginia* and *The Vicar of Wakefield*. Gothicism and sensibility loomed large in the fiction Neal savored as a boy.[7]

All of his life Neal was a voluminous letter writer with an astonishing facility for what he called "talking on paper." It was this facility that, in his view, prepared him for authorship—"and there was nothing left for me but authorship, or starvation, if I persisted in my plan of studying law." Throughout his career he advocated a natural eloquence that would break loose from constricting and inhibiting artificiality. Studying grammar as a preparation for speaking or writing was, in his view, like learning all the rules of horsemanship before mounting the saddle. He scorned writing that "was too well written by half—much too classical—after the manner of Dr. Blair and Allison."[8]

His earliest literary productions were attempts at verse that showed little concern for naturalness, designed as they were to impress a succession of pretty girls. His first effort ("a downright imitation") was an acrostic which never got beyond the first line. Young John, at ten or eleven, was wretchedly in love with a girl named Lucy; having achieved a promising first line, he labored in vain with the second, for he could think of only one word that

7. *Wandering Recollections*, pp. 109, 111–12.
8. Ibid., pp. 341–42.

began with *u*: uncle. Like Mark Twain's Emmeline (who "hung fire on a rhyme for . . . Whistler"), the young versifier was stuck and never "finished that acrostic, nor attempted another." But unlike Emmeline (who went into a rapid decline), Neal shifted his ground and tried something "in the epitaph line" for a girl whose pet robin had been throttled by a cat. In the winter of 1814 he had "another paroxysm" brought on by someone named Olivia. A year or so later, in Baltimore, Neal was associated with "a set of handsome, clever, and very pleasant young women" who met weekly as a club to listen to the writings of its members. Some of the sketches and poems Neal wrote for this group appeared in an ephemeral publication called *The Wanderer*.[9]

His first serious efforts as a writer grew out of his association with the Delphians, founded on August 31, 1816, by seven men, among them Dr. Tobias Watkins, John Pierpont, and John Neal. John Earle Uhler has suggested that the great flowering of New England in the decades before the Civil War has completely overshadowed an earlier "efflorescence" in Philadelphia and Baltimore. The Delphian Club made a significant contribution to American letters from its founding to its dissolution in 1825. It did so rather casually. Each Saturday the members gathered for the advancement of literature, and a jolly night out. Impromptu epigrams and epitaphs, elaborate puns, quips and assorted high jinks occupied much of the evening and were followed by "a supper of 'testaceous bivalves,' . . . or simply of cheese and crackers, with whiskey and cigars as a supplement." Each of the members was assigned a "clubicular" name. Watkins and Pierpont were Pertinax Particular and Hiero Heptaglott. Because of his impetuosity and fiery temper—and a name his comrades mistakenly believed to be Irish—Neal was christened Jehu O'Cataract. In a more serious vein, a member would read an essay or poem on a subject assigned at the previous session. Many of these efforts were published in *The Portico*, a monthly founded by Dr. Watkins and Stephen Simpson. Others appeared in the

9. Ibid., pp. 183–87.

Journal of the Times, a Baltimore newspaper edited by Delphian Paul Allen.[10]

Each Delphian was solemnly granted an academic degree and title. Neal was designated Professor of Jocology and opened his "First Annual Lecture" with a ponderous figure: "Like the elephant that shattered his skull in launching a ship, merely because his powers had been overrated, I shall present my forehead to the formidable machinery of this science, and strain as he did, to the utter annihilation of my strength, until, like him, I have launched my joke, or fractured my skull." There follows a mock-learned survey of jokes through the ages—interspersed with touches of ribaldry: "What know we of the Egyptians, but of their worshipping onions—and building pyramids? What of the spartans but their eating black broth? and wrestling naked— young men and women—knee to knee—knuckle to knuckle—&c. to &c. in publick? And, what are these, but jokes?" The science of punning is thoroughly scrutinized; a single example will serve: "Recovered: re-covered, i.e. covered again. Hence we say, when a woman is getting better of a lying-in, she is re-covered. Consult Solomon Fitz Quizz [Paul Allen]." [11]

This high-spirited ribaldry accompanied serious concerns. The first number of *The Portico* announced to its readers that "Dependence, whether literary or political, is a state of degradation, fraught with disgrace; and to be dependent on a foreign mind, for what we can ourselves produce, is to add to the crime of indolence, the weakness of stupidity." The victorious conclusion of the second war with England had intensified national pride and fired anew the campaign for a national literature. During those boisterously optimistic years, such journals as *The Portico* proclaimed "zealously if often naively . . . that America could as readily demonstrate her power in the literary as in the military

10. Uhler, "The Delphian Club," pp. 305–07, 315, 331; *Wandering Recollections,* pp. 174–75.

11. Delphian Club Records, Delphiad 16, Session 1, April 3, 1819, Maryland Historical Society.

sphere." [12] Native writers, however, were not produced by procla-
mation. The Delphians were, on the whole, a genteel and conserva-
tive group of citizens responsive to neoclassical models and ideals
(as the names of their club and magazine indicate) as well as to
new romantic voices. They liked to think of themselves as more
daring and original than they were. Byron was their professed
hero (he was invited to become an honorary Delphian), but the
poetic effusions that graced the pages of *The Portico* were largely
derivative of the English school of sentimental verse. It was John
Neal who took up the cudgels for Byron in a bold and dashing
fashion—Byronic and distinctively American.

When Tobias Watkins urged Pierpont to write a critical essay
on Byron for *The Portico*, Pierpont refused because he felt un-
qualified. Neal, who had debated Watkins on the relative merits
of Byron and Moore, volunteered for the assignment and be-
dazzled the Delphians by reading all of Byron's works and pro-
ducing a 150-page critique in four days. His essay, published in
three installments, was supplemented by others on *Childe Harold*
and *Manfred*.[13] His first critical flight displays the easy assurance
that characterizes most of his prose. He was dealing with a subject that spoke to his own condition: Byron's struggle against
terrible odds to achieve his goal as an artist. *Childe Harold* is
"full of deep philosophizing sadness: the picture of a man whose
mind has been blighted by neglect; of a pride that has been
trodden upon with heartless severity—of a heart whose warmest
sympathies have been noted but by curiosity, and returned only
by unkindness." [14] The "shipwrecked," fatherless, self-educated

---

12. Benjamin T. Spencer, *The Quest for Nationality: An American
Literary Campaign* (Syracuse, N.Y., 1957), p. 75.

13. "Criticism: Lord Byron," *Portico* 2 (1816):304–15, 476–85; 3
(1817):53–62; "Childe Harold's Pilgrimage, Canto third . . . ," *Portico*
3 (1817):173–84; "Criticism: Manfred . . . ," *Portico* 4 (1817):260–74.
For accounts of *The Portico*, see F. L. Mott, *A History of Magazines* (New
York, 1930), pp. 183–84; and John C. McCloskey, "A Note on the *Portico*,"
American Literature 8 (1936):300–304.

14. "Criticism: Lord Byron," *The Portico* 2 (1816):386.

Quaker boy now, in his young manhood, recognizes a spirit attuned to his own boundless loneliness and desperate ambition.
But commingled with Neal's romantic identification are a native
shrewdness and a flair for the epigrammatic:

> Byron never touches Greece but he blazes.

> A wildness that never wanders—a calmness that is never
> still.

> His heaven has clouds; but clouds have charms: for who
> can abide eternal day?

> Fools only are affected by seeing others laugh or weep
> without knowing the cause.

Neal's intense feelings about Byron found further expression
in two *Portico* poems, "Fragment in Imitation of Byron" and "To
Byron." His Byronism is also displayed in two long poems, "The
Battle of Niagara" and "Goldau, or the Maniac Harper," written
at Pierpont's suggestion. A literary adventure Neal undertook to
publicize "Niagara" provides a revealing glimpse of a young
author, cloaked in Byronic mystery, in search of an audience.

In June of 1818 Neal journeyed to Philadelphia, assumed
the name of George E. Percival, hired a hall, and arranged for
the sale of two hundred tickets to what he hoped would be a
triumphant public recitation of extracts from his unpublished poem
—a recitation that would rouse Philadelphia and make the literati
aware of a blazing new poet in their midst. The posted advertise-
ments warned the public, "heaven forgive me! that *'no more than
two hundred tickets would be sold!'* " and invitations were scru-
pulously distributed to the chief critics. On the fateful evening,
at the appointed hour, the poet left his hotel for the hall. He
hoped for a full house, for he was in the Athens of America, a
metropolis of 130,000 inhabitants. But in the unlikely event of
a disappointing turnout, he had rehearsed a witty castigation of
this benighted city where poets are ignored while jugglers, rope
dancers, ribbon swallowers, and the like perform night after night
to capacity audiences. He arrived to find the hall in darkness; not
a single ticket had been sold! "The next day," wrote Neal, "I left

Philadelphia; have not been there since, and never mean to go, if there be any way on earth to get round it." [15]

The Portico did not pay its contributors; Neal's ill-fated invasion of Philadelphia was prompted, in part, by an urgent need for money to finance his law studies. In the summer of 1816, "after considering the matter for ten minutes or so," he dashed off a first novel—at first entitled *Judge Not by First Appearances* but renamed *Keep Cool* at the suggestion of a publisher who wanted a title people could remember. The book proved unacceptable in Boston, where Pierpont attempted to have it published, and Neal was overjoyed to sell the copyright to Joseph Cushing of Baltimore for two hundred dollars.[16] For a time he soared as a full-fledged professional author. But two ambitious efforts in poetry, *The Battle of Niagara* and *Otho*, the latter a verse tragedy (both published in 1818), brought him little fame and no money. He took on hack jobs: he compiled a *General Index to the First Twelve Volumes of Niles' Weekly Register* (1818) and wrote much of Paul Allen's *History of the American Revolution* (1819) after Allen failed to meet his publisher's deadline. For several months, in 1819, he was literary editor of the *Federal Republican and Baltimore Telegraph*. While carrying on such labors, Neal was cramming law for twelve hours a day, seven days a week, and writing poems and novels—for relaxation.

"But how could you do such things? They are incredible," Will Adams asks Hammond (both alter egos of the author) in Neal's autobiographical novel, *Errata*. "By system—perseverance. I began to carry the bull while it was a calf." Most people study by nodding over their books, imperfectly absorbing about twenty or thirty pages in a day consisting of three or four hours work and an equal number devoted to daydreaming and other diversions.

---

15. Neal recounts his Philadelphia adventure in an essay, "To the Reader," prefacing *The Battle of Niagara*, 2d ed. (Baltimore, 1819), pp. xxx–xxxvi (cited hereafter as *Niagara*). The Philadelphia story is also told in a letter to John Pierpont, June 8, 1818, Pierpont Papers, The Pierpont Morgan Library (cited hereafter as PML).

16. *Wandering Recollections*, p. 197.

"I would sooner," continues Hammond, "digest my own heart three or four times a day—with all its bitterness, than starve my spirit on such a rascally diet." By gradually increasing the quantity of his reading, not bothering to load his memory with details readily available in reference works, he is eventually able to read and retain three hundred pages a day of law and miscellany. This labor done, he would turn to writing "when other men were revelling—when all the world were asleep;—and then, not as to a labour or a study; but as to a relaxation. It was excitement and intoxication to me—with the eye of God, only, waking above me." [17]

In January of 1820 Neal completed his studies, passed his examinations, and was admitted to the Maryland bar "against a strong combination, who were opposed to me on several grounds —first, that I was a broken merchant; secondly, that I was uneducated; and, thirdly, that I was a Yankee." He rented an office at 26 Chatham Street and claimed to have developed a prospering practice during the next few years.[18] But he seems during this period to have been much more intensely involved with literature than with law. It was a stormy time in his emotional life, one in which he impulsively resigned from the Delphian Club and broke with the Quakers, and in which he was entangled in the love affairs that precipitated the breakup of his close friendship with John Pierpont.

"Two volume novels thrown off in a month!" exclaims Fred Lewis Pattee, adding: "Hard to believe—until one reads the novels." [19] The four novels that Neal produced between October 1821 and March 1822—*Logan, Randolph, Errata,* and *Seventy-Six*—are indeed hasty and slipshod; but they have distinctive qualities that need to be reckoned with. Linked as they are to events in his troubled private life, they have a wildness and

17. *Errata*, 2:133–35, 111.

18. *Wandering Recollections*, p. 215; MS. Autobiography.

19. Introduction to John Neal, *American Writers: A Series of Papers Contributed to Blackwood's Magazine* (1824–1825), ed. F. L. Pattee (Durham, N.C., 1937), p. 5.

demonic passion unmatched in any of Neal's later writings. The intimate record that has survived of Neal's friendship—and break —with Pierpont explains much about the man and his work during this period.

3 John Pierpont
Closest Friend and Confidant

You know me—you, of all the world & thank God!

NEAL TO PIERPONT, FEBRUARY 1, 1819

*I have learnt . . . that the man is a fool,
who ever puts himself into the power
of any human being, man or woman.*

NEAL TO PIERPONT, FEBRUARY 1, 1823

A century after John Pierpont's death his voluminous correspondence has come to rest in the Pierpont Morgan Library. In a score of folders spanning the five decades of their friendship are the hundreds of letters Neal dashed off to his "earliest and best friend." The greatest number boiled out of Neal in the years immediately after Pierpont's move to New England. They reveal a joy and despair, an almost desperate intimacy that led, perhaps inevitably, to the rupture in their friendship in 1823. They were estranged for almost three years, and their relationship, when it resumed, was never again to be what it had been. Neal's youthful tumult—largely responsible for the break—subsided with the years, especially after his marriage in 1828. In the long years that remained to them, Neal's closest friend was never again to be so close, and Neal was never again to try for the same intense intimacy with anyone.

During the turbulent period of their business success and failure, it was the younger man, the self-educated Yankee trader, who led the way for his friend—poet, scholar, lawyer, but no business man. After the postwar crash wiped them out, Neal wrote Pierpont: "you are at that age when such misfortunes are most terrible—the sapling may be prostrated with little damage to the oak itself—but when the oak falls, a thousand dependences fall

24

with it." Such sententiousness from a footloose young bachelor
may have struck the family man as gratuitous. An insensitivity
toward Pierpont and a veiled hostility toward his wife survive in
Neal's suggestion five decades later (in an obituary tribute)
that his friend might have been one of the great lawyers of
America if he had not married so early.[1] Neal's attitude toward
his friend alternates between the patronizing and the deferential;
for a time Pierpont seems to have encouraged both roles. But
two temperaments so dissimilar—the one rash and impetuous, the
other cautious and discreet—were bound to fall out.

The gulf between them in literary matters became apparent
when Pierpont attempted to find a Boston publisher for Neal's
first novel, *Keep Cool*. Pierpont reports back with suggestions for
revision that reflect not only his own and the publisher's views
but also those of Mrs. Read, the publisher's wife. She complains
that "there is not quite *love* enough in it to suit the ladies." On
the other hand, both Read and Pierpont agree that the female
characters are too earthy and susceptible. "You must not," urges
Pierpont, ". . . doom to the bar-room, a book which without
those defects might and would grace the toilet of beauty and be
read and listened to, and applauded in the drawing room."[2] At
this stage in their relationship Neal was compliant and dutifully
rewrote the novel. Though now much tamer about sexual matters
than it had been, the revised version was still unacceptable to
Read (or his wife) and was eventually brought out by a Baltimore
publisher.

Pierpont's *Airs of Palestine* seems today a tepid work, highly
derivative of Chateaubriand and Wordsworth. But on its publication in 1816 it had been praised as a work "destined to a permanent place among the classics." Neal reviewed the poem, joining
the chorus of praise but pointedly calling attention to the limita-
tions of a poet who seeks "to delight, to elevate us with a calm
and cheerful approbation; not to overwhelm us in wonder." He

1. Neal to Pierpont, April 17, 1816, PML; "John Pierpont," *Atlantic Monthly* 18 (1866):651–52.
2. Pierpont to Neal, January 6 and 24, 1817, PML.

wishes to "reserve some rich epithets . . . for the genius that succeeds him." [3] That genius would be John Neal. When Pierpont encouraged Neal to try his hand at poetry, suggesting the Battle of Lundy's Lane as a subject for a long poem, Neal responded enthusiastically. He kept his *Battle of Niagara* a secret to surprise his friend with a published book. In this he succeeded remarkably well.

When *The Battle of Niagara* (including the long poem, "Goldau") appeared in 1818, it created something of a stir among the Delphians and elicited a scattering of admiring comment from the reviewers, though its public reception was far less favorable than that of the *Airs*. Its impact on Pierpont was electrifying. He informed his wife that "either of them ['Niagara' or 'Goldau'] contains more of the greatness and madness of poetry than *any* other poem that was ever written in America." To Neal, after expressing his admiration and awe, he announced an extraordinary decision: "Whatever else I may do, John, I don't mean to write poetry *any more.*" And, after a fashion, he kept his word. Pierpont did, in fact, continue to write poems throughout his long life, but he limited himself almost entirely to "the wares of a verse-wright, made 'to order.' " [4]

Pierpont's response to Neal's poems is linked to his feelings about Neal, and about himself. The older man is always the prudent guide and mentor and relishes that role; but he also admires and perhaps occasionally envies his young friend's adventurousness and freedom. In his own poetry he senses an

3. In "Savanarola of Hollis Street," John T. Winterich observes: "Had there been a Pulitzer Prize for poetry in 1816 the judges would have decided in favor of John Pierpont without leaving their seats." The assessment that places the *Airs* among the classics is that of James Hall, quoted in John T. Flanagan, *James Hall: Literary Pioneer of the Ohio Valley* (Minneapolis, 1941), p. 112. Neal's observations on the poem are in his review, "Airs of Palestine . . . ," *Port Folio*, 5th ser., 2 (1816):528.

4. Pierpont quotes from a letter to his wife while writing to Neal, September 9, 1818, PML; his renunciation of poetry is in the same letter. His deprecatory self-assessment is in his Preface to *Airs of Palestine and Other Poems* (Boston, 1840), p. v.

excessive tameness. Compared to Neal's poems, he confesses to his wife, "The 'Airs of Palestine' . . . is more correct, and more harmonious; more polished in the structure of the verse, but immeasurably more *tame.*" He also finds this excessive tameness within himself and, on occasion, turns to his wild young friend as mentor. Shortly after assuming the ministry of the Hollis Street Church he writes Neal exultantly about a sermon he has just delivered: "it would have done your soul good not because I was eloquent . . . , but because I was what you would have wished me, *manly, frank,* direct."

Neal swells to such treatment and pours out his heart to a friend who can be both mentor and admirer. He floods the mails with lengthy confidences about his amorous involvements and is duly grateful for Pierpont's cautionary pronouncements. He is alternately rhapsodic about Pierpont's deep understanding and impatient with what he believes to be his neglect. "What is a labyrinth to everybody else," he cries out to his friend, "you hold an unerring clue to—the intricacies of my heart & brain. You know me—you, of all the world & thank God!" And when Pierpont fails to write, he finds his silence "unaccountable . . . —unkind, even amid the multiplicity of your business," and warns that their friendship cannot long survive such neglect.[5] He needs to know that his friend is always close at hand to talk to and confide in. *"This is all confidential.* I would not be known to any but you on earth," he says, proceeding in this instance to give his friend a racy account of his ill-fated attempt to give a public reading of his poetry in Philadelphia. Just one year later, Neal incorporates this *"confidential"* Philadelphia story into his chatty introduction to *The Battle of Niagara: Second Edition Enlarged* (1819). What was a mortifying secret told with greatest caution to his closest friend is now spread over six printed pages.

A partial explanation of Neal's public exploitation of his

5. Pierpont to Neal, September 9, 1818, and April 26, 1819; Neal to Pierpont, February 1 and December 27, 1819, PML.

own great secret is that the personal account is now transmuted
into art. The sixty-seven-page introduction to *Niagara* is designed
to stir up the reader by its outrageous candor. (He confesses,
for example, that some of the short poems reprinted in the volume
are pretty awful stuff, "a sort of she-poetry," included only because "I want a copy for myself—in a more portable shape.")
His adventure quickly becomes the occasion for an amusing dia-
tribe against Philadelphia: "brother poets, if you have a mind
'to pick up a penny' in the way of your profession; heaven help
you! . . . shun the American Athens, as you would shun a poor-
house, or else dress yourself up like a harlequin . . . proclaiming
ribands to be swallowed, glasses gingled—with a thing called a
poem between the acts." [6] But there is another explanation.
Mockery and self-mockery frequently hover over the surface of
Neal's serious emotions—even the most intense and private. In
his criticism and fiction this tendency is reflected in a rapid
oscillation of mood, in a fusion of the serious and flippant, comic
and tragic. To Pierpont, he tries to explain these emotional turn-
abouts as inner necessity: "Forgive me!—I am *very* serious—
but, really, if my eyes were running over,—if my very heart were
bursting, I must relieve myself by saying or doing something
ridiculous." Again, he cries out in inarticulate rapture at the
news of Pierpont's appointment to the Hollis Street Church, interrupts his emotional stammerings to interpolate a question in
parenthesis about grammatical usage, and just as abruptly resumes
his stammerings.[7]

There is a deep need to protect himself from unguarded
emotion. He tells his friend of a strange feeling of oppression
that comes over him when he is the recipient of an unexpected
kindness; somehow such friendly overtures penetrate a defense
he has built all around him—"a kind of solitude within me that
I shuddered to feel disturbed by common visiters." Only Pierpont
may penetrate this defense: "You were the only one on earth—

6. Neal to Pierpont, June 8, 1818, PML; *Niagara*, pp. xxxv–xxxvi.
7. Neal to Pierpont, July 2, 1820, and February 1, 1819, PML.

aye the only one—for whom I felt any strong anxiety, and you too, were the only one who might steal into my retirement without being rebuked." He cannot bring himself "to kneel or pray" or share Pierpont's religious convictions, for, he says, "I have no creed but this—I believe all may do their duty—and therefore all *must*." But "I can feel." [8]

He can feel, but is all too keenly aware of the fact that emotions, however intense, may spring from self-deception. He reflects cynically about the benevolent and protective feelings aroused in him by Mrs. Howard, a beautiful young woman he has befriended. Would he be so eager to help her if she were not so beautiful? The answer is no. "The devil take our fine sentiments I say. The very rascal who would drive his curricle over an ugly, dirty old woman, would burst his own heart-case in sobbing with a young and beautiful (& tidy) one." (Here Neal anticipates Melville's questions about Pierre and the beautiful Isabel: "How, if accosted in some squalid lane, a humped, and crippled, hideous girl should have snatched his garment's hem, with—'Save me, Pierre—love me, own me, brother; I am thy sister!' ") [9]

Only Pierpont is exempt from the distrust he feels for others —and himself. The Boston pastor becomes the sole repository for all his confused and troubled emotions and for his accounts of the entanglements and escapades that accompany them. "I will relate to you as madly romantick a freak as you ever heard of," he writes, prefacing an account of an "elopement" with a "rich Dutchman's daughter" (*"related* to the Gov. of Pennsylvania"): "We were pursued to New York. At New Jersey (Trenton) I had to jump out of a 2 story window to escape a bullet." The gratification he receives from confiding such adventures to his friend is explicitly identified in another letter:

8. Neal to Pierpont, February 22, 1819, PML.

9. Neal to Pierpont, November 13, 1820, PML; *The Writings of Herman Melville*, ed. Harrison Hayford et al. (Evanston and Chicago, 1968–), vol. 7, *Pierre* (1971), p. 107.

So far I have written—almost in a fever—expecting a girl every moment—*for advice*—. It is evening and the time is already passed. The only way to relieve me—I knew was this—time appears shorter when I am writing you, than at any other time—.

She hasn't come. The hour is past. And I am—all resignation! having made about as good use of this sheet of paper as I would of her, in getting rid of my lasciviousness.

The girl was probably Mrs. Howard; when she moved to Boston several months later to pursue an acting career, Neal played with the idea of sharing his mistress with his friend: "Hourra!— 'Abraham'—stop, I have it—cant you say to a poor creature, (when necessary)—as *he* did—let there be a *piece* between my *seed* & thy *seed?*" [10]

It was Neal's involvement with Pierpont's young sister-in-law, Abby Lyman Lord, that eventually led to the break in their friendship. He was, for a time, a boarder in the household of Joseph Lyman Lord, his former business partner (Pierpont's brother-in-law). His room was next to that of Abby, Lord's fourteen year-old sister. One night Neal entered the girl's room and bed but fled when she awakened with a cry. Several years later, Neal (in a thinly disguised fictional account) insisted that he had meant the girl no harm but had merely wanted to teach her a lesson by placing her in his power; she had been guilty, he said, of some rather shamelessly provocative behavior. Because such an explanation would have seemed implausible even to his closest friend, Neal substituted an even more implausible lie in his letters to Pierpont: On some past occasion, he wrote, Joe Lord had kissed his old flame May Anne Dawson, "by my own desire and yet I never forgave him." On the troublesome night in question Neal had dreamed that the newly-married Joe "came and asked me to try the strength of his fair one—that he led me to her bed—and then I dreamt how I jumped in—and how she squalled—and here

10. Neal to Pierpont, July 6, 1818; March 4 and November 13, 1820, PML.

I waked." He had escaped from Abby's bed to his own room
safely and had not been suspected; he was informing Pierpont
so that he might act as he thinks right about telling Abby's mother,
"for if A. yet thinks of it with terrour and believe it *reality*—
she will carry it with her to the grave . . . —besides it will
render her timid and suspicious of her senses. You know even
if she was not a child—she would have nothing to fear from
me—unless I had been a devil— . . . *you* know me." Pierpont advised that the matter be left alone for the time being.
Abby suspected the truth, he noted, but was also half-convinced
that she had been dreaming. He would say nothing "till I see
her: and then if I think that justice either to her or you demands
it I shall inform her of the truth—or what I believe was the
truth of the matter." [11]

Neal's involvement with Abby seems to have contributed to
the Lord family's decision to return to Boston early in 1819. In
February Pierpont reported, in terms congenial to Neal's penchant
for witty obscenity, that Abby had a new attachment: "I think
[she] is mortgaged to Mr. Green, or at least that he has a lien
—(not lying)—upon her. He has the reputation of a clever
man—He has neither your genius nor your passion—But I am
told she loves him—strangely ductile is the metal of a female
heart." Neal's reply protested indifference somewhat excessively.
Forgetting (or remembering) the sleepwalking episode, he insisted that "I never have—nor ever shall lose an hours sleep
on her account." He was not ashamed of the fact that he "did
like her exceedingly" and could have *loved* her," but now
Mr. Green had his consent "heart and soul." Neither Abby nor
Neal had any grounds for reproach, for he had striven "not
to win her affections—not to encourage the yearning and clinging
of a young heart" but to discourage such feelings on her part. He
was nevertheless convinced that one hour's conversation with her

11. Neal to Pierpont, June 5 and July 6, 1818; Pierpont to Neal, July
26, 1818, PML. This episode surfaces in Neal's novel *Randolph* ([Phila-
delphia], 1823), 1, 115–76, and in his postscript to *Errata*, 2, 345–47.

would suffice "to take her out of his [Green's] arms—almost at the very altar." He hoped never to "cross her path—or her slumber. Yet I fear I shall." [12]

Abby Lord was still very much in his mind two years later when Neal announced that he had found a woman "entirely qualified, I religiously believe, . . . to make me just such a wife as I ought to have." His beloved, the daughter of artist Rembrandt Peale, had "a fine person—and a countenance *'not handsome'* like all my heroines you know!—but uniting a good degree of loftiness and innocence—." Rosalba Peale, he reported, resembled Abby Lord but was "a *better* person." Miss Peale's accomplishments and shortcomings are the theme of several letters; but the young lady eventually "found me out, and sent me adrift—for which I am afraid she has never been sufficiently thankful." [13] His courtship of Rosalba was at an early stage when Rembrandt Peale, visiting Boston to arrange an exhibition of his huge canvas "The Court of Death," called on Pierpont with a letter of introduction from Neal. In May of 1821 Peale sketched from life a striking pencil portrait of the minister (reproduced following p. 148). Pierpont complained that his countenance was too severe, but Neal found it an excellent likeness.[14] The affair with Rosalba seems to have been still flickering in 1823 when Neal posed for two portraits of himself, one painted by Sarah Miriam Peale, gifted young cousin of Rembrandt, the second attributed to Sarah Peale but probably by Rembrandt Peale or another artist in the Peale circle. In the one signed by Sarah Peale, Neal meditates pensively over an open book, his free hand poised delicately aloft. The second (reproduced as the frontispiece of this book) is a bolder and more characteristic portrait of the artist as a young man in love—more or less. The Peale portraits of Pierpont and

12. Pierpont to Neal, February 28, 1819; Neal to Pierpont, March 18, 1819, PML.

13. Neal to Pierpont, March 18, April 5, October 22, 1821, PML; *Wandering Recollections*, p. 357.

14. Pierpont to Neal, May 23, 1821, PML.

Neal are an enduring legacy of Neal's attachment to Rosalba.[15]

Pierpont remained a sympathetic and loyal friend through all these crises of the heart. But considerable strain was produced when Neal tried to involve the "Savanarola of Hollis Street"— already in deep trouble with his congregation because of his unorthodoxy—with his protégée, Mrs. Howard. Neal, apparently uneasy about the relationship, had subsidized the young woman's move from Baltimore to Boston and a theatrical career. For reasons now obscure, he enlisted Pierpont and Joseph T. Buckingham to serve as intermediaries for his letters to her. This was bad enough, but the minister finally balked when he was urged to befriend Mrs. Howard. It would be difficult enough for someone in his walk of life to have anything to do with an actor; an actress was out of the question. When Neal persisted, the mild-mannered Pierpont—in language unusually emphatic—informed his friend that he wanted "to hear and see nothing more" of the woman. On May 12, 1822, Neal launched an extraordinary eight-page reply summarizing and justifying his involvement. He claimed that, aside from a six-and-a-half-week period of sexual intimacy, his motives had consistently been "the hope, a proud and virtuous and disinterested hope, of saving a fellow creature." Even the sexual stage of their relationship was more the result of a "dormant" moral sensibility on his part than of vice; his curiosity led him into "a species of intemperance . . . no more *serious* . . . than occasional intemperance in drinking." As soon

15. J. Hall Pleasants conjectures that the frontispiece portrait was painted by Sarah M. Peale in about 1835 while Neal was visiting Baltimore. But Neal's cloak in the portrait, with its distinctive metal clasp, is identical with that worn by Neal in the portrait signed and dated: "Sarah M./Peale/ 1823." Neal was persona non grata in Baltimore after 1823; the two portraits seem to be the productions of the same year, 1823. The unsigned and undated frontispiece portrait is quite dissimilar in style from the Sarah Peale portrait and is probably the work of Rembrandt Peale or another artist in the Peale circle. I am indebted to Mildred Steinbach, of the Frick Art Reference Library, for transmitting the late Dr. Pleasants's opinion.

as he found "that she was not so utterly abandoned, as such women usually are," he "undertook her reformation." [16]

The now shaky friendship deteriorated drastically when Neal and Abby Lord renewed their involvement amidst gossip that injured her reputation and undermined her engagement to Mr. Green. Infuriated by reports that the Lord brothers (Joseph and Erastus) were circulating malicious stories about him, Neal notified Pierpont that he would cowhide them on sight. Torn between family and friend, Pierpont stood by his family. He continued, however, to hold open the possibility of a reconciliation. They would remain friends, Neal replied, "but I cannot feel toward you as I have felt—and never shall so feel again toward any man, I hope and believe." Pierpont had done his duty as a family man and preacher in setting himself "above the weaknesses and confidences of human passion." But in so doing he had stifled forever the deep feeling that existed between them. Hereafter Neal would trust and confide in no man:

> You have shown me that it is foolish . . . to *confess* that one has been a scoundrel: but that, if a man must be a scoundrel, or if he have been a scoundrel—or *villain*— it is better to hold his tongue. He that is honest *beyond other men* . . . in telling his own shame—will, one day or other learn, as I have, that he had better be *more* of a villain—and hold his tongue. . . . I do not hesitate to say that the manner in which I have been treated, for my foolish confidence in the magna[ni]mity of men, has made not only *my temper,* but *my heart,* more suspicious and unkind, and therefore, worse.[17]

Even as he wrote, a time bomb was ticking that was to blow up any semblance of friendship that remained. Into his novel *Randolph* (essentially completed in early 1822 but revised and enlarged prior to its publication in late July 1823) Neal had

16. Neal to Pierpont, November 13, 1820; Pierpont to Neal, November 8 and December 15, 1820. Pierpont's repudiation of Mrs. Howard is quoted by Neal in his lengthy letter (to Pierpont) of self-justification, May 12, 1822, PML.

17. Neal to Pierpont, June 16 and July 7, 1823, PML.

incorporated details extremely compromising to the Lord family. At great length the Byronic hero-villain Edward Molton describes and justifies his visit to the bed of a fourteen-year-old girl in whose household he is a boarder. Abby Lord is not identified by name, but the man she became engaged to (Mr. Green) is referred to as "Mr. G." Joseph Lord is, in the novel, the girl's brother "Joe," the object of Molton's contempt as a hypocritical libertine and "the blockhead who is the author of all this mischief." [18] This personal attack on the Lords would be transparently clear to the family and to all others acquainted with the gossip circulating freely in Baltimore and Boston.

Randolph was published anonymously and with great secretiveness in Philadelphia. On October 3 Neal wrote what was to be his last letter to Pierpont for more than two years; in it he inserts a paragraph designed to make certain that John and Mary Lord Pierpont, all the Lords, and all his enemies would read the novel. Without explicitly admitting to its authorship, he says that it "is attributed to me." It has been described as "libellous, blasphemous and obscene. . . . Copies are here and I have read one. It is the boldest thing of the age—undoubtedly with a great deal of trash in it, tha[t] will be intelligible to but a few & unaccountable to others;—nay, perhaps to the few intelligible only, and not justifiable except on the ground of self defence, a justification." [19]

The mask dropped completely a month later when *Errata* was published with Neal's name in the copyright notice and a postscript defending *Randolph* against those outraged by its revelations: "It has been said of Randolph that it contains too much *private history*. Ah!—how know the people that there is any *private* history in it? How came such *private* history to be so universally known." The answer is that the author made the mistake of revealing a secret transgression because "he could neither eat nor sleep, till he had confessed the wrong, and made atonement for it."

18. *Randolph*, 1:157–69.
19. Neal to Pierpont, October 3, 1823, PML.

The consequence, the postscript laments, was apparent forgiveness disguising hatred and secret vindictiveness. The only recourse was to write a book that would pass for a novel to some but would be, for those who had been exposed to the gossip, "a refutation of the vile and wicked calumny." [20]

The bomb in *Randolph* exploded not only for Pierpont and the Lords but also for the young naval officer and poet Edward C. Pinkney, whose father was ridiculed rather outrageously in the novel. William Pinkney, Baltimore lawyer and statesman, is not only criticized for professional incompetence and dubious ethics but, worse, labelled "a notorious sloven"—with details about his habitual nose-picking while addressing the court. This eight-page insult was compounded by an unforeseen occurrence while the book was in press: Pinkney died. There was time for Neal to soften or delete his criticism, but he settled instead for a footnote deploring Pinkney's demise but insisting that truth remained truth and must stand. Young Pinkney challenged Neal to a duel. When the author persisted in declining the honor, Pinkney distributed printed cards bearing this message:

> The undersigned, having entered into some correspondence with the reputed author of "Randolph;" who is, or is not, sufficiently described as JOHN NEAL, a gentleman by indulgent courtesy;—informs honourable men, that he has found him unpossessed of courage to make satisfaction for the insolence of his folly.
>
> Stating thus much, the undersigned commits this Craven to his infamy.
>
> EDWARD C. PINKNEY.
>
> *Baltimore*, Oct. 11, 1823.

While all this was going on, Neal was seeing *Errata* through the press. To the previously mentioned postscript he appended an "Editorial Notice" giving his version of the affair and reproducing their correspondence and Pinkney's final denunciation (with annotations).

Windsor Daggett has suggested that Neal's refusal to fight a

20. *Errata*, 2:345–47.

duel and his being posted as a coward did no permanent damage
to his reputation, but his scurrilous commentary on William Pinkney
"created a stir in Baltimore" and "set the teeth of the writing
fraternity for the rest of his life." In addition to Pinkney's challenge,
there were several anonymous threats, and for a time Neal made
it a point to show himself at public gatherings in order to face down
any show of violence.[21] There was no violence. But the poisoned atmosphere unquestionably contributed to Neal's precipitous decision,
exactly one month after the publication of *Errata*, to leave Baltimore
and seek his literary fortune abroad.

21. Neal's critique of William Pinkney is in *Randolph*, 2:235–44. For
an account of the Neal-Pinkney "duel," see T. O. Mabbott and F. L. Pleadwell, *The Life and Works of Edward Coote Pinkney* (New York, 1926),
pp. 25–29; their account is based on Neal's versions of the affair in his
"Editorial Notice," *Errata*, 2:349–64 and *Wandering Recollections*, pp. 229–
36. For Daggett's observation, see his *A Down-East Yankee from the
District of Maine* (Portland, 1920), p. 7.

4 England
Flight or Invasion?

But what sent me to England?
I wish I could tell you.

WANDERING RECOLLECTIONS

At Oxford, on the thirtieth day
of January 1824, I heard uncaged birds
singing all about me,
as I wandered among the trees.

"YANKEE NOTIONS"

"Baltimore was done with Neal," observes F. L. Pattee; and Neal with Baltimore, he might have added. Long before *Randolph* exploded, Neal had been exhibiting signs of restlessness. In January of 1820 he suddenly resigned from the Delphian Club where he had spent so many convivial evenings. Pierpont urged him, in vain, to reconsider this "precipitate" and "unreasonable" response to the Club's rejection of a friend he had proposed for honorary membership.[1]

It was in this year also that Neal began his practice of law; but before long he became disgusted with it and with "the whole tribe of lawyers in America, from the highest to the lowest." In language influenced by the views of Jeremy Bentham (to which he was exposed while studying with Professor David Hoffman of the Maryland Law School), Neal slashes out at the hypocrisy and corruption "rising up on every side of our Federal institutions because of the law in America" and the "army of lawyers . . . crowding up to all high places and seats of power." [2]

1. F. L. Pattee, Introduction to *American Writers*, p. 12. For Neal's resignation from the Delphian Club, see Uhler, "The Delphian Club," pp. 315–16; also Neal to Pierpont, January 11, 1820; and Pierpont to Neal, February 6, 1820, PML. Neal's rejected friend is identified in the Pierpont-Neal correspondence as William B. Walter.

2. Neal's disillusionment with law and lawyers in America is conveyed in his autobiographical essay "Yankee Notions," *London Magazine*,

Bored and disgusted with the law, Neal turned to writing as an outlet for his turbulent emotional life and, eventually, as a pathway to the fame that had come to Washington Irving and Fenimore Cooper. The four novels published in 1822–23 reflect his preoccupation with the theme of sexual guilt—a preoccupation that must have contributed to young Hawthorne's fascination with them. Neal himself called *Logan*—the first in the series—not a novel but a "wild, fiery, protracted dream . . . a great void, peopled with phantoms." The novels that followed (in order of composition, not publication)—*Randolph* and *Errata*—strike out at real and imagined personal enemies. Having thus discharged his wildest inner feelings, Neal was now free to respond to Cooper's just-published *The Spy*. "I had got charged to the muzzle," Neal was to write later, "with the doings of our Revolutionary fathers, while writing my portion of 'Allen's History,' and wanted only the hint, or touch, that Cooper gave in passing, to go off like a Leyden jar, and empty myself at once of all the hoarded enthusiasm I had been bottling up, for three or four years." [3] The result was *Seventy-Six*, completed on March 19, 1822, a novel that was to establish Neal's reputation in the early 1820s as Cooper's chief rival.

David Kaser has observed that "In 1822 neither author nor

n.s. 4 (1826):446–47; Neal was living in Bentham's household when he wrote this essay, but his interest in Bentham's views can be dated back to 1819 when, in a letter to Pierpont (February 1, PML), he discusses the feasibility of his bringing out a translation of Bentham's *Théorie des peines et des récompenses*. See also *Wandering Recollections*, p. 301, and Neal's Introduction to Bentham's *Principles of Legislation* (Boston, 1830), pp. 42–43.

3. For his timetable of composition see Neal's letter to Carey and Lea, February 26, 1822, quoted in Earl L. Bradsher, *Mathew Carey: Editor, Author and Publisher* (New York, 1912), pp. 125–26. His production schedule is also detailed in a footnote to the sketch of himself in *American Writers*, p. 168; Neal must have revised and enlarged *Randolph*, for it contains references to *Seventy-Six*. Hawthorne's addiction to Neal's novels is referred to in a letter from his Bowdoin College classmate Jonathan Cilley; the letter, dated November 17, 1836, is quoted in Julian Hawthorne, *Nathaniel Hawthorne and His Wife* (Boston, 1885), 1:145. Neal's description of *Logan* is from *Randolph*, 2:223; for Neal's statement about Cooper's influence see *Wandering Recollections*, p. 224.

publisher wholly trusted the other" and that it was John Neal who was one of the first American writers "to put complete faith in a publishing house." It was a disheartening experience. H. C. Carey and I. Lea published *Logan* after a year of maddening printing delays, marked also by the firm's trepidation concerning profanity, "wildness," and "incoherence"—traits "not well calculated for the novel readers of our day." His series of novels (*Logan, Randolph, Errata, Seventy-Six*), Neal informed Carey and Lea in 1822, were "materially *American*." They would outstrip the emerging American Scott, he implied, and would represent a formidable challenge to the reigning grandmaster, the author of *Waverley*:

> I am impatient . . . and therefore I would have you come down upon them (the publick) clap after clap, before they can get their breath. They are startled at the celerity of the Scotch novelist—Let us appal them—if we can! [4]

Troubled by the wildness, incoherence, and profanity of *Logan*, the Philadelphia publishers begged off from any further involvement with Neal and his volatile, unreadable, would-be masterpieces.

Neal turned for assistance to the author of *The Spy*. In October of 1822 he forwarded to Cooper the manuscript of *Randolph* (then titled "Walpole") along with a copy of *Logan*.[5] Cooper's reply has not survived, but it was apparently unfavorable for Neal was forced to make his own arrangements for the publication, in 1823, of *Seventy-Six, Randolph,* and *Errata*. This rebuff must have rankled and might have contributed to Neal's determination to eclipse the soaring reputation of the "American Scott." It explains,

4. David Kaser, *Messrs. Carey & Lea of Philadelphia: A Study in the History of the Booktrade* (Philadelphia, 1957), p. 73. Neal's voluminous correspondence with Carey and Lea is at the Historical Society of Pennsylvania; the letter expressing concern about *Logan* is dated October 1, 1822. Neal to Carey and Lea, February 26, 1822, Historical Society of Pennsylvania, Philadelphia; quoted inaccurately in Earl L. Bradsher, *Mathew Carey: Editor, Author and Publisher* (New York, 1912), 125–26.

5. For Neal's overture to Cooper see his letter of October 18, 1822, Cooper Collection, Yale University Library.

in part, the ferocity of Neal's later attacks on Cooper in *Blackwood's Magazine.*

Though the four novels elicited anger and derision, some of the reviews verged on—or soared beyond—the ecstatic. "In all the productions of the human understanding, that we have ever heard of," writes one reviewer about *Logan,* ". . . we remember nothing, we *know* nothing, we can *conceive* of nothing equal to this romance." The critic concludes his devotions with an expression of "astonishment that the *still life* of the Pioneers, should be read and applauded in the same age that produced *Logan!*" A lady admirer is said to have become so infatuated with Neal's pungent style that she lost her taste for all other books and died with a copy of *Seventy-Six* in her hand. One British critic, however, likened the style of *Logan* to "the raving of a bedlamite" and recommended that its author be consigned to "the wholesome restraint of a straw cell and a strait waistcoat." Still another attacked the "inelegant and peculiar" language of *Seventy-Six,* but found energies in it that were "rough" but "powerful . . . like much of its author's vast continent, not cultivated but fertile." To both praise and abuse Neal responded with delight. After reading a review complaining of the "horror, torn flesh, &c. &c." in *Seventy-Six,* he was so happy he "tried to wear a natural expression of the face for a day or two, but could not . . . and whenever anybody looked at me, though it were in a church, I smiled in spite of my teeth." [6]

The great success of *The Spy* at home and abroad had been heady news to literary nationalists bristling at Sydney Smith's taunt: "In the four quarters of the globe, who reads an American

6. The ecstatic review of *Logan* is from the *Columbian Observer,* undated clipping in Neal's scrapbook, John Neal Papers, the Houghton Library (cited hereafter as HL). Neal identifies the reviewer as S. Simpson, editor of the *Observer.* For the admirer who died with a Neal book in hand, see *Wandering Recollections,* pp. 227–28. The other reviews are in the *Magazine of Foreign Literature* 1 (1823):102, and the *Monthly Review Enlarged* 102 (1823):212; quoted in William B. Cairns, *British Criticisms of American Writing, 1815–1833,* University of Wisconsin Studies in Language and Literature, no. 14 (Madison, 1922), pp. 208, 209. Neal's response to these criticisms is described in "Yankee Notions," pp. 448–49.

book?" At the time Smith posed his infuriating question, Irving's *Sketch Book* was a recent publication, and *The Spy* and the first of Cooper's *Leather-stocking Tales* were still unwritten. But even after Irving's international reputation seemed assured and our American Scott had scored triumphantly with *The Pioneers*, there were those who felt that an authentic native literature was still very much in the making. While James Kirke Paulding found it necessary to defend Cooper against the charge of "vulgarity" leveled against him by J. G. Percival and other genteel sensibilities,[7] other critics insisted that Cooper, like Irving, was far too tame and imitative. They looked toward bolder and more vigorous writing; toward a new literature emblematic of their vast new continent.

Many English readers found *The Spy*, as did one reviewer, strong stuff—"Yankee to the back bone." The work satisfied their eager interest in America while simultaneously advocating—in the words of another British critic—"The best interests of virtue and religion" in a style consistently "light and agreeable." While Neal's wild incoherencies and "inelegant and peculiar" style scarcely promised a similar success, he was occasionally linked with Cooper, in terms favorable to both, and to the developing American novel. "America begins to be prolific in Novels," observed a British reviewer, who then proceeded to deal out even-handed praise to the "well-written sketches of character and scenery" in *The Spy* and *The Pioneers* and to the "energy and freshness" of the battle scenes in *Seventy-Six*. The enterprising Whittakers of London pirated *The Spy* "at great profit to [themselves], but at none to anyone else." A year later they brought out *Seventy-Six* in three handsome volumes. At about the same time another London firm, A. K. Newman and Company, reprinted *Logan* in four volumes.[8]

7. See Marcel Clavel, *Fenimore Cooper and His Critics* (Aix-en-Provence, 1938), pp. 149–51.

8. The reviews cited are in *The Spirit of Literature* 1 (1830) :425; *Monthly Review Enlarged* 102 (1823) :212; *Literary Gazette* 8 (1824) :501. Quoted in Cairns, *British Criticisms of American Writing*, pp. 118, 210, 226. For the Whittakers' publication of *The Spy*, see Robert E. Spiller and P. C.

"A London publisher! think of that. I knew nothing of London publishers." In England Neal was to learn that Newman and Company was a disreputable firm, "people who manufacture a certain sort of literary ware by shiploads," and that the Whittakers were not much more highly regarded. But in Baltimore, in late 1823, Neal was convinced that *Randolph* and *Errata* would be even better received in England than *Logan* and *Seventy-Six* "because they were bolder and, if possible, yet more out of the common way." While dining with Henry Robinson, a Briton who now made his home in Baltimore, Neal heard once again, "more in sorrow than in anger," Sydney Smith's all too familiar taunt: "Who reads an American book?" Neal informed Robinson that he would answer that question abroad. "Irving had succeeded; and, though I was wholly unlike Irving, why shouldn't I?" Cooper was being well received, and Neal, "without crossing his path, or poaching upon his manor," was certain he could do something "so American, as to secure the attention of Englishmen." The date of this dinner party is not recorded, but it must have followed very closely the publication, on November 10, of *Errata* with its postscript identifying him as the author of *Randolph*—and completing the destruction of his friendship with Pierpont. On November 15 Neal wrote to Mathew Carey, Philadelphia publisher and ardent nationalist: "I am going to London, Paris, Rome, & perhaps over the continent. If I *should* choose to *publish* in London, who is the best man, think you?" During the next few weeks Neal closed out his affairs in Baltimore and borrowed enough cash to pay his passage and keep him for a few months in England, where he "could live upon air, and write faster than any man that ever yet lived." The *Franklin*, under Captain Graham, was scheduled to leave Baltimore on December 1; after numerous delays, the ship finally set sail on December 15, "a wet, heavy, damp, rascally day." [9]

Blackburn, *A Descriptive Bibliography of the Writings of James Fenimore Cooper* (New York, 1934), p. 5. The British publication of Neal's *Logan* and *Seventy-Six* is discussed in his "Yankee Notions," pp. 447–49.

9. Neal's most reliable account of his leave-taking is in "Yankee Notions," pp. 447–50 and "Yankee Notions," no. 2, *London Magazine*, n.s. 5

During the long voyage Neal filled his diary with descriptions of the stormy sea and with wry observations about his fellow passengers and himself. "Steward sea-sick, but like everybody else, ashamed to acknowledge it. Why? For the same reason that leads young men to smoke cigars till they are white in the face; and all men to drink more wine than they ought, and appear to know more about all sorts of debauchery than they do. They are afraid of being thought *raw*." [10] Despite the foul weather and his own seasickness, he found it possible to notice a beautiful Irish girl ("Pity she dwells in the steerage though. I would share a cabin with her") and to work on a new novel, eventually to be titled *Brother Jonathan*, but then called *The Yankee*. He wrote a preface (later discarded) "while the noises overhead were like the perpetual roar and thunder on every side of the ship, above and below—a cannonade in the sky echoing to a cannonade in the water." And while the ship careened through these seas, he resolved "to make Jonathan Evans a *real* Yankee; he was not so when I first made the book." In all of his previous novels he had sought through natural eloquence and passionate characterization to convey truths rarely recorded in print. He had frequently sounded the cry for an authentic American literature but was himself split down the middle in his creative efforts; he carried with him on board the *Franklin* not only the draft of *Brother Jonathan* but also a copy of his Byronic verse tragedy, *Otho*, a work he planned to revise for a London production. In a heavy sea off the coast of Newfoundland, Neal attempted his first full-scale Yankee character.

The ship is buffeted by terrible storms. On December 27, the winds swoop in from all directions so that the struggling vessel "stops— . . . shudders fore and aft, so that I can feel the shudder through every part of her; springs forward, with a convulsive motion, her sails flapping like the huge wings of any other mighty

---

(1826):71–72; in *Wandering Recollections*, p. 239, he adds the detail that his decision was triggered by Henry Robinson's repetition of Sydney Smith's famous question. Neal's letter to Mathew Carey, November 15, 1823, is in the University of Pennsylvania Library.

10. Neal reproduces his voyage diary in "Yankee Notions," no. 2, pp. 79–89.

bird in distress (a wounded eagle, or a condor shipwrecked . . . among the clouds of South America. . .)." They ride out the storm—for "one might as well try to pick up quicksilver, as overthrow a fine ship at sea." Three days later, with seas again crashing on deck "like ten thousand trumpets and thunder in proportion," Neal busies himself with the wrestling match episode in *Brother Jonathan* (chapter 9): "I work it up much as it now stands, from a little sketch, a mere outline of a page or two; finish it in the very thick of the gale." On January 4 the sea changes to a muddy green. Soundings at eight fathoms bring up a fine grey sand: "I look upon it with extraordinary pleasure; it is the land of Europe—of another world."

On January 8, twenty-three days after leaving Baltimore, the *Franklin* docked in Liverpool. Neal's impressions of the bustling port are tinged with "childish curiosity" and malicious wonderment. He circles round and round Nelson's monument, puzzles over the figures at the base, sketches it; he saunters through the markets and, seeing shrimps for the first time, "would as lief eat a handful of huge fleas" after they had turned red; he encounters a ballad singer and notes that you never see one in America, "and God be praised for it, you never hear one there." He walks the streets of Liverpool deep in mud and suggests that "mud and air . . . are so much alike, that perhaps I mistook the one for the other." [11]

Neal's tour of English villages from Liverpool eastward was at first equally disappointing. Leamington was a lovely exception, as were also the ruins of Kenilworth, "overgrown with the . . . greenness of summer in late January." It was unseasonably warm, and he understood why England is likened to a garden in fall and winter when "At Oxford, on the thirtieth of January 1824, I heard uncaged birds singing all about me, as I wandered among the trees." [12]

London—his home for the next three years—was no garden; it was February, and the weather detestable. He looked at famous

11. "Yankee Notions," no. 3, *London Magazine*, n.s. 5 (1826):181–97.

12. "English Scenery—Villages: Leamington, Warwick-Castle, Kenilworth," *The Yankee and Boston Literary Gazette*, n.s. 1 (1829):133.

landmarks in disbelief: "Could *that* be St. Paul's? and *that* the bank of England? Was that unshapely column, hung with fog, and dripping with unwholesome dampness, the Monument we had been told so much of." His account of a pilgrimage to England's most sacred shrine might, suggests F. L. Pattee, be entitled "Mark Twain in Westminster Abbey":

> I saw no sceptered shadows gliding hither and thither among the pillars and tombs; no crowned or headless apparitions parading slowly in the "dim religious light." . . . I saw a crowd of people, with their hands in their pockets, running about after a guide, all bareheaded and most of them with lips blue and teeth chattering—perhaps with awe—perhaps with cold. I saw . . . a group of waxen images—war heroes and kings fairly set up for show in the habiliments of the toy-shop among the sepulchres and solitudes of Westminster-Abbey! Who would not have come over the waters for a peep at such a spectacle in such a place? and who would not, if such a thing were told of the barbarians of the South-Sea, or of the Dutch, who would not speak of it as altogether characteristic of their barbarous condition, or deplorable want of taste.[13]

Neal's first lodgings were in Providence House, quiet and respectable, but rather too "sanctimonious and methodistical" for his taste; he felt aggrieved at being subjected to family prayers at meals and outraged when he was locked out at midnight. Charles Robert Leslie, the American painter, helped him find quarters more suited to a literary man. To his great delight he found himself in "the very lodgings—two rooms on the first floor of a house in Warwick-Street, Pall-Mall—which had been occupied by Washington Irving for a long while and where he had written the 'Sketch-Book.' " [14]

13. [John Neal], *Authorship: A Tale* (Boston: Gray and Bowen, 1830), pp. 3–5.

14. For details concerning Neal's arrival in London and his Warwick Street lodgings see *Wandering Recollections*, pp. 240–43; see also, Irving T. Richards, "John Neal's Gleaning in Irvingiana," *American Literature* 8 (1936) :170–79.

In such an environment he *must* succeed. But the first months were disheartening. His efforts to arouse interest in the republication of his novels were rebuffed. The Whittakers, to whom he submitted *Randolph,* rejected the work despite praise for its "great originality" and "powerful writing." It was too much a vehicle for digressive critical essays—essays which seemed to *them* the best part of the work but, alas, not suitable for "our *Novel* readers." [15] In some desperation Neal turned to the journals beginning with *Blackwood's Edinburgh Magazine,* "the cleverest, the sauciest, and most unprincipled of all our calumniators." By getting possession of that "blazing rocket-battery" he could effectively answer the "swarming whipper-snappers" who were filling British periodicals with lies and distortions about America. But how was an obscure Yankee to break into so famous a journal? He had by this time "good reason to believe, that communications from an American, if he did not abuse America, would go into the Balaam-basket." [16] The answer was the kind of Byronic subterfuge Neal had always delighted in, though never before had he embarked on a venture quite so fantastic—and, for a blazing season, so successful.

15. Letter to Neal, April 13, 1824, HL.
16. *Wandering Recollections,* p. 246. An indication of the prevailing anti-American climate is the fact that the gentle and inoffensive Washington Irving had recently been subjected to newspaper ridicule when he (an *American* writer) was nominated to a committee planning a Shakespeare memorial. See Benjamin Lease, *"John Bull* versus Washington Irving: More on the Shakespeare Committee Controversy," *English Language Notes,* vol. 9 (1972), in press.

5 The Carter Holmes Affair

"Carter Holmes"—was not so much a
nom de plume *as a* nom de guerre. . . .

JOHN NEAL, "WILLIAM BLACKWOOD," 1865

You are exactly the correspondent that we want.

WILLIAM BLACKWOOD TO "CARTER HOLMES,"
APRIL 20, 1824

I have seen Mr. Blackwood
and found him somewhat in a turmoil.

LANGDON ELWYN TO JOHN NEAL, FEBRUARY 10, 1826

In April of 1824 William Blackwood, proprietor of the lively and flourishing Edinburgh magazine bearing his name, received a curious letter from a stranger who gives his name as Carter Holmes. "I am a traveller," the letter opens, "and for a time, at least, a sort of wandering Jew. I am about to traverse Europe in a direction and in a manner not often attempted in this age of adventure—on foot and alone." The date of his departure is uncertain, he says, and "In the mean time, I must have some sort of employment to keep me out of mischief." He asks whether he can become an occasional contributor ("I like the bold familiarity, temper, talent and spirit [of the journal]") and encloses an article, "Sketches of the Five American Presidents, and of the Five Presidential Candidates, From the Memoranda of a Traveller." He assures Blackwood that he writes from first-hand observation and with "no hostility toward the people of the United States," and he suggests that his proposed articles meet a real need, for "There never was a time, when information concerning either of the Americas would be sought with so much avidity, as at the present." "I shall adopt a fictitious name for the present," writes the mysterious correspondent, ". . . but have no objection to leave my real name with you under seal, to be given up, on any suitable occasion." Some fifteen months and thirty-six letters later, on the eve of their first face-to-face encounter,

"Carter Holmes" drops the mask: "I *will* sign my true name now./ John Neal." [1]

Neal's two-year association with Blackwood and *Maga* (*Blackwood's Magazine*) is an extraordinary chapter in the history of American letters and Anglo-American literary relations. It is doubtful that William Blackwood was for a moment or for long taken in by Neal's British disguise, but he heartily liked his work and welcomed him warmly. "You are exactly the correspondent that we want," he wrote "Carter Holmes" on April 20, 1824, "and I hope you will continue to favor us with your communications, and you may depend upon being liberally treated." A draft for five guineas was enclosed. "Five guineas!" exclaims Neal forty years after the event—"twenty-five dollars cash, for a paper I had flung off at a single sitting, and which at home would have been thought well paid for with a 'Much obliged,' or, at most, with a five-dollar bill." [2] The jubilant "Holmes" proceeded to dash off more articles with

1. "Holmes" to Blackwood, [April] 7, 1824; Neal to Blackwood, June 27, 1825, Blackwood Papers, National Library of Scotland (cited hereafter as NLS). Neal's first letter is misdated "March 7." Other American writers, including Nathaniel Hawthorne and Sidney Lanier, were to make overtures to *Blackwood's Magazine* in later decades—with less spectacular results. See my articles, "Hawthorne and *Blackwood's* in 1849: Two Unpublished Letters," *Jahrbuch für Amerikastudien* 14 (1969):152–54; and "Sidney Lanier and *Blackwood's Magazine:* An Unpublished Letter," *Georgia Historical Quarterly* 53 (1969):521–23. Details concerning Poe's "profitable engagement" with *Blackwood's*, as he referred to it in an 1839 letter to a friend, have not yet come to light. See *The Letters of Edgar Allan Poe*, ed. John Ward Ostrom (Cambridge, Mass., 1948), 1:116.

2. Copy of letter from Blackwood to "Holmes" (in Blackwood's hand), April 20, 1824, William Blackwood and Sons Limited letter books (cited hereafter as Blackwood Letter Books). Neal reprints this letter in "William Blackwood," *Atlantic Monthly* 16 (1865):662; his comment on Blackwood's generosity appears in the same essay, p. 663. Neal's basic rate, which so pleased him at the outset, was ten guineas a sheet (sixteen pages). Two months after his debut as a contributor, "Holmes" requested an increase to sixteen guineas a sheet but was firmly notified by Blackwood that the going rate was a "fair remuneration" if he wanted to continue their association.

his usual rapidity; between May 1824 and September 1825 fourteen of his contributions were published, making him one of *Maga*'s most prolific contributors during this period.

F. L. Pattee has expressed bewilderment at "the complete surrender of *Blackwood's* to the swashbuckling young American." But Neal had chosen a journal he had come to know well in Baltimore and to whose critical tenets he was sympathetically attuned. And there were temperamental affinities: Blackwood was a shrewd, volatile Scotsman who, in 1818, used a hazel sapling to thrash an angry reader seeking vengeance with a riding whip. With the help of his literary editors, John Wilson ("Christopher North") and John Gibson Lockhart, Blackwood created a magazine full of controversy and high spirits. Vituperation was an active ingredient, and the first eighteen volumes of *Maga* have been aptly described as "riotous" and "blackguardly." William B. Cairns observes that "Neal's slashing style and the somewhat sensational nature of his utterances fitted well with the manner of *Blackwood's*." [3]

Some of Neal's contributions are treated with extraordinary deference by the editors. "A Summary View of America" (in the December 1824 issue) has an introductory note by "Christopher North" proclaiming that this longest review in the history of *Blackwood's* (thirty-six double-column pages) "contains more facts, more new reasonings, more new speculations of and concerning the United States of America, than have yet appeared in any ten books . . . upon that subject." And after the appearance of the fifth and final installment of "American Writers"—an explosive series of commentaries, alphabetically arranged, on 120 American authors living and dead (with most space given to John Neal)

3. For Pattee's reaction to the "surrender" of *Blackwood's* to Neal see *American Writers*, p. 16. An account of William Blackwood's "duel" is to be found in Frank D. Tredrey, *The House of Blackwood, 1804–1954* (Edinburgh, 1954), pp. 32–33. A. L. Strout's description of *Maga* is quoted from his *A Bibliography of Articles in Blackwood's Magazine, Volumes I through XVIII, 1817–1825* (Lubbock, Texas, 1959), Introduction. For the affinity between Neal's style and *Blackwood's*, see Cairns, *British Criticisms of American Writing*, p. 16.

—William Blackwood expresses his pleasure in terms that emphasize the kinship between *Maga* and "Carter Holmes"; it is a vigorous kinship that puts them both at far remove from the genteel sensibilities of Washington Irving:

> You have finished your series in capital style. The whole is spirited and most original. Many may differ from you in some points, but beauties or blemishes, no one will pretend to say that they are not your own; and may I add that I hardly know any work except Maga where you could have felt yourself so much at your ease in most fearlessly saying what you thought right of men and things. Washington Irving once told me he considered my Maga as a daringly original work. It was too much for his delicate nerves.[4]

Neal's opening installment had set the tone by announcing that, with few exceptions, "there is no American writer who would not pass just as readily for an English writer." The exceptions are Charles Brockden Brown, James Kirke Paulding, and John Neal. There follows a discussion of the stifling effect of early fame on creativity. In the past, observes Neal, posing as an Englishman, the English ignored American writers; now they were going to the opposite extreme of overrating some of them and endangering the writers' careers by doing so. He concludes with brief commentaries on a dozen writers at the top of the alphabet. William Cullen Bryant "is not, and never will be, a great poet. He wants fire—he wants the very rashness of a poet." The prose style of William Ellery Channing is "remarkable for simplicity, clearness, and power." His diction is "of the heart—not of the schools. It is, as it were, a language of his own—a visible thought."[5]

4. North's preface introduces "A Summary View," *Blackwood's Edinburgh Magazine* 16 (1824):617–52. "American Writers," in five installments, is in *Blackwood's Edinburgh Magazine* 16 (1824):304–11, 415–28, 560–71; ibid. 17 (1825):48–69, 186–207 (see also single volume, *American Writers*, in works cited). Blackwood's letter praising the series is dated February 19, 1825, Blackwood Letter Books; an extract is quoted in "William Blackwood," p. 668.

5. *American Writers*, pp. 29–44.

Blackwood sums up his reaction to this first essay in a word: "excellent." He must have savored both the racy, idiomatic flow of Neal's language and the provocative candor of his views. He trusts that "Holmes" will "put forth all [his] strength on the 2d part." He calls attention to the way "Tickler [J. G. Lockhart] has tickled Washington Irving" in the current number, but he urges Holmes not to be influenced and to give his "own sentiments freely." In his "Letters of Timothy Tickler, Esq. No. XVIII" (in the same number as the first installment of "American Writers"), Lockhart praises faintly the "occasional flashes of a gently-pleasing humour" in *The Sketch Book* and damns the work in its entirety as "insipid." The *History of New York*, he notes, is far superior to any of Irving's later productions, and Lockhart hopes "this elegant person" will come to recognize "the enormous, the infinite, and immeasurable superiority of his American sketches over all his European ones." If he does not, Lockhart continues, he may keep the good opinion of "the Mayfair bluestockings, and their half-emasculated hangers-on," but must inevitably lose all favor with "really intelligent and manly readers."

Neal's long discussion of Irving in the January 1825 issue is remarkably similar in outlook. His highest praise is also reserved for *Knickerbocker's History*, a work "bold—and so altogether original, without being extravagant, as to stand alone, among the labours of men." He finds it far superior to the enormously popular *Sketch Book*, a "timid, beautiful" work, a mixture of "bold poetry" and "squeamish, puling, lady-like sentimentality." [6]

Neal wrote rapidly and carelessly; the quality of his criticism and fiction is wildly uneven. Nelson F. Adkins characterizes his commentary on Fitz-Greene Halleck as "difficult to match for hope-

6. Blackwood to "Holmes," September 21, 1824, Blackwood Letter Books; [John Gibson Lockhart], "Letters of Timothy Tickler," no. 18, *Blackwood's* 16 (1824):294, 296; *American Writers*, p. 135. Neal adds, somewhat inconsistently, that the "happy," "natural" world of humor in *The Sketch Book* makes him wish he could have written it himself—far more than any other work by Irving. Lockhart's authorship of the "Timothy Tickler" article critical of Irving is established by Strout, *A Bibliography of Articles in Blackwood's Magazine*, p. 123.

less inaccuracy and unabashed egotism." Stanley Williams and Tremaine McDowell, on the other hand, find the evaluation of Irving's
Knickerbocker's History the most intelligent to appear since the
publication of the book in 1809.[7]

Blackwood's enthusiasm for Neal's spirited commentaries was
somewhat dampened by Neal's harsh treatment of Cooper, dismissed
in half a column as an imitator of Scott ("not so much, in any one
thing—as altogether"), "a man of sober talent—nothing more." In
a later, longer essay ("Late American Books"), Neal expressed
disappointment in Cooper's failure to write a truly American book.
Lionel Lincoln is vastly inferior to *The Spy*, and neither is the
great American novel that shall some day appear—"a brave, hearty,
original book, brimful of descriptive truth—of historical and familiar truth; crowded with real American character; alive with
American peculiarities; got up after no model, however excellent."
Cooper deserves praise for turning to American materials, but these
have not yet received the large and courageous treatment they
require; he is likened to Aladdin scampering away in fright when
the doors to a great untouched treasure fly open at his accidental
touch. There are those now at work, Neal suggests, who will not
be frightened away, who "will go deep—very deep—into the very
foundations of that, which they have begun to explore." When Blackwood expressed the view, before the essay was printed, that he
"perhaps [hit] poor Cooper rather hard," Neal's cool and cocky
rejoinder is that "I would be kinder—but could not." But he does
agree to delete a passage comparing Cooper and himself (to
Cooper's disadvantage) not because it is, as Blackwood suggests, in
bad taste but as "a bit of unworthy pleasantry—a puff, which I
should have been the first to acknowledge." [8]

Among the three American writers Neal claims would not

7. Nelson F. Adkins, *Fitz-Greene Halleck* (New Haven, 1930), p. 75;
Stanley Williams and Tremaine McDowell, eds., *Diedrich Knickerbocker's
A History of New York*, by Washington Irving (New York, 1927), Intro-
duction.

8. *Americans Writers*, pp. 70–71, 205–13; Blackwood to "Holmes,"
April 14, 1825, Blackwood Letter Books; "Holmes" and Neal to Blackwood, April 19 and July 30, 1825, NLS.

pass just as readily for Englishmen, James Kirke Paulding receives mixed praise as a man of "good, strong talent" with an unhappy disposition that leads him to sarcastic humor. His *Koningsmarke* (1823) is a satirical affair that "cuts up the city of Washington speculators in good style; with no pathos; no passion—but is full of meaning." Much more space and enthusiasm is devoted to Charles Brockden Brown, America's first professional author, whose tragic career epitomizes for Neal America's terrible neglect of her artists in life and in death. An imitator of Godwin, with "no poetry; no pathos; no wit; no humour; no pleasantry; no playfullness; no passion; little or no eloquence; no imagination," he nevertheless overpowers the reader. He is like a person who is utterly convincing despite—perhaps because of—the stumbling way in which he reports an incident: "You feel . . . as if you had just parted with a man who *had* seen it—a man . . . who had been telling you of it—with his face flushed." [9] Predictably the one author among the 120 discussed who comes closest to fulfilling the role of a truly American writer in subject and language is John Neal.

He has his faults. Neal's works, according to Neal, "were not written . . . for the appetite of the age. They were the feverish productions of a man, who could not be idle—whose very trifling was always desperate, or serious." But with all their faults and follies, "there was only one man, alive, when they appeared, who could have written them." *Logan*, he writes, is so crowded and incoherent that nobody can read it entirely through. But "Parts are without a parallel for passionate beauty;—power of language: deep tenderness, poetry." *Seventy-Six* needs pruning but is nonetheless "one of the best romances of the age . . . told with astonishing vivacity." *Randolph* is "as courageous a book as ever was, or ever will be, written"; and *Errata* is "a powerful work—loaded with rubbish—full of deep interest, nevertheless." The seventeen columns in *Blackwood's* that Neal devotes to himself invite dismissal as an amusing exercise in flamboyant egotism. But beneath the bravura

9. *American Writers*, pp. 172–73, 56–68, 152–69.

surface and free-flowing braggadocio is a fresh and prophetic critical intelligence. William Blackwood sensed this. When one of his favorite contributors and advisers, William Maginn, complained that the "American Writers" series is "a tissue of lies from beginning to end," the publisher stoutly defended his mysterious Yankee. He informs Maginn that his opinion differs from his own and those of friends in Edinburgh and London. Everything he has heard convinces him that "there are not manny [sic] articles I have had which have done so much for Maga as these of this writer." This American is a "singular person certainly, but no one can read his articles without seeing that he is a person of power and originality." Blackwood's high opinion was shared by David Macbeth Moir, another prolific *Maga* contributor, whose advice was frequently sought out by the publisher. Moir praises the vigor and fluency of the author's style and "its knowledge of a subject concerning which we sit in darkness." "American Writers," he asserts, displays a more intimate grasp of American literature than anything else which has appeared on either side of the Atlantic.[10]

Blackwood's enthusiasm for Neal's critical prose also extended to his fiction—but with serious reservations that eventually spelled trouble. Shortly after launching his "American Writers" series, Carter Holmes wrote that "I have a novel [*Brother Jonathan*] nearly ready for you which is altogether American—scenery—incidents—characters." The completed manuscript was forwarded to Edinburgh in early October 1824. A month later came the reply—a crowded five-page letter accompanied by an anonymous four-page critique written at Blackwood's request by "a friend whose opinion I value much" (D. M. Moir). The novel cannot be brought out as it now stands, Blackwood informs Holmes. It is a powerful, interesting, and original work—but also a distressingly indecent one: "I felt perfectly savage at you sometimes for plunging your characters without any strong necessity into so much vice and wickedness." He cites in some detail several episodes deleted

10. Ibid., pp. 168–69; Maginn to Blackwood, undated letter, NLS; Blackwood to Maginn, March 7, 1825, Blackwood Letter Books; Moir to Blackwood, three undated letters, NLS.

from the version finally published; his letter consequently provides us with the only surviving clues as to what the novel was like before its revision. Echoing Pierpont's response to *Keep Cool*, Blackwood reminds Holmes that "the pictures you give of seduction &c. are such as would make your work a sealed book to nine tenths of ordinary readers." He speaks as the father of a large family in reminding the author that "it is not fit for young people to read of seduction, brothels, and the abandoned of both sexes," for there must be "pollution to the minds of the young in any such details." Moir's accompanying critique is similar in substance and tone. After paying tribute to the novel's power ("of a kind that is unhackneyed and original"), he charges it with two fatal flaws: first, its sacrifice of "ease and gracefulness," of "a sense of propriety and decorum," to sprawling and prolix "metaphysical ingenuity" and exaggeration; second, its pervasive indecency. Moir invokes the omnipresent "circle of female readers" to condemn the presence in the novel of "elaborate plans for female seduction" and "pictures of male profligacy which startle while they astonish, and nauseate while they create interest." [11]

In a manner not often observed in the course of his long life, Neal responded with an eagerness to please. *"The novel shall not be published in its present state,"* he assures Blackwood, and in a

11. "Holmes" to Blackwood, September 29, 1824; his letter accompanying the novel is dated October 7, 1824, NLS. Neal had mentioned his novel earlier and was told it would have to be considered for the next season ("Holmes" to Blackwood, April 23, 1824, NLS; Blackwood to "Holmes," May 17, 1824, Blackwood Letter Books). Blackwood's long letter of criticism is dated November 8, 1824, Blackwood Letter Books. The unsigned critique that accompanied it is among the Neal Papers, HL. Neal mistakenly believed his anonymous critic to be John Wilson (Christopher North); see his "William Blackwood," p. 665. I an indebted to James S. Ritchie of the National Library of Scotland for identifying its author as Moir through a handwriting comparison. Moir's authorship was confirmed by my subsequent discovery of a copy of the critique headed "Remarks on Brother Jonathan / By △," loosely inserted in the Blackwood Letter Book for 1824–26. Moir's contributions to *Maga* were signed "△". Neal quotes from Blackwood's letter in "William Blackwood," pp. 665–66, but omits all references to his concern about indecency.

series of letters announces that he is rewriting it word for word; that
he "shall now spare no pains upon it" and "would rather die, than
fail"; that he is grateful to the publisher for not bringing it out in
its original state. Into the revision, completed in late March 1825,
Neal claims to have introduced a great *"variety of power, . . .
character,* and *style"* and also more truth "peculiar to America,
and descriptive of the Americans" than is to be found in the sum
of all other books published in or about America—except for
histories. This time Blackwood accepted *Brother Jonathan* for
publication—but rather unenthusiastically and with a request that
Neal revise the manuscript once again before turning it over to the
printer. For the author's guidance Blackwood enclosed another
critique from a friend "whose judgement I value more than that
of any one I know, almost." According to this critique, the novel is
"quite as clever and interesting as any of Coopers, and . . . the
character of Edith [the heroine] is, throughout, a work of true
genius." The anonymous critic is troubled by the author's style but
responsive to his displays of extraordinary power: "The style has
the same eternal effect of italics—& breaks—& affectation; but in
many passages & descriptions, I have met with *nothing* more
beautifully strong and original." [12]

Neal was certain that Blackwood's trusted and influential
friend was none other than Sir Walter Scott. It must have seemed
to him a whimsical twist of fate that could lead Scott to read his
great American novel and find it—a work written to eclipse the
productions of the "American Scott"—*"quite* as clever and interesting as any of Coopers." The identity of Blackwood's adviser
has eluded identification, but it seems certain that Neal was wrong:
he was not Scott.[13] He was unquestionably a trusted friend, and his

12. "Holmes" to Blackwood, November 11 and December 24, 1824;
March 22, 1825, NLS. Blackwood to "Holmes," April 14, 1825, Blackwood
Letter Books; quoted, in part, in "William Blackwood," p. 669. A transcription of the critique, in Neal's hand, is in the Neal Papers, HL. It is
headed "copy Sir W. S." (see following note).

13. The critique Neal believed to be Sir Walter Scott's was part of a
letter to the publisher which Blackwood forwarded on April 14, with the

high praise explains the publisher's decision to bring out a novel about which he had serious misgivings.

Still another attempt to remove the defects charged to his book "would be destructive to [its] wholeness and character," warns Carter Holmes. Some exaggeration is needed in fiction, he argues, pointing to "an *heroick* style in prose, as in poetry—painting—sculpture or the drama." But he agrees to the gigantic task of another revision, for he is eager to cooperate; the final editorial decisions, however, must be his: "I wd not be obstinate, and, yet, I wd rather be obstinate than servile." [14]

On the eve of publication Blackwood came down to London, and for the first time Neal dropped his pen name to send a hasty note to the Somerset House on Sunday morning, June 26, signed with his "true name." Blackwood called on Neal at his Warwick Street lodgings, and during this first meeting the author received his pay in cash—the balance due on two hundred guineas (an additional hundred guineas to be forthcoming after the sale of a thousand copies). That evening Neal joined the publisher and William Maginn for dinner at the Somerset House. The American liked the plain straightforward Scotsman as much as he disliked the cold reserved Irishman; he had no way of knowing that Maginn had already conveyed to Blackwood his keen distaste for both Neal and his writings. He attributed the strained atmosphere to the Irishman's desperate need for a drink.[15]

The June issue of *Maga* announced the imminent publication in Edinburgh of "The Tales of the Crusaders, by the Author of Waverley, 4 vols." and "Brother Jonathan; or, the New Englanders, 3 vols." "I am glad that Sir Walter Scott is coming up in *four volumes*," wrote Neal to Blackwood; "It will be a sort of passport, or *excuse* for the great length of Bro. Jonathan." Unfortunately the

---

signature cut away; "Holmes" transcribed and returned it, remarking (in his letter of April 19, 1825, NLS) that he recognized the handwriting.

14. "Holmes" to Blackwood, April 19 and 28, 1825, NLS; see "William Blackwood," p. 669, for extracts from the letter of April 19.

15. Neal to Blackwood, June 26 and 30, 1825, NLS; "William Blackwood," pp. 670–71.

popularity of the wordy Author of Waverley could not insure the popularity of a wordy and unknown American. Two thousand copies were printed, but fewer than five hundred were sold. *Brother Jonathan* was a "total failure," and the firm took a heavy loss.[16]

The reviews were mixed. In a commentary that must have left its mark on Blackwood, one critic expressed regret that a writer capable of such superb descriptions of New England wrestling matches and quilting frolics should "wilfully devote three huge close-printed volumes to the adventures of profligates, misanthropes, maniacs, liars, and louts, for such are the serious personages of 'Brother Jonathan.' " [17] But another reviewer found in the work "a vigour and pathos" which were only to be found in novels of the first rank.[18] An extraordinary fifty-page essay-review proclaimed that the novel, if it was the author's first, signaled the appearance of one "destined to occupy a permanent place in the very foremost rank of his age's literature." But, the same reviewer shrewdly added, "if [he] has written two or three such works, we almost despair of his ever writing a better." [19] Four years after the novel's publication a critic for the *Edinburgh Literary Journal* found the novel "full of vigour and originality," abounding in "descriptions of scenery, and illustrations of the natural passions of the human heart and soul, worthy of that prodigious continent, whose hills are mountains, and whose mountains are immeasurable." [20]

16. Neal to Blackwood, June 18 and 30, 1825, NLS; Blackwood to A and R Spottiswoode and to Longman and Dickinson, both letters dated April 23, 1825, Blackwood Letter Books; Blackwood to John Chesterton, November 19, 1828 (copy), NLS.

17. The review cited is from *British Critic* 2 (July 1826) :406, quoted in Cairns, *British Criticisms of American Writing*, p. 213.

18. *The Literary Chronicle and Weekly Review*, 102 (July 16, 1825) :449, quoted in Cairns, *British Criticisms of American Writing*, p. 210.

19. P. G. Patmore, ed., *Rejected Articles* (London, 1826), pp. 311–12.

20. *Edinburgh Literary Journal*, 1 (May 9, 1829) :386, quoted in Cairns, *British Criticisms of American Writing*, p. 213.

Neal did not fail to call Blackwood's attention to the favorable criticisms, but the financial failure of *Brother Jonathan* marks a turning point in their relationship. "Upon my word, I care more for you in the matter than I do myself," Neal wrote about the poor sale of his novel. All was not yet lost, he assured the publishers, for he would spare no effort "to make my future books good enough to sell this." Blackwood was too canny a publisher to be taken in by such optimism and too sensitive a Scotsman not to be mightily provoked by the American's explanation of the disaster—one that implicitly put the blame on him: "I worked it up too much. I nearly re-wrote it after you saw the m.s. Had I been less careful, I should have been more natural and easy, and attractive." [21]

During his revision of *Brother Jonathan*, Neal had unveiled a grand plan to the publisher designed not only to insure the success of the novel but, more important, to help make *Maga* vastly more popular in America. *Maga*, he proposed, should publish a series of North American tales written by himself. These, along with occasional literary critiques and essays on American affairs, would be eagerly looked for in the United States and would secure for *Blackwood's* "a pre-eminence over the *native journals*." While the novel was in press, he wrote again about his scheme and its revolutionary potentialities: "They are making prodigious efforts in America now, for the promotion of native literature. Your Maga, I hope and believe, will become a sort of *dictator*. I wish it for many reasons: for your sake; my own—& for that of America. It will operate a reform there." [22]

To spur Blackwood's approval of his plan, Neal wrote and submitted a preface to his projected series of tales and also several

21. Neal to Blackwood, July 30, September 1 and 28, 1825, NLS.

22. "Holmes" to Blackwood, March 22 and May 10, 1825, NLS. Neal was encouraged to make his proposal by Blackwood's request for confidential information about Messrs. Wilder and Campbell of New York, who had arranged with the publisher to distribute *Maga* in the United States on a trial basis. See Blackwood to "Holmes," February 19, 1825, Blackwood Letter Books. Neal's reply, February 27, 1825, NLS, hints at the grand plan which he later elaborated.

stories. One of the stories—probably titled "New-England Witch-craft" and later expanded by Neal into the novel *Rachel Dyer*—the publisher found "very striking and powerful"; it was paid for and set in type but, because of its great length, not printed ("it would have destroyed it to have divided it"). But John Neal, after the failure of *Brother Jonathan,* had lost the electrical appeal of Carter Holmes. Blackwood rejected his preface and new stories, and he ignored Neal's repeated inquiries about the publication of his witch-craft story. The American therefore turned to other magazines.

After several months of silence Neal wrote a stiff note asking for the return of the proof sheets of his story. "Publicity is a part of the recompense for which I stipulated," he reminded his former friend and patron. Blackwood coldly replied that he could have the story "with pleasure" when he returned the twelve guineas he was paid for it. The publisher took the occasion to convey his un-happiness about Neal's references to *Maga* in the current issue of the *European Magazine and London Review.* In his "Reply to Mr. Mathews: By a Native Yankee," Neal had breezily identified him-self as a writer for *Blackwood's* and cited several of his contri-butions. "This is neither customary nor delicate . . . and I hope it will not be repeated," says Blackwood.[23] A *Maga* contributor either wrote exclusively for *Maga* or, when he strayed or was cut loose, had the tact not to mention it publicly.

The native Yankee immediately took pen in hand and, in eight explosive pages, blew to smithereens any remaining vestiges of this remarkable rapprochement between American and Scottish letters. Blackwood, he suggested, had been frightened away from Neal's bold writings by "your Delta" (D. M. Moir), a man not truly fitted for *Maga* either as poet or critic—"too pigeon livered by far." The North American tales had been written to prepare the public for *Brother Jonathan,* and Blackwood's failure to publish them contributed to the failure of the novel. Did Blackwood believe

23. "Holmes" to Blackwood, November 24, 1824, NLS; Blackwood to "Holmes," April 14, 1825, Blackwood Letter Books; Neal to Blackwood, September 1, 21, 28, October 10, 1825, January 31, 1826, NLS; Blackwood to Neal, February 6, 1826, Blackwood Letter Books.

him to be a hack writer who would be satisfied by pay without publication, "to be made use of, and let fly, and pulled back, as by a thread whenever you thought proper?" Since the publisher would owe him, if he did not already, one hundred guineas (for *Brother Jonathan*), Neal proposed that he now pay him fifty pounds and return the proofs of "New-England Witchcraft" to clear his account. As for Blackwood's surprise at his lack of delicacy in mentioning *Maga* in a rival magazine, "I shall speak of you and your magazine, wherever and whenever it shall appear to me good to do so, without consulting other folks about their notions of delicacy." He had sought to do *Maga* a favor by mentioning it and continued to feel gratitude toward it and Blackwood for publishing papers "which nobody else wd. have had the courage to publish," but no one could address him in such a style without rebuke. "I have seen Mr. Blackwood and found him somewhat in a turmoil," wrote a friend to Neal on the day his letter reached Edinburgh. Young Langdon Elwyn was not surprised at the rift, for he never believed that two persons so different in temperament could long remain friends: "A Scotchman and a man of feeling cannot suit, they are what Chymists call incompatible." [24]

The Carter Holmes affair was not quite over. Neal returned twelve guineas for the proofs of his story, but in May he wrote Blackwood for the hundred guineas he claimed was still due him by the terms of their *Brother Jonathan* contract. Again he expressed his gratitude to the publisher and *Maga* for helping him when he was "sorely pushed," but warned that he was "not of a disposition to be put aside or trifled with, even by those I regard." Blackwood's reply, by return mail, was terse. He could only account for Neal's letter by supposing him "to labour under a fit of temporary insanity." He paid what Neal asked for his book and warned that he would not communicate further about it. Three years later a London lawyer, attempting to collect a hundred guineas for Neal, was told somewhat more gently that his client's claim was a specimen of

24. Neal to Blackwood, February 9, 1826, NLS; A. M. Langdon Elwyn to Neal, February 10, 1826, HL. Neal had given young Elwyn a letter of introduction to Blackwood in October.

his "impudence and extreme folly" and deserving only of "silent contempt." Since he was addressing a stranger, Blackwood continued, he would tell him what his employer well knew: Blackwood sustained a loss because of the total failure of the book; the contract required the sale of one thousand copies for further remuneration, but instead fewer than five hundred were sold.[25]

Forty years later Neal wrote again to the editor of *Maga* (now John Blackwood, son of the founder) recalling his involvement with the firm long years ago and inquiring whether he would be interested in more articles about America. He cited Christopher North's tribute to his "A Summary View of America" and quoted an extract from William Blackwood's letter congratulating him on the completion of his "American Writers" series. He did not quote from other, less complimentary, letters but added a postscript: "My correspondence with Mr. B. was under the name of Carter Holmes." Nothing came of the overture. It seems to have been prompted by Neal's reminiscence of William Blackwood in the *Atlantic Monthly* in which he pays warm tribute to the publisher as an "extraordinary man" and to *Maga*—with all its faults and follies "always full of earnestness and originality and tumultuous life." In his article Neal acknowledged that, in his quarrel with Blackwood, "I was chiefly to blame, but not altogether." He attributed their break to the publisher's displeasure with his references to *Maga* in the *European Magazine*: "He wanted all his contributors to himself, either in fact or in appearance." Neal played down the financial failure of *Brother Jonathan* and omitted any reference to Blackwood's and Moir's concern with what they believed to be the indecency of the book. Instead he repeated the

25. In his Preface to *Rachel Dyer* (Portland: Shirley and Hyde, 1828), p. v, Neal claims he paid for the proofs. For the controversy concerning the *Brother Jonathan* contract see Neal to Blackwood, May 15, 1826; Blackwood to Neal, May 17, 1826; John Chesterton to Blackwood, October 4, 1828; Blackwood to Chesterton, October 10, 1828; Chesterton to Blackwood, October 21 and November 14, 1828; Blackwood to Chesterton, November 19, 1828, NLS (all of Blackwood's letters are copies in his own handwriting).

charge (that must have rankled William Blackwood four decades earlier) that the book failed because excessive revision had removed all its "freedom and naturalness." [26]

The failure of *Brother Jonathan* and Blackwood's rejection of his North American tales were mortal blows to Neal's campaign for a literary fame that would equal or surpass that of Irving and Cooper. He later asserted that his novel had been scheduled for republication in America but had never appeared because the sheets forwarded to Charles Wiley (Cooper's publisher) had been suppressed. The firm's records have not survived to document this claim. In any event Neal's most ambitious novel was scarcely noticed in his native land. He did, however, claim for his campaign a victory of a different kind:

> When it is remembered, that, up to this period, May, 1824, no American had ever found his way into any of these periodicals, and that American affairs were dealt with in short, insolent paragraphs, full of . . . downright misrepresentation, as if they were dealing with Fejee Islanders, or Timbuctoos, it must be admitted . . . that my plan was both well-conceived, and well-carried out.

But whatever satisfaction he could derive from his successful invasion of *Maga* and other periodicals, his grand dream of the great American novel and an international fame was shattered. After his break with Blackwood, he "gave up the idea of astonishing the natives [in America]." [27] By the time he returned home in June 1827 he was no longer the chief rival of Cooper.

For almost a year and a half prior to his return Neal had set aside literary campaigns for an intense involvement with utilitarianism. He had been introduced to Jeremy Bentham's writings while studying law under Professor David Hoffman and had

26. Letter dated from Portland, September 15, 1865, HL; "William Blackwood," pp. 672, 671, 668–69.
27. "William Blackwood," p. 670; *Wandering Recollections*, pp. 251–52.

unsuccessfully attempted, in Baltimore, to interest a publisher in subsidizing a Neal translation of Bentham's *Théorie des peines et des récompenses*. Despite his great admiration for the philosopher and the fact that Bentham lived just a few hundred yards from his Warwick Street lodgings, Neal did not meet the great man until November 1825. After distinguishing himself in a debate with some young Utilitarians (including eighteen year-old John Stuart Mill, "with a girlish face and womanly voice . . . yet a formidable antagonist"), Neal was invited to dinner at the Hermitage. The philosopher was impressed with the brash American, and Neal soon after moved from lodgings surrounded by the aura of Washington Irving to rooms in Bentham's home "occupied not long before by Aaron Burr." There he lived for more than a year working on a translation of Bentham's *Traités de législation* and assisting the Utilitarian cause in a variety of ways as "a Down-East Yankee at the court of King Jeremy."

Eventually, however, the atmosphere clouded. Neal quarreled with Bentham's housekeeper and, worse, with his secretary, John Bowring ("the busiest of busybodies and the slipperiest"). As editor of the *Westminster Review* Bowring arbitrarily inserted a passage into an article by Neal ("United States"), making it appear that the author was attacking American literature ("the very reverse of what I did say . . . and for which I have had to suffer from that day to this among my countrymen"). Bowring's intense dislike for "the rough republican" may have colored his account of what Bentham said about Neal and his novel: "Neal's 'Brother Jonathan' is really the most execrable stuff . . . Neal is a nondescript . . . I might as well have had a rattlesnake in my house as that man." On record, however, is the letter Bentham wrote to Neal in early April 1827 (from one room to another) rejecting his young disciple's request for money "to enable you to try your fortune, or see the world, or both, at Paris." He would supply what is necessary for the price of a passage "to your own country" but "the money will not be receivable by you or to your use till you are there." "From what I have witnessed," the philosopher concluded, "I can not but think that for talents such as yours the country that gave birth to them is the most appropriate theatre." Very soon after, on April 14, Neal sailed for home—arranging his itinerary to include a one-month stopover in Paris.[28]

28. For this episode see Neal's diary and account of his stay in the Bentham household reproduced in Neal's Introduction to *Principles of Legislation: From the MS. of Jeremy Bentham* . . . , tr. John Neal (Boston: Wells and Lilly, 1830), esp. pp. 41–55; also Neal's "Jeremy Bentham," *Atlantic Monthly* 16 (1865):575–83; and *Wandering Recollections*, pp. 51–57, 273–75, 300–301. Neal's involvement with utilitarianism is treated comprehensively in Peter J. King, "John Neal as Benthamite," *New England Quarterly* 39 (1966):47–65. For Neal's quarrel with Bowring see Benjamin Lease, "John Neal's Quarrel with the *Westminster Review*," *American Literature* 26 (1954):86–88. For Bentham's opinion of Neal and his novel as reported by Bowring see Bowring's edition of *The Works of Jeremy Bentham* (Edinburgh, 1843), 10:555–56. Bentham's letter to Neal, headed "J.B. to J.N." and dated "April 1827," is in the Neal Papers, HL; Neal has added a marginal comment: "J. Bowring owed me 200£ at the time this was written. . . . The letter is full of strange errors. . . ." For Neal's departure from England see "Trip to Paris," *The Yankee and Boston Literary Gazette*, n.s. 1 (1829):157.

II
intimations and absurdities,
1816-1826

6 Yankee Poetics

*Yes, I do . . . believe that we
shall see poetry done away with—
the poetry of form, I mean—
of rhyme, measure, and cadence.*

RANDOLPH

From Neal's voluminous and scattered critical writings during the first decade of his literary career emerges a rough-hewn but fairly consistent set of principles concerning the nature and function of American literature. He was indeed, as Alexander Cowie suggests, an "eager apostle" and "a colorful critic . . . during the difficult days when American writers were just beginning to *be* American." [1] Like a host of other critics clamoring for literary independence after the War of 1812, he absorbed some of the ideas of the Scottish common-sense philosophers and associationist aestheticians—ideas that encouraged the quest for nationality in literature. [2] But literary nationalism for Neal's *Portico* colleagues—and for most of the other early advocates of cultural independence—meant writing about new subjects in the same old way, a way that was not up-setting to conventional standards of style or morality. Hugh Blair's tenets are reflected in this typical assessment from *The Portico*:

1. *The Rise of the American Novel* (New York, 1948), pp. 177, 165.
2. See William Charvat, *The Origins of American Critical Thought, 1810–1835* (New York, 1961), pp. 27–58 and passim; Benjamin T. Spencer, *The Quest for Nationality: An American Literary Campaign* (Syracuse, N.Y., 1957), pp. 73–101; Robert E. Streeter, "Association Psychology and Literary Nationalism in the *North American Review*, 1815–1825," *American Literature* 17 (1945):243–54.

"The diction is often low and unsuited to the subject; the construction of the sentences frequently ungrammatical, and the phrases sometimes vulgar." John Pierpont's *Airs of Palestine* is indebted to Byron's *Hebrew Melodies,* but Pierpont gags at the licentiousness of *Don Juan:* "[Byron] is already corrupt, and if he writes much longer he will make others so." [3] From such fastidiousness Neal stands boldly apart. "There seems a kind of style and expression peculiarly appropriated to the subject of morality," he complains, labeling such discourse as frigid and hypocritical. Moralistic novels, like those of Maria Edgeworth, "aim to instruct the publick" while romances, through exaggeration, "take captive the hearts of the mighty." Neal prefers the romance. Byron's attacks on conventional morality are vindicated by his genius: "We get to approve crime, it is made so dazzlingly glorious by his magick." [4] The elegance and gentility of Washington Irving represented an ideal to most American critics of the early 1820s—including the literary nationalists proud of his international fame. Harold C. Martin has suggested that "The first sharp deviation from this Irvingesque graciousness is to be found . . . in the work of John Neal, the Ezra Pound of early nineteenth century criticism." [5]

On the eve of his precipitous departure from Baltimore, Neal described himself as "a compound of contradictory properties" which threatened to destroy each other. As a self-educated Yankee who has lived long in the South, he was too impetuous and emotional for the North and too methodical for the romantic tempera-

3. Review of *"Researches on America . . . ,"* *The Portico* 2 (1816): 110; see also John C. McCloskey, "The Campaign of Periodicals after the War of 1812 for a National American Literature," PMLA 50 (1935), 267–68. Pierpont's displeasure with Byron's licentiousness is expressed in a letter to Neal, October 9, 1819, PML.

4. For Neal on the style of moralists see his "The Moralist," *Federal Republican and Baltimore Telegraph,* March 20, 1819, Neal's scrapbook, HL. For Neal on Byron's immorality see "Criticism: Lord Byron," *The Portico* 3 (1817):61.

5. "The Development of Style in Nineteenth-Century American Fiction," in *Style in Prose Fiction: English Institute Essays, 1958,* ed. Harold C. Martin (New York, 1959), p. 128.

ment of the South. But, he wryly observes, "oil and water have been mixed heretofore; and why may not fire and water be mixed —or snow and fire, poetry and mathematics, literature and law, truth and falsehood, great wisdom with great folly?" Neal's "compound of contradictory properties" is a crude variation on Coleridge's view of great art springing from a "reconciliation of opposites"—from a harmony achieved by resolving the antagonism between emotion and control. Whitman sensed this tension, says F. O. Matthiessen, but "evaded the problem . . . in his eagerness 'to let nature speak, without check, with original energy.' " His eager evasion resulted in a great American poem. Neal, a decade before Poe and three decades before Whitman, failed. But F. L. Pattee, who finds Neal and Whitman very similar in personality, fails to look beneath the surface when he calls Neal "a mere literary David Crockett . . . who believed he could roar himself into a classic."

"Critics may talk as they please," observed Whittier in 1830, "but for ourselves we *do* like the bold, vigorous and erratic style of Neal. We could fall asleep over the delicately rounded period and the studied and labored paragraph, but the startling language —the original idea, standing out in bold relief of all its native magnificence, rouse up our blood like a summoning trumpet-call." It was more than a sense of personal gratitude that prompted Poe to regard Neal as one endowed with a "philosophical and self-dependent spirit which has always distinguished him, and which will even yet lead him . . . to do something for the literature of the country which the country 'will not willingly,' and cannot possibly 'let die.' " [6]

Neal's enthusiastic reception by *Blackwood's Magazine*—so

6. "Yankee Notions," *London Magazine*, n.s. 4 (1826):445–46; F. O. Matthiessen, *American Renaissance* (New York, 1941), pp. 566–67; Fred Lewis Pattee, *The First Century of American Literature, 1770–1870* (New York, 1935), p. 283; *Whittier on Writers and Writing: The Uncollected Critical Writings of John Greenleaf Whittier*, ed. E. H. Cady and H. H. Clark (Syracuse, N.Y., 1950), p. 46; "Marginalia" [1848], in *The Complete Works of Edgar Allan Poe*, ed. James A. Harrison (New York, 1902), 16:131.

puzzling to Pattee—stems in part from the fact that he brought to
the journal a point of view to a considerable extent derived from
it. A. W. Schlegel's principle of effect was enthusiastically adopted
by J. G. Lockhart at the time he joined the editorial staff of *Maga*
in 1817; *Blackwood's* was widely read and contributed significantly to the spread of Schlegelian doctrine in Baltimore and Philadelphia.[7] Margaret Alterton has documented Poe's intensive study
of *Maga* while he was developing his critical theory; some of the
numbers he studied featured portions of Neal's "American Writers"
series and his "Late American Books." Neal had come to know
Blackwood's well before becoming a contributor, and it is not
surprising that his poetic theory foreshadows and influences Poe's.[8]

7. Evidence of the keen interest in Schlegelian doctrine is to be
found, for example, in the pages of the *Port Folio* which published in six
numbers between 1817 and 1819 a discussion of and five extracts from A.
W. von Schlegel's *A Course of Lectures on Dramatic Art and Literature*,
trans. John Black, 2 vols. (London, Edinburgh, and Dublin, 1815). See
Hanna-Beate Schilling, "The Role of the Brothers Schlegel in American
Literary Criticism as Found in Selected Periodicals, 1812–1833: A Critical
Bibliography," *American Literature* 43 (1972):566–69. Neal was a contributor to this Philadelphia monthly magazine in 1816 and was closely
associated with it until he quarrelled with its editor, John E. Hall, in 1823.
It is true, as Dr. Schilling suggests (pp. 564–65), that American critics
(including Neal and Poe) sifted Schlegelian doctrine for those concepts
that served their needs and that the word "influence" should be used
cautiously. For other studies of Schlegel's importance in America, see
the following note.
    8. For Schlegel's importance, see Charvat, *The Origins of American
Critical Thought*, pp. 56–57; Alterton, *The Origins of Poe's Critical Theory*
(Iowa City, 1925), pp. 7–45. For Poe's indebtedness to Schlegel, see Albert
J. Lubbell, "Poe and A. W. Schlegel," *Journal of English and Germanic
Philology* 52 (1953):1–12. Poe's psychological concept of effect is discussed in Walter Blair, "Poe's Conception of Incident and Tone in the
Tale," *Modern Philology* 41 (1944):228–40. Neal's influence on Poe is
briefly examined in J. J. Rubin, "John Neal's Poetics as an Influence on
Whitman and Poe," *New England Quarterly* 14 (1941):359–62. For a
provocative exploration of Poe's involvement with *Blackwood's* in terms of
his search for an audience, see Michael Allen, *Poe and the British Magazine Tradition* (New York, 1969).

In his criticism, Neal is primarily concerned with effect, with the varied responses of readers to varied literary stimuli. Man's faculties, according to Neal (and most of his contemporaries), consist of the *brain,* the *blood,* and the *heart.* Brain writings are excluded from the scope of true literature because they are the products of artificial effort and skill. The blood is aroused to sublimity by those mysterious, grand, indistinct manifestations of nature which suggest the unknown and unknowable. The heart is stirred to sympathy by the vivid, realistic, unadorned manifestation of another heart. The central problem of authorship, according to Neal, is concerned with the ways in which the writer incorporates into his work qualities analogous to those in nature.[9]

The productions of the blood poet are peopled with supernatural entities or human beings cloaked in mystery. Their setting is nature at its grandest and most mysterious. Pierpont's *Airs* lacks greatness because it has "finish and distinctness, sunshine and tranquility." In contrast, "That is *great,* that is *sublime,* which operates upon you like the appearance of a mountain enveloped in clouds . . . when you cannot see its *outline* or measure its altitude . . . —our terrour[,] our tumult when we are excited attributes eternity—boundlessness to everything mysterious." Decades later Poe was to say much the same thing in a different way: "We can, at any time, double the beauty of an actual landscape by half closing our eyes as we look at it."[10] Anticipating Poe's famous denial of the possibility of a long poem, Neal argues that it is impossible to read a poem as long as one of the Waverley novels, for "in the confusion of such a beautiful and confounding exhibition of power and brightness, your senses would lose all their

9. This account draws on my "Yankee Poetics: John Neal's Theory of Poetry and Fiction," *American Literature* 24 (1953) :505–19.

10. See Neal's "Should not all supernatural agency . . . cease with the credibility that gave it interest?" Delphian Club Records, year 3 (1818), sess. 111, Maryland Historical Society, and his review of Pierpont's "Airs of Palestine," *Federal Republican and Baltimore Telegraph,* March 25, 1819, Neal's scrapbook, HL. Poe's statement is in "Marginalia" [1849], *Works,* 16:164.

activity: they would reel under it; and retain no distinct impression at all." Poe probably read and was struck by this passage from *Randolph;* in his *Literati* he refers knowledgeably to Neal's *Errata* and *Seventy-Six,* and to *The Battle of Niagara,* whose preface includes a similar observation. What is certain is that both Neal and Poe were responsive to what Charvat calls *"Blackwood's* doctrine of the short poem, adopted from Schlegel."[11]

The poet of the blood transcends nature as he sees and hears things with other senses during these visitations; his spontaneous utterances strike fire within us, arouse us to a sense of the poet within all of us: "We might have died, without thinking that we were combustible, but for something that had jarred all our blood, like an earthquake."[12] Neal believed, however, that a significant transformation was taking place in the literature of his time, a shift from grandeur and magnificence to realism and passion, from poetry of the blood to literature of the heart. In the poems of the future "man must be the hero—and his heart the world which is convulsed in his career: the passions of man are the most terrible ministers—more terrible—infinitely more so, than the familiars of Milton's angel."[13] Sympathy—the response of one heart to another —is a powerful force in literature because it is a powerful force in life:

> Call up a mother, who has just lost her infant—bid her tell the story—look at her—study her. There is no weary-ing preparation. She repeats the same thing, over and over again, a hundred times.—There is no poetry; no play of the imagination, in what she says. There is not even the simplest observance of rule—her sentences

11. The quoted passage is from *Randolph,* 2:187. In his Preface to *Niagara,* p. xlviii, Neal observes that "the reason given [by a reviewer] why Niagara is fatiguing is a just one—the imagery is too high wrought, crowded and thronging." For Poe's comments on Neal's novels and *Niagara* see "The Literati of New York City," no. 2, *Godey's Lady's Book* 32 (1846):271. Charvat, *The Origins of American Critical Thought,* p. 57.

12. *Randolph,* 2:186.

13. "Should not all supernatural agency . . . ," Delphian Club Records.

> are short—broken—exclamatory—familiar—colloquial
> —vulgar, it may be, and ungrammatical. But your tears
> follow—and your heart heaves to it.[14]

Shakespeare is most moving when most simple—when through spontaneous touches of natural eloquence the man only is heard, not the poet and dramatist. Such a poignant moment occurs "when Lear rebukes the angels of the storm, and then submits uncomplainingly *for they were not his daughters*; or where he first meets mad Tom, and enquires if he too, had given crowns to his daughters, and will not believe that ought else beneath the skies could so subdue a man." [15]

A new literature of the heart will leave the old false forms behind. In *Randolph* (1823) and "American Writers" (1824–25) Neal boldly prophesies the organicism of Emerson and Whitman. The day is rapidly approaching, he says, when the poetry of conventional meter must give way to a mightier poetry in prose. He suggests that "rhyme, or blank verse, or *regular* rhythm, is altogether as artificial, unnatural, and preposterous a mode of expression, for the true poet; as the use of a foreign idiom . . . to the true home-bred man." He looks toward the time when new poets will learn

> that *poetry* is always poetry—however it may be expressed; that rhythm, cadence (regular cadence)—rhyme
> —alliteration, riddles, and acrostics, are all beneath poetry; that better poetry has been said in prose, than ever has been said—or ever will be said—either in blank verse or rhyme. Poetry and eloquence have a rhythm and cadence of their own; as incapable of being soberly graduated by rule, as the rambling, wild melody of an Aeolian harp.

The new prose-poetry will reflect the vitality and variety of live talk. He deplores the prevailing tendency of writers to employ an inflexible style, either in "the sleepy milk and water-school of

14. *Randolph,* 2:206.

15. "What Is the Chief Excellency of Shakespeare?" *The Portico* 5 (1818):417.

Addison" or "intemperate and florid": "No matter what may be the theme, their language is the same." Seven decades before Mark Twain's corrosive commentary on "Fenimore Cooper's Literary Offenses," Neal lashes out at the same target in remarkably similar terms:

> [Cooper] is afraid of his dignity, perhaps; . . . afraid, if he put bad grammar into the mouths of people, who, as everybody knows, talk nothing else, in real life, that he himself may be charged with bad grammar. We are sorry for this. It is a great error; but one which we hope to see done away with on every side, before long—every-where—by everybody. Truth is not vulgarity; nor is truth refinement.[16]

Truth is neither vulgarity nor refinement; neither is it un-alloyed bliss or sorrow. In life tears and laughter may be the almost simultaneous manifestations of the same inner turmoil. Neal says of his *Rachel Dyer*: "The mixture of nonsense and sublimity, of tragedy and farce did not occur from a want of self-denial in the author, but from *design*." Just as the profound poignance of *Lear* is intensified by a simple and spontaneous touch, so "the tragic might be heightened by the comic if it were interspersed ju-diciously." This view may have reached Neal through *Blackwood's* or from an encounter with John Black's 1815 translation of Schlegel's *Lectures*. In his lecture on Shakespeare Schlegel observes that "The comic intervals everywhere serve to . . . preserve the mind in the possession of its serenity, and to keep off that gloomy

---

16. *Randolph*, 2:187; *American Writers*, pp. 89–90; *Randolph*, 2:174; *American Writers*, p. 213. Neal expresses a similar viewpoint in his prolific writings about art and architecture. In *Randolph*, 1:65, more than seventy years before the prophetic utterances of Frank Lloyd Wright, Neal decries the deceptive use of materials in a Baltimore church: "a piece of exquisite deception—manufactured of *lime-stone*, wooden-bronze, and pine-marble; that is, . . . plastered and stuccoed, till the eye is completely deceived into a notion that it is stone." For Neal's importance as a pioneer critic of American art see *Observations on American Art: Selections from the Writings of John Neal*, ed. Harold E. Dickson (State College, Pa.: Pennsyl-vania State University Press, 1943), Introduction.

and inert seriousness which so easily steals upon the sentimental, but not tragical, drama." [17]

Authentic emotion (alternating freely between pathos and farce) through a flexible style incorporating live talk is part of a larger concern: the depiction of authentic character. Neal rebukes those authors who, looking at literary models rather than life, construct diverting surfaces instead of live characters capable of eliciting sympathy. He calls attention to the artificiality of a Bulwer novel in which characters are created "by the eternal repetition of a few favourite words. . . . They are too Cooperish by half." The heart "assents" only to those who possess true individuality and "the affecting signs of humanity." In America it is in New England that one finds such authentic individuality. No other part of the country has preserved such complete homogeneity of character: all its people are alike in that they are all different, that is, uncompromising individualists.[18]

These New Englanders are not always admirable. Neal classifies the Yankee in ethical terms as "unperverted" and "perverted"; each of these may be—to the extent he is exposed to the larger world—"illuminated" or "unilluminated." The Yankee character, he suggests, "is formidable; unperverted and unilluminated, it is remarkable for sobriety, invincible steadiness and good faith. But illuminated and perverted—or perverted alone, it is either destructive and wasting, or the perfection of rascality." Frequent

17. Neal's comment on *Rachel Dyer* is in "Rachel Dyer," *The Yankee and Boston Literary Gazette* (hereafter referred to as *The Yankee*) 2 (1829):39. The observation about the comic intensifying the tragic in Shakespeare is made in a summation of the views of A. W. Schlegel and others in Karl S. Guthke, *Modern Tragicomedy* (New York, 1966), p. 31; A. W. von Schlegel, *Lectures on Dramatic Art and Literature*, trans. John Black, 2d ed. (London, 1886), p. 370.

18. For Neal on Bulwer see his review of *The Disowned*, *The Yankee* 2 (1829):86; for Neal on the New Englander see his "Character of the Real Yankees: What They Are Supposed to Be, and What They Are," *The New Monthly Magazine and Literary Journal* 17 (1826):253–56; and "Sketches of American Character . . . ," *The European Magazine and London Review*, n.s. 1 (1825):374–75.

satiric targets are satanic Yankees who "go about the business of worldly thrift and absolute fraud, precisely as they go about their worship"; but Neal is also eager to see literary justice done to the unperverted Yankee—illuminated and unilluminated.[19]

Individual though he may be, the Yankee is also representative of mankind in his vigorous display of traits common to all men; he is, as a result, capable of eliciting sympathy in all men. It is not inconsistent, then, for Neal to deplore the excessive regionalism of Scott's fiction when it is so local and particular that characters are unintelligible to any but Scotsmen. Nor is it inconsistent for him to call for the occasional depiction of authentic characters not fixed in the New England milieu. His appeal is grounded in psychology rather than chauvinism. America, he claims, possesses materials most rewarding for literary representation, and New England is held to be a uniquely rich segment of America. Other regions of the world have produced admirable, individualistic peoples, for example, Scotland, but historical circumstances have made Americans and New Englanders better exemplars of traits common to all mankind and the best possible exemplars to American readers.[20]

However authentic and individualistic he may be, the character of the New Englander does not emerge under static conditions: "Without affliction; without trial, discipline, and sorrow, where was there ever a great man?—or a great virtue? Not upon this earth. The strongly rooted are known only in the strong wind." But the fictional re-creation of affliction and trial cannot be achieved through conventional plot, that is, an artificial patterning of events

---

19. "Character of the Real Yankees," p. 256.

20. *Randolph*, 1:217–18; Neal, "United States," *Westminster Review* 5 (1826):194. Neal also looks to the West as a rich source of vigorous, colloquial tales. See his "Story-Telling," *The New-England Magazine* 8 (1835):9. Neal's interest in the evocative power of regional realism seems to have been first whetted by James Kirke Paulding's *Letters from the South* (New York, 1817), which he read with enthusiasm shortly after its appearance; see his review of "Paulding's Works," vols. 5 and 6, *The New-England Galaxy*, October 31, 1835. The *Letters* struck him as "hearty and positively American; peculiar, vigorous and healthy."

that leaves all loose ends neatly tied at the close of the story. Events in real life—chaotic, disjointed, incomplete though they may be—stir the spectator when they involve real people. These qualities need to be preserved if fiction is to have its proper effect. To insure arousing the maximum degree of sympathy, Neal suggests that the writer subordinate all characters to one central figure. The psychological principle is analogous to that invoked in his argument against excessive length in poetry of the blood. Just as the senses "reel" if subjected to an excess of "power and brightness," so does the heart "dissipate" its sympathetic response if there are several leading characters of equal importance. The affinity between fictional character and reader is strengthened when it flows in a single channel, and is weakened when diverted into several tributaries.[21]

A pioneering study by J. J. Rubin in 1941 offers evidence that Neal's poetics had an influence on Whitman and Poe.[22] Whitman was a contributor to the journal *Brother Jonathan* during Neal's involvement with that flamboyant periodical. A copy of Neal's *Rachel Dyer* was in the library at Jamaica, on Long Island, where Whitman worked as librarian and printer; its preface, Rubin points out, "reads like a challenge to the later author of *Leaves of Grass.*" Whitman may have also read, in the preface to *The Down-Easters*, Neal's appeal to American writers to adopt and use the American language; and he may have also seen in the pages of the *New York Aurora* the opinions of "our own superb and glorious Neal" on the universality of the poetic impulse. *Sartain's Union Magazine* published a contribution by Whitman, following it with Neal's "What is Poetry?" and Poe's "The Poetic Principle." "It is not strange," observes Rubin, "that there are passages in 'The Poetic Principle' which are reminiscent of Neal's papers."

That Neal could influence two writers so dissimilar points to his importance as a transitional figure—and to the "contradictory properties" in contention within him. In his poetry and fiction Neal

21. *Randolph*, 2:57; review of *The Idle Man, Baltimore Morning Chronicle*, August or September 1822, Neal's scrapbook, HL.
22. "John Neal's Poetics as an Influence on Whitman and Poe."

attempts what may be the impossible task of accommodating Schlegelian doctrine to other influences: Gothicism and Godwinism (as reflected in Charles Brockden Brown); the sensibility of Richardson and Sterne; Byronism and the Storm and Stress revolt against didacticism and abstract generalization. In the 1830s Poe was to draw on *Blackwood's* and the Schlegelian principle of effect while perfecting his tightly constructed tales. More than a decade earlier Neal was moved by this same doctrine to break loose from conventional literary patterns and produce what F. O. Matthiessen has called "the slipshod volumes of John Neal . . . , a kind of cross between Byron and Cooper, 'the damned ranting stuff' that Hawthorne had relished so much on its appearance while he was an undergraduate." [23] A closer look at these works may help explain young Hawthorne's fascination with them. With all their crudities and absurdities, they are a significant foreshadowing —in ways the works of Irving and Cooper are not—of the coming of Hawthorne, Melville, Whitman, Twain.

23. *American Renaissance*, p. 201.

7 Yankee Byronism
Keep Cool and
Other Early Works

*Where is there a society in the whole world
that has not polished down all the ruggedness,
distinctness, asperity, and angular expression,
of its members into a general uniformity
—uninteresting and fatal?*

KEEP COOL

The gulf between Neal's prophetic vision of a native literature and his own capacity to fulfill that vision is painfully apparent in his first novel, *Keep Cool* (1817).[1] Its preface proclaims associationist doctrine in bold Whitmanesque prose: "The time will arrive, when the production of American science and genius, will bear some proportion to the scale of their inspiration . . . when our posterity will wonder that we could ever have doubted the everlasting charter of greatness that is written upon our barriers;—our cataracts—our rivers—and our mountains." But what follows these brave words is a seesaw succession of Shandean antics and Richardsonian melodramatics. There is another preface, this one a burlesque review calling attention to the weaknesses of *Keep Cool*; and there is a review of the review, castigating it as "a laborious effort to conceal the most disgusting vanity under a veil of pleasantry. The author cannot think, that what he calls faults in this *novel*, are really so, or he would have removed them." The opening portion of the story itself continues in the manner of Sterne, centering on Charles Percy, a former Army captain who is amusingly foppish and susceptible to all the ladies. Suddenly and unaccountably he is transformed into a passionate, jealous lover

1. *Keep Cool: A Novel*, 2 vols. (Baltimore: Joseph Cushing, 1817). All references are to this edition.

81

who provokes a duel in which he is fatally wounded. Percy's involuntary antagonist is the Byronic Colonel Henri Sydney, an Englishman, who does penance for his deed by fleeing civilization to live among the Indians. After two years of voluntary exile—and many adventures—he returns to kneel at a portrait of Percy and is silently joined by the lovely Laura St. Vincent. (She has been described earlier: "That form so ethereal, so visionary, bending over a superb harp— . . . her rich locks floating like a dark mist around her.") They kneel together "in speechless gratitude to Heaven," and the "Fair Reader" is notified in an arch afterword that the Hero and Heroine are married and have blessed the world with a brace of as beautiful cherubs as ever shook their curling heads in the sunshine.

Absurd sentimentalism is somewhat counterbalanced by absurd humor. "Keep Cool, reader" is an intermittent refrain reminding us (rather superfluously) not to take things too seriously. Early in the novel Captain Percy takes charge of a Shandean boardinghouse dinner, signalling the various courses as if they are phases of a military operation. In the midst of a book full of sentimental rant, a character cries out: "I may be romantick; but I would blow my brains out this very moment if I thought mine was the sickening, snivelling romance of *novels*" (1:73). Shortly after what seems a typically lush description of the ethereal heroine entrancing her admirers with a harp recital, we are given this breezy vignette of the aftermath:

> Laura was still the theme of every tongue; every lady in New-York, who was able to spare sixty, seventy, or a hundred dollars, had bought either a harp, or a substitute; and from one extremity to the other of the city, at all hours, day or night, foul weather or fair, in every by-alley and crooked street, you would see a window up, and something wrapped in a white, flowing, fantastical dress—rattling, and thrumming, and shrieking over a harp—and nine out of ten, would have a wreath of scarlet flowers, with a spring hook, like a bracelet, to be loosened at pleasure. (1:106)

The playful piling on of phrases and clauses and the easy, malicious colloqualism in sentences like this prompted a contemporary reviewer to complain about the author's "too great a fondness for colloquial phrases and expressions, and too little attention to the proper connexion of his sentences." In a later age, if he had encountered it, Mark Twain might have relished such a sentence as much as he cheerfully detested the genteel style and "singularly dull" word-sense of Fenimore Cooper. In this century F. L. Pattee has called Neal "the first in America to be natural in his diction," a judgment given some support by his first novel—with all its shortcomings.[2]

Keep Cool has been described by Arthur Hobson Quinn as an "immature and wandering" attack on duelling and defense of the Indians. Concerning its immaturity and digressiveness there can be no doubt; but a basic question exists about the didacticism of this or any other Neal novel or tale. Neal's fictional characters bristle with ideas and opinions, frequently Neal's own, but the consequence—when they have bristled successfully—is a sympathetic identification of the reader with what Hans-Joachim Lang has called the "moral energy" of the character, not an acceptance of his view. Neal's doctrine of effect establishes the greater importance of the manner in which an idea is presented over the intrinsic value of the idea itself: "So, *one* powerful thought, though it be not the very best in the world, will be remembered forever, when judiciously applied, where many that are better, if crowded together, will be forgotten as soon as heard." A contemporary critic of *Keep Cool* suggests that Echo (a poet-genius who discourses on many subjects) strikes us as "a perfect original" in part because he possesses "such a power of making the worse appear the better reason" that the reader is simultaneously pleased and surprised. This critic for the *Western Spy,* in 1822, may be more closely attuned than Quinn to the Schlegelian doctrine of

2. "Keep Cool," *The Portico* 4 (1817):169; Samuel L. Clemens, "Fenimore Cooper's Literary Offenses," *North American Review* 161 (1895): 1–12; Pattee, ed., Introduction to *American Writers*, p. 12.

effect that underlies Neal's criticism and fiction.[3] The numerous causes set forth so passionately in Neal's first novel and in the works that follow are far less important than the effect—the moral energy generated among the characters who argue them. And most important among these characters is the novelist-narrator who hovers over them all and who, as in *Keep Cool,* can defend their amorphousness with a rationale both sly and cogent: "Where is there a society in the whole world that has not polished down all the ruggedness, distinctness, asperity, and angular expression, of its members into a general uniformity—uninteresting and fatal?" (1:55).

Keep Cool went virtually unnoticed, and Neal now turned to poetry. He was immersed in law studies and a laborious hack job—compiling an index to *Niles' Weekly Register*—but when Pierpont read aloud an account of the Battle of Lundy's Lane, his imagination took fire. He confined himself to his study to produce in six days an 854-line epic, *The Battle of Niagara.* While he wrote (he later reported) his consciousness was pervaded as if by a visitation from another world and he felt an exhilaration "that I cannot describe, scarcely wish to experience again, but hope I shall never lose the memory of." [4]

Although *Niagara* does not conform to the Schlegelian doctrine of the short poem, it has all the other characteristics Neal ascribes to a work designed to arouse the "blood." Two sets of characters act out the tumultuous events: mortal beings, human and animal, and such entities as Thunderer, spirit of the sun; Ontario, spirit of the Lake; and a host of other spirits, "unseen—and unknown—but thick as stars." The poem opens with a description of a giant eagle mounting the skies to commune with Thunderer. Through

3. Arthur Hobson Quinn, *American Fiction: An Historical and Critical Survey* (New York, 1936), p. 48; Hans-Joachim Lang, "Critical Essays and Stories by John Neal," *Jahrbuch für Amerikastudien* 7 (1962) :208; the writer for the *Western Spy* is quoted in "American Literature," *Boston Commercial Gazette,* October 4, 1822, Neal's scrapbook, HL.

4. *Niagara,* p. xxviii.

the eyes of the wheeling bird we see a troop of American horsemen silently traversing a mountain path toward the enemy camp. The men are uniformly tall, gallant, and fearless and their leader is "a warrior of flame!—on a courser of night." In the midst of battle his sword flashes above all others like "a bolt of heaven" as he rides "firm and high . . . all bone—all strength." In keeping with such idealized treatment, none of the soldiers is identified by name, for as Neal points out in the preface, "as yet, we have no *names*, except that of Washington, that can give dignity to any poem" (p. xii). Perhaps to counteract the danger of fatiguing the reader with too prolonged a display of power, Neal alternates gay and somber horsemen in the opening canto, scenes of martial intrepidity and domestic tenderness in the second, exultation and portent in the third. The foreboding atmosphere with which the fourth canto opens is followed by the climactic battle, carried out amidst hovering visitants. The brief final canto describes the field the morning after and is a dying fall to the tumultuous alarums of battle that precede it.

Setting and language similarly augment this poem of the blood. Here Neal pictures the great cataract at which the battle is fought:

> Bounding off—all in foam—from the echoing height—
> Like a rank of young war-horses terribly bright
> Their manes all erect!—and their hoofs in the air!
> The earth shaking under them—trumpets on high—
> And banners unfurling away in the sky—
>
> (p. 84)

In his characteristically candid preface, Neal confesses that the anapestic tetrameter couplets of the opening portion of the poem were written under the mistaken notion that they were iambic pentameter; it took him some time to "get fairly from the gallop of that, into the majestick jog of the heroick." About the heroic verse to which he shifts, he writes, "I made it rugged intentionally— because I do, from my soul, hate the sing song of Pope, 'two up and two down.' " In answer to critics who deplore the subordination of thought to imagery and metaphor in *Niagara*, he replies: "What is imagery but the . . . manner of thinking." Descriptive poetry—in contrast to the terrible simplicity of the language of passion—arouses the blood to the "awful, sublime, and terrible" through metaphor (pp. xxx, lviii–lx).

In Whitmanesque fashion, Neal proclaims *Niagara* to be "no neutral, no hermaphrodite." Despite—perhaps because of—its faults it is, he feels, an intuitive product of genius (p. xviii). But aside from Pierpont's awestruck response and a scattering of praise from the critics, there was little in its reception to dissuade Neal from his announced intention of giving up poetry for prose—the poetry of the future. Some of the praise elicited by the poem reflects the chauvinistic spirit of the times. One critic sees in its scenic grandeur and great events a worthy celebration of American troops victorious over "the boasted conquerors of Napoleon's legions" and deserving of the admiration of "all true-hearted Americans." None of Neal's contemporaries refers to a quality readily apparent to William Ellery Leonard, its Byronism. According to Leonard, Neal's style occasionally conveys the spontaneity and vigor of Byron—"a concrete reality, a vividness" that make *Niagara* one of the few examples of good Byronic poetry among numerous self-conscious imitations.[5]

Neal's verse tragedy *Otho* (1819) was also written under Byron's spell; his preface acknowledges a debt to "all Byron's heroes, little and big," to *The Corsair* as well as *Manfred*—and also to Maturin's *Bertram*, which he had recently seen portrayed by the great tragedian Thomas Cooper. His hero, Neal informs us, "is desperate—like Bertram, I admit; but to me this desperation seems to have a more elevated—a more terrible sublimity in it."

---

5. Joseph T. Buckingham praised the poem in the *New-England Galaxy*, August 13, 1819, Neal's scrapbook, HL; the chauvinistic tribute to *Niagara* is in a review in the *Baltimore Patriot and Mercantile Advertiser*, August 6, 1819, Neal's scrapbook, HL; Leonard, *Byron and Byronism in America* (Boston, 1905), p. 50. Leonard adds that Neal's Byronic style "was oftener burlesque exaggeration." Neal was sensitive about being called by others an imitator of Byron; see his letter to Pierpont, December 15, 1818, PML.

When Pierpont complained about the obscurity of the play (it needed "a sky-light or two" cut into it), Neal sent him a plot summary—itself rather dense. Otho is a bastard who loves Ala. When she rejects him, he disappears but continues to watch over her in various disguises. The numerous complications that follow culminate in a grand death scene. Neal claims that Otho is "a generous spirit" who acts heroically but talks simply. There is an occasional display of declamatory power, but never when Otho "feels, truly and deeply, and intensely." A brief excerpt, typical in language and tone, will convey the wide gap between plan and execution:

> *Otho is seen walking about* [in his prison cell] *in great agitation.*
> *Feeble light:*
> OTHO. No, No, I cannot sleep!
>   Would that mine hour
> of pulseless sleep had come!—that I might die,
> and pour my blood out, like a brooding curse,
> Upon the land that nourished me for death.[6]

Otho reflects Neal's deep involvement with British and European romanticism at a time when he, and many others, were making their shrillest demands for a truly native literature. W. E. Leonard observes that many American Byrons "lived on to do better work in the period following, but . . . they grew away from Byron." The Byronic-Gothic elements that dominate Neal's earliest writings persist throughout his career. His continuing penchant for elaborate mystification springs, in part, from a deeply rooted

6. Neal's comments are in his preface to *Otho* (Boston: West, Richardson and Lord, 1819), pp. iv–viii; for the exchange concerning the obscurity of *Otho*, see Neal to Pierpont, December 27, 1819, and Pierpont to Neal, January 5, 1820, PML; the quoted passage from *Otho* is on p. 52. Charvat, *The Origins of American Critical Thought*, pp. 124–25, points out that, among American critics after the War of 1812, "John Neal was almost alone in his admiration of Maturin's *Bertram*." At about the same time that Neal was praising *Bertram* (in *The Portico* 3 [1817]:421–29), a writer for *The Port Folio* attacked it as "a disgusting imitation of the Schiller-Byron school."

emotional commitment to the writings of Charles Brockden Brown. It is also a legacy of his time: The *Portico* review of *Keep Cool* complains that the author has omitted "most of the essential qualities that give *popularity* to a Novel. He has introduced no impenetrable mystery to keep alive the anxiety and terrour of his readers." [7] *The Portico* did not survive to report on the remarkable series of novels that Neal produced in 1822–23, novels heavily freighted with impenetrable mystery, with anxiety and terror, and with much more.

7. Leonard, *Byron and Byronism in America*, p. 55; *The Portico* 4 (1817):162–63.

8 "Damned Ranting Stuff" *Logan* and *Seventy-Six*

What sort of book have you written, Hath?
I hope and pray it is nothing like
the damned ranting stuff of John Neal,
which you, while at Brunswick,
relished so highly.

JONATHAN CILLEY TO NATHANIEL HAWTHORNE, 1836

In 1816 Pierpont's concern about the licentiousness of *Keep Cool* prompted Neal to revisions designed to make the book more agreeable to feminine readers. Five years later, *Logan* [1] showed no such restraint. "It is not a nice story," wrote Alexander Cowie. He observed that "sensuality, colossal hatred, delirum, rape, insanity, murder" are, among other ingredients, "the stuff out of which Neal weaves a Gothic tapestry never quite paralleled by Charles Brockden Brown or Poe." The "interminable" dream world of *Logan*, says Neal, is "without moral or design—but alive with some tremendous apparitions." [2] The novel is linked to *Niagara* as a prose poem of the blood seeking to convey an overpowering sense of the sublime—and of the horrible. It represents Neal's most ambitious effort to bridge the gap between poetry and prose.

The setting is the pre-Revolutionary frontier. A loose tissue of events and hallucinations (scarcely a plot) revolves about Logan, chief of the Mingo Indians—actually an Englishman of high birth pledged to revenge the massacre of his Indian wife's family. Harold, proud Byronic hero, is Logan's son, though they are (until a grand recognition scene) unknown to each other. Both love the same Indian girl, Loena, but Harold also comes to love Elvira,

---

1. *Logan: A Family History*, 2 vols. (Philadelphia: H. C. Carey and I. Lea, 1822). All references are to this edition.
2. Cowie, p. 167; *Wandering Recollections*, p. 223.

beautiful young wife of the elderly governor. While presumably dying of wounds inflicted by Mohawks who had seen through his Indian disguise, Logan secures Harold's promise to carry on his campaign of extermination against the white man. Harold embarks for England to plead the cause of the Indians before Parliament and encounters on shipboard Elvira (now widowed), her little son, Leopold, and a mysterious young man, Oscar. Little Leopold turns out to be Harold's son, conceived when Harold visited Elvira's bed while she was dreaming of her husband. Oscar turns out to be Harold's brother—and a former lover of Elvira. At the close of the novel, Harold and Loena return to the site of Logan's death. There Harold is shot down by Logan—not dead after all, but a madman haunting the woods. Loena falls dead on the corpse of Harold, and Logan "like some wild beast strangling in his own blood . . . gives up the ghost"—this time for good. Oscar goes mad and dies when Elvira confesses her secret shame.

High pitched absurdity from beginning to end. And yet an extraordinary poetic dimension is conveyed in many passages. Oscar, about to murder his sister in a fit of temporary madness, speaks to her as follows:

> "The whole world sleeping below me, like the beings of another planet. The stars hovering around me and over me; the heavens turning round about us, over our heads and under our feet; and we, standing as in the centre of the universe, maintaining our sublime and solitary sway, over the fish of the sea, and the beast of the field, and the fowl of the air . . . when all our united force, all our wisdom, and all our policy, cannot stay or impede the smallest of yonder lights in its journeying." (2:134–35) [3]

In their incantatory repetition of participles (*sleeping, hovering, turning, maintaining, journeying*) and their Biblical evocation of

3. Oscar has been instructed by a mysterious voice to conduct his sister to a mountain top and there to sacrifice her. At the close of the quoted rhapsody he asks her to kneel with him in a final prayer, but another voice cries *"Forbear!"* Neal, here and elsewhere, borrows from Brockden Brown's *Wieland*.

man and cosmos, these cadenced periods are an important anticipation of Whitman.

Cowie has suggested that some of the scenes in *Logan* reveal
a psychological penetration "distinctively suggestive of Poe"—
more specifically, the extravagantly gruesome Poe of *The Narrative
of Arthur Gordon Pym*.[4] He calls attention to Harold's nightmares
after he has revenged himself by raping Elvira, the governor's
wife. The rape itself is a variation on Neal's account of his dream-
visit to the bed of Abby Lord; in the novel it is Elvira who dreams
she is in the embrace of her husband. When she wakes to find
Harold standing at her bedside, "A horrible apprehension of the
truth broke upon her." Harold flees to do desperate penance for his
crime—a protracted penance filled with trances and hallucinations:

> A flaming jewel lay before him. He touched it. It crum-
> bled, and grew dark. Another!—it dissolved while he held
> it, like the ice that departs in a vapour!
> "It is a dream! all, all a dream," thought Harold
> even in his sleep: and he struggled to wake. [His dream is
> now transformed into an ecstatic vision.] . . . He felt
> himself rising from the earth! . . . The blue sky opened,
> and he entered. . . . The spirit of Elvira passed him!
> She was dead—She touched his heart with her rotten
> fingers! He screamed! and awoke. The echo of his scream
> came back to him from the skies. (1:176–92)

On the ship journeying to England the lovely Loena seems to appear before him: "She would lay her hand upon his shoulder—
he would turn; his eyes running over with heaven and love, to
press her beautiful mouth—he would turn—and the blue face of a
dead woman, with eyeless sockets, and bare teeth, would touch
his lips." Later, while lying in his berth, Harold is suddenly and
preternaturally aware of the ravening horrors separated from him by
the thickness of a plank. His blood runs cold as he envisions a
shark gorged "with the festering garbage" of the deep, perhaps
"fattened on some floating and swollen human body." He experiences an apocalyptic vision of the "measureless, bottomless soli-

4. Cowie, *Rise of the American Novel*, pp. 168–69.

tudes of the ocean upturned"—its voracious creatures "exulting in the certainty and nearness of their appointed meal" (1:291–97). Here Neal reaches beyond *Pym* toward the nether world of *White-Jacket* where, suspended between life and death after his great plunge from the yardarm, the young sailor is brushed by coiled fish and unfathomable terrors.

By February of 1822 Neal's deepest and most private emotions had found release in *Logan* and in the drafts of two other novels, *Randolph* and *Errata* (revised and published the following year, shortly before his departure for England). The pre-Revolutionary struggle between the settlers and Indians had served, in *Logan,* as a point of departure for a prose-poetic rhapsody of the blood. His research for Allen's *History of the American Revolution* and the success of Cooper's recent novel of the Revolution now suggested exciting possibilities for deploying historical events in a passionate narrative of the heart. Neal praised *The Spy* as "a capital novel" but deplored its wooden style (devoid of all "peculiarity—brilliancy—or force") and its contrived plot ("rather too full of stage-tricks and clap-traps"); he could and would do better in *Seventy-Six.*[5]

The opening sentences of *The Spy* and of *Seventy-Six* set side by side reveal the gulf between Cooper and Neal—between conventional romance and storytelling:

> It was near the close of the year 1780, that a solitary traveller was seen pursuing his way through one of the numerous little valleys of Westchester. (*The Spy*)

> Yes, my children, I will no longer delay it. (*Seventy-Six*)

Cooper expertly orients us in time and place and arouses our curiosity. Neal gives us someone talking—we know not who or what about. We eventually learn that we are reading a communication

5. A two-volume edition of *Seventy-Six* was published in Baltimore in 1823 by Joseph Robinson. A three-volume edition was published the same year in London by Whittaker and Company (see Works Cited). All textual references are to the three-volume Whittaker edition.

from an old man, Jonathan Oadley, informing his children and
their children of his intention to leave them a record of Revolutionary times as experienced by one who was there. "My style may
often offend you," writes Oadley. He hopes it will so that they will
the better remember it. Ranging from "plain and direct" to
"roused and inflamed" (but never "pleasant and graceful"), his
style will always be the *"talk on paper"* of "an uneducated,
plain soldier." It will be a unique record; there are many histories of the Revolution but no first-hand accounts, "not one,
where the mighty outline of truth is distinctly visible—no, not
one." [6]

This "mighty outline of truth" opens as the Oadley household
—as yet untouched by the war swirling around it—debates
whether its young men should volunteer for service. Archibald
Oadley (Jonathan's brother) passionately pleads the cause of the
Revolution, but his father—though proud of the boy's spirit—will
not permit him to enlist because of his delicate constitution; John
and his cousin, Arthur Rodman, are given leave to go. On the
eve of his departure, John makes a farewell call at the home of his
beloved, Clara Arnauld; he is accompanied by Archibald, who
loves her sister, Lucia. Because of the proximity of Hessian mer-
cenaries, the boys stay overnight. When they return to their own
home in the morning, they find it in ashes, their mother raped,
their father wounded. Archibald pursues the Hessians and kills
the rapist. His father cries out a grateful consent to Archibald's renewed plea: "Yes . . . and I will go with you, lead you . . .
into the presence of Washington, buckle a sword upon my thigh,
and stand by you . . . to the last drop of my blood!"

The scenes of battle that occupy much of the novel are given
added intensity as witnessed and reported by Jonathan. Poe's
verisimilitude is foreshadowed in some of the descriptions. Even
more harrowing than the blood and muck of a corpse-strewn field is
a detailed account of the death of a horse during the crossing of the
Delaware. As their boat hits bottom on the Jersey shore, Archibald

6. *Seventy-Six* (London: Whittaker and Co., 1823), 1:1–11.

leaps into the icy water to avoid the hooves of a rearing horse. Several horses plunge in after him. He leads them ashore—all except one that blindly swims out into the river. Through the sleet and darkness the brothers watch the horse struggling to save himself: "at last he grew desperate—the rattling of his nostrils became incessant—his blows upon the ice—one uninterrupted struggle, then, poor creature, a long, loud half suffocated neigh—a few more struggles, and he passed under the ice, as we supposed, for we heard a sound as if it came from the bottom, long afterward, afar off, and dying away in the distance and darkness." Archibald and John are by this time battle-hardened veterans who have carried off a field the corpse of their father without showing their grief. But they are moved to tears by the death of a brute (1:325–28).

The tumultuous battle scenes counterpoint a love story, restrained when compared to that of *Logan*, but frenzied by any other standard. Jonathan's engagement to Clara Arnauld is endangered by his susceptibility to seductive Ellen Sampson (also engaged to another). On one occasion, John forgets Clara when confronted, in a secluded room, by Ellen's lovely bosom and "beautifully moulded shoulder." They embrace passionately, but he recovers in time to tell her how lucky she is that he is an honorable man (2:123). At the close of the novel Clara forgives John his weakness; and Ellen renounces her impetuous ways to find happiness in marriage. Archibald's relationship with Lucia Arnauld, however, ends in tragedy. Piqued by Archibald's jealousy, Lucia encourages the advances of a dashing officer, Clinton, until he succeeds in seducing her. Her downfall comes about when she wakes from a dream about Archibald to find herself in Clinton's arms. Archibald kills Clinton in a duel and returns from heroic service in the war to die of his wounds—and of grief. Lucia, dying of remorse, is forgiven by the dying Archibald. They marry and, the ceremony over, he falls dead.

Seventy-Six might well have been the most appealing of "the damned ranting" romances by Neal that young Hawthorne relished so highly. More than the others of this period, it displays some control in manipulating historical events to enlarge and intensify its drama of the "heart." The mental anguish of Archibald and Lucia as they totter about with their fatal secret toward a grand denoue-ment—triumphant death for him and penitent survival for her—must have appealed mightily to the impressionable collegian who, a few decades later, was to render so much more masterfully the agonies of Arthur Dimmesdale and Hester Prynne. And while *Seventy-Six* is largely free of the hallucinatory frenzy and Gothic excess of *Logan,* its touches of the marvelous and the emblematic may also have stirred the youthful Hawthorne. The night before the death of the elder Oadley, a mysterious rapping is heard (3: 61). On another occasion, shortly after seeing a bloody corpse, Jonathan has a dream, a nightmare vision of war: Fire rains from the sky and the earth shakes to endless columns of marching men in shining blood-spattered mail; there is an explosion, and he finds himself sinking in a bottomless swamp, surrounded by reptiles and corpses (2:261–63). Neal occasionally reaches beyond Hawthorne to animal imagery and metaphor suggestive of the art of Stephen Crane: "We had now been at Morristown four days—the enemy had fallen back, fold upon fold, coil upon coil like some vast serpent, whose development had been suddenly checked by a fur-nace" (2:1).

Provoked by Cooper's wooden dialogue to new advances in colloquial realism, Neal was rebuked—in an otherwise favorable re-view of *Seventy-Six*—for his mistaken belief that oaths and "irre-ligious exclamations" necessarily belong to the vocabulary of sol-diers. The reviewer may have had in mind such lively and unin-hibited talk as this (spoken by Clinton): "I wheeled, made a dead set, at the son-of-a-bitch in my rear, unhorsed him, and actually broke through the line" (2:11). Also noteworthy are Neal's first serious efforts to reproduce Yankee vernacular through a minor character named Hanson, a frontiersman turned soldier.[7] Here, in

7. "Seventy-Six," unidentified clipping in Neal's scrapbook, HL. For examples of Yankee vernacular in the novel, see *Seventy-Six*, 1:94; ibid., 3:219–21, 228–34.

the midst of a rambling account of a battle engagement, is Hanson
telling of Archibald Oadley's escape from the enemy:

> "Well—(the yankees, and Hanson was a yankee,
> had the practice of prefacing almost every remark, and
> every question, and every answer, then, as now, with a
> *well*, or a *why*)——after he got well, they let him go out
> on parol; and, one night some of 'em run off; and, he
> might a' gone—but he would'nt—out 'pon honour, he
> said—so he would'nt—never mind 'em—they braced him
> up—served him all the same as the rest—now look out,
> said he—I'm clear o' my word, now—keep me if you can
> —so, not a week after, we escaped—see here—(showing
> his wrist—) I had a bayonet through, there—and here,
> and here—the balls whistled like hail; they sent hundreds
> arter us, through the bushes—but we got clear——
> guns!" (3:230)

9 Private Corridors
Randolph and *Errata*

On every page [of Randolph] *are sentences*
which sound to me just as if you were talking them
and I can picture to myself
your exact tone gesture and expression
in uttering them.

ROBERT CARTER TO JOHN NEAL, 1843

I love religious people;
particularly them that wear petticoats,
and tumble, and roll about, in their extacies;
and them, too—if they have sweet voices—that whoop,
and haloo, and bawl, in their devotions;
there is somewhat so reverential and composing—
so august and dignified in it.

ERRATA

After completing *Logan,* Neal wrote drafts of two new novels, *Randolph* and *Errata,* but set them aside to respond to the challenge of Cooper's *Spy.* He returned to *Randolph* after the publication of *Seventy-Six* in February 1823, adding to it new matter designed to refute his slanderers and embarrass his enemies.[1]
He claimed for the work a new approach fusing into the novel fiction, criticism, travel, and a good many other ingredients; it was this "compound nature" that occasioned its rejection by the London publishers who had brought out *Seventy-Six.*[2] Neal's "new kind of novel" actually differs very little in format from the long outmoded epistolary romance.

Randolph centers on the efforts of lovely Sarah Ramsay to discover the truth about the mysterious hero-villain Edward Molton

1. See p. 39 and n.3.
2. See above, p. 47.

97

—suspected of being a seducer and murderer. Much of the novel is given over to Molton's elaborate refutations of the numerous charges against him. For example, he did enter the room and bed of a fourteen year-old girl ("She had the appearance of a fresh, healthy girl of sixteen") but only to give her a lesson she would never forget by placing her in such a situation that "she should not dare, on her own account, to call out, or resist me." When she wakes and does cry out, he beats a temporarily successful retreat. Out of concern for the poor girl's peace of mind (she might be troubled all her life as to whether the visitor was "an apparition or reality"), he confides in her brother-in-law, "my most intimate friend, a good and wise man." Because the truth would never be believed, he confides a lie: he says he visited the girl while walking in his sleep as a result of a jealous dream provoked by the girl's brother Joe. Later, troubled about his lie, he tells the whole truth, and the family—which had accepted the lie—now cruelly repudiates him (1:115–76).

Edward Molton's account parallels in extraordinary detail Neal's account, in two letters to Pierpont, of his visit to Abby Lord's bed.[3] *Randolph* is, however, more than a private vehicle for self-justification. Molton defends himself with a sardonic self-mockery that suggests, as William Ellery Leonard puts it, a character "drawn rather more after Byron himself than after any one of his heroes." [4] Molton takes pleasure in angering a friend by confessing that he occasionally peeked through the keyhole at the young girl whose bed he invaded; his behavior, he insists, was truly civilized: "I am no listener at key-holes; but I hold it to be something brutish and insensible, to pass by any opportunity of seeing a beautiful woman, (nature's masterpiece,) naked, without profiting by it" (1:162).

The candor of these revelations led one reviewer to describe the novel as "a daring and naked exposure of what people in gen-

3. Neal to Pierpont, June 5 and July 6, 1818, PML. See above, pp. 30–32.

4. Leonard, *Byron and Byronism in America*, p. 49.

eral, cannot avoid *thinking*, but dare not express." [5] He suggests further that the central concern of *Randolph* is with "that passion which brought 'evil into the world, and with it all our woe:'—A passion which this book shows us in sunlike rays, should never be *trifled with*—never indulged without solemn consideration, and never excited wantonly, wickedly, or for the purposes of vanity, revenge, or lust." Neither the reviewer nor Neal makes it very clear when the passion should be indulged; Molton's views and actions vacillate wildly between Benjamin Franklin's sexual credo ("Rarely use venery" and never to "the injury of your own or another's peace or reputation") and D. H. Lawrence's celebration of the "passional impulse."

Molton tells of an encounter with a stranger on a stagecoach— "a fine looking woman" with a child—whom he recognizes as a "respectable" married woman. Before they reach his destination, his "veins ran lightning," and by the time he alights (at Salem) "her hand trembled—her frame shook—and there was a pulse to her finger-ends." She consents to an assignation in Boston but he, after a sleepless night, decides not to be "the destroyer of a husband's honour" and "the blaster of a family's peace" (1:295–96). Virtue, or prudence, triumphs; but the fact of sexual attraction as a force among "respectable" men and women has rarely been so candidly treated in nineteenth-century American fiction. Molton speaks out boldly against hypocritical prudishness ("the woman, who could be corrupted by *Don Juan,* could never be prevented from reading it") and utters the ultimate heresy: "many a fallen woman is more pure—because she has withstood more temptation, than many, who are yet upright" (2:165). For the most part, however, Molton's Byronic displays of irresistible power over women are qualified by a Nealian proclivity for conquest without consummation.

Molton's shocking revelations are made known to Sarah Ramsay through the letters of an intermediary—a cousin who is soon won over to an acceptance of Molton as a great and good man.

---

5. Undated and unidentified review, Neal's scrapbook, HL. /58006

While traveling in Maine, Sarah is stalked by a mysterious deaf and dumb man, and falls in love with a protector, kindly Spencer Randolph—whose name gives the novel its title. She does not know that she has herself been on trial. A grand denouement reveals that Edward Molton, the deaf and dumb man, and Spencer Randolph are one and the same person: Sarah—"her magnificent black hair" falling "in loose and glorious profusion, all about the floor, where *he* knelt *with* her"—buries "her shame and sorrow, for ever and ever, in the bosom of Edward Molton."

Such melodramatic absurdities counted for little to James Russell Lowell as he listened, in 1843, to a reading of *Randolph* by his friend Robert Carter.[6] What delighted young Lowell were Neal's "dashing sketches" of his contemporaries—inserted at intervals as letters from Molton to a British friend. (Twenty years earlier young Pinkney had been outraged by one of these sketches.) Lowell's magazine *The Pioneer* had just collapsed after three numbers designed to provide its subscribers "with a rational substitute for the enormous quantity of thrice diluted trash" of the popular magazines, and he was "particularly tickled" by Molton's devastating assessments of editors ("a cowardly, mercenary set") and their periodicals. Especially amusing to him was Molton's commentary on the prestigious *North American Review*: "Even he [Robert Walsh, Jr.], who has the impudence to set himself up, as one of the guardians of American literature, . . . is consuming his strength . . . in the monthly *compilation* of a museum, made up, God help our patience! of the refuse haberdashery of Great Britain" (1:109).

Among the poets and prose writers of America, John Neal is singled out by Molton for extended discussion. This self-educated Yankee, "whose whole life has been a tissue of wild and beautiful adventure," is impossible to know well because of talents "so various, contradictory, and capricious." The incoherency of *Logan* and

6. Lowell's reaction to the reading is described by Carter in a letter to Neal, March 29, 1843, HL; the letter is reproduced in Benjamin Lease, "Robert Carter, James Russell Lowell, and John Neal: A Document," *Jahrbuch für Amerikastudien* 13 (1968):246–48.

Seventy-Six may be accounted for, Molton suggests, by their attempt to reproduce the fragmented syntax of living speech. The only other novelists worthy of notice are Charles Brockden Brown (whose dramatic technique makes "very trifling incidents of importance enough to occupy your whole heart and soul") and Cooper. Brown, unfortunately, is too slavish an imitator of Godwin; and Cooper follows Scott so closely, that if he included "some good tedious Scotch dialogue . . . , few people would be able to detect the counterfeit." Further, like Scott, he is barren of invention: "Whenever the author is in a scrape [in *The Spy*] . . . he sets fire to the chief mansion house—or introduces General Washington." Praiseworthy are his descriptions (of nature, not the human heart) and his humor; but he lacks the qualities of paramount importance to a writer: "originality—passion—poetry—and eloquence" (2:207–24).

In his letter to Neal describing Lowell's enthusiastic response to the critiques in *Randolph*, Robert Carter pays his own tribute to another aspect of the novel: its colloquialism. "On every page," he observes, "are sentences which sound to me just as if you were talking them and I can picture myself your exact tone gesture and expression in uttering them." The colloquialism that young Carter so admired in *Randolph* is a central characteristic of Neal's next novel, *Errata*, written, says the author, to show "how people talk, when they are not talking for display." "Get your heart full of the subject," he suggests, "and you cannot help talking well." [7]

Errata, or the Works of Will. Adams is in some ways the most powerful of Neal's novels because its colloquialism truly springs from a "heart full of the subject": his childhood and young manhood. Parts of the book are autobiography so thinly disguised that real names are used—for example, his account of a flogging at the hands of Stephen Patten, his Portland schoolmaster (1:59–62). Neal later claimed that he had drawn on his early life in Portland without malice or bitterness in order to create "a rude, rough story"

7. *Errata*, 1:v–xiii.

so exaggerated and embellished that it could not possibly be mistaken for autobiography.[8] This scarcely explains why Will Adams, from whose point of view most of the story is told, should identify young Neal's schoolmaster by his real name.

The novel is nevertheless the product of a poetic imagination rather than a literal record. The evocation of a loveless, desperate childhood in the opening chapters is a creditable anticipation of Dickens. Will's young life is a series of whippings at the hands of his Quaker father—a nightmare relieved only by his mother's furtive affection. On the night of her death the boy steals into her room and tries to pull her hands apart—"for I had no true notion of death." For this, and for shrieking aloud, he says, "[my] father whipped me, at the bed side of my poor dead mother, until I foamed at the mouth; and she,—ah, she never raised her hand, nor uttered a single moan." Soon after, his little dog, now his only solace, is put to death: "there he lay!—washed up on the beach, among the drift wood; and shells; and white ridges of sand, with a great stone about his neck, and a rope almost gnawed off, in two or three places—so that he must have been a long while a dying" (1: 27–30).

Will's father turns him over to an uncle, a butcher, who takes almost equal pleasure in torturing animals and whipping the boy until his trousers are drenched in blood. One summer night Will sneaks off to the river to wade out and join a group of youngsters cavorting on a raft at some distance from the wharf. He cannot swim and can neither enter the water nor leave the raft as the tide keeps rising about his feet. The other boys leave and, standing alone in the rising water, he is certain that nothing can save him from drowning. But he is curiously unafraid and feels "a pleasant, drowsy, and cool thrilling, through all my blood." He peers into the clear dark water and sees large fish moving slowly or mooring at the bottom and multitudes of tiny fish sporting like birds in the air. There is an awful stillness like that of death, and he experiences a great pull "as a strong hand pressing me into the

8. *Wandering Recollections*, p. 327.

water, by main force." A sudden cry interrupts his dangerous revery. Another boy, caught in the eel grass at the bottom, is struggling for his life. Will plunges into the water and strikes a sunken log. His right arm is numb, broken, but he manages to catch at "a head of human hair floating about [his] face" with his left hand. "Well, I saved the life of a human creature. And what was my reward? I was whipped nearly to death for it; but I swore then, by the blood of my own heart, that it should be for the last time. It was for the last time" (1:38–44).

Will grows up a moody, occasionally exuberant, young man with an eye for the girls and a hatred of hypocrisy. He tells of a revival meeting in a large tent where forty or fifty people, on a hot night, jump and shout and agitate their limbs. The women show modesty in occasionally "adjusting their dresses; but without opening their eyes; losing their place; or stopping in their trance." In the midst of this hubbub he is outraged to see several louts toying wantonly with a lovely child. He is about to rescue her when "a pretty, rosy, dimpled country girl" catches his eye and—outrage forgotten—he succeeds in drawing her off to a solitary place. There they are interrupted and rebuked by two of the elders for "disturbing their solemnities." "Their *solemnities!*" cries Will —"tents full of legs and arms. . . !" (1:274–77).

Will's robust approach to the girls gives way with dizzying abruptness to intense feelings of guilt; he is suddenly and inexplicably transformed into a blood relative of Harold in *Logan* and Archibald Oadley in *Seventy-Six*. He has become a boarder in a Quaker household. When his romantic involvement with Caroline, a Quaker girl, is broken up by her parents, she knocks on his door the night before his scheduled departure. Alternating between faint and delirium, she clings to him—ignoring his prudent reminder of their danger. During a clinging faint, her bosom becomes exposed, and he nervously replaces the thin handkerchief covering it. Then, losing control, he presses his "passionate mouth to her bosom." The results are impressive: "I felt her heart stop; and her head reel. She turned cold instantly all over. . . . My voice rattled in my chest. I was dying." There are footsteps and voices at the door, and

Will pleads with Caroline for forgiveness. She falls on *his* bosom and grants it. "O, it was musick to me—it was the voice of humanity, to a shipwrecked and famished creature upon a desolate rock." Caroline's parents burst into the room, and Will falls unconscious. Three months later he regains consciousness in a madhouse. Caroline is a patient in the next room. He recovers but she dies. On her deathbed, in the presence of Will and her parents, Caroline proclaims her innocence (1:286–325).

Adams is nursed back to health by Albert Hammond, a dwarf, whose life story occupies much of the concluding half of the novel; like Will's, it parallels Neal's. He was a clerk in a drygoods store, then entered into a disastrous business venture in Boston, New York, and a "city of the south." When his partnership collapsed, he turned to the study of the law, supporting himself by writing criticism and novels. His disquisitions and anecdotes are disordered and colloquial—much like Will's. Adams' account of a revival meeting is matched by Hammond's earthy descriptions of New England customs—including a raising and a husking (2: 50–51). He quarrels frequently, on one occasion with a Kentucky roarer, who challenges the dwarf frontier style: "Do you know *what* I am? Steam-boat!—run agin me, run agin a snag...jam up...got the best jack knife, prettiest sister, best wife, run faster, jump higher, and whip any man in all Kentuck, by Gaud!" (2:175). (Such tall talk had, by 1823, made its way into newspapers, sermons, and song; [9] this was its first appearance in a novel.) Hammond's own talk is laced with vernacular wit and profanity. He tells of a hotel in Virginia where he was given a garret "with a bed hot enough to roast any thing but bed bugs, and they were gasping for breath." When he finally managed to doze off, "do you think the sons of bitches didn't send up a negro wench to wake me, with a plate of green pears! pears that you could not bore into, with a gimlet" (2:179).

Superimposed on this ill-assorted but lively collection of anec-

9. Walter Blair, *Native American Humor* (*1800–1900*) (San Francisco, 1960), pp. 30–31.

dotes is a clumsy Gothic plot revolving about the pathological jealousy of Will Adams. He informs his new love, Emma, "I would as
soon my wife should go to bed with another man, as to be kissed by
him," however innocently. After their marriage Will comes upon
Hammond innocently kissing his wife's hand. He shoots the dwarf
and flees the country. Following a number of gruesome adventures
(that again foreshadow *Pym*), Will returns to his native land
to find his wife and child dead—and he goes mad once again. This
time he is not nursed back to health by the dwarf (who has survived) but dies insane. Hammond alone remains to conclude their
story.

As in *Logan*, these absurdities are somewhat redeemed by occasional penetrating and poetic explorations of the dream world of
Will Adams. As a whipped, starving schoolboy he dreams of walking through a strange house, observing with minute particularity
signs of desolation and disorder in every room (1:100–101).
Years later, during his courtship of Caroline, he dreams of another
visit to the house. This time he encounters in one of the rooms a
seated girl "with fair hair, and agreeable eyes, watching me with an
air of perfect indifference." He tries to speak to her, but the
words stick in his throat. He notices that she is wearing a dress
so thin as to reveal her "fine bosom; and, particularly, her right
breast, which was surprisingly beautiful and natural—unsustained
by any corset or stays, almost as if it had been naked" (1:217–20).
He next dreams of the house during an emotional collapse brought
on by a jealous frenzy: he has just learned that his sister Elizabeth
loves Hammond. In his delirium he finds himself lying in bed in the
same desolate house: "a soft face lay near to mine, upon the same
pillow— . . . I thought it was Elizabeth; and tried again and
again to kiss it, but it constantly vanished" (2:215–16). The
final vision of the house comes shortly after he discovers Hammond
kissing his wife Emma. In a dizzying revelation he recognizes
Emma as the seated girl he had encountered in his earlier dream;
and he knows the dream house to be a desolate replica of the
house in which he now lives. It is a prophetic vision of the catastrophe awaiting him (2:311–12).

As a whole *Errata* must be labeled—along with *Logan* and *Randolph*—an incoherent failure. But in numerous passages it anticipates the wit and realism of Twain and the psychological depths of Poe and Melville. The evocative power of the opening chapters (dealing with the childhood of Will Adams) make them worthy of comparison with the masterpieces of nineteenth-century American fiction—and with the charged prose of Faulkner and Wolfe. The Doppelgänger and incest motifs in the recurrent dreams of Will Adams are prophetically suggestive of the worlds of William Wilson, Roderick Usher, and Pierre Glendinning. This power and these hints are, unfortunately, pretty much lost in the prevailing confusion.

10 A "Vast Conglomeration" *Brother Jonathan*

It is extremely powerful—and,
what is more to the purpose,
its power is of a kind
that is unhackneyed and original.

D. M. MOIR TO WILLIAM BLACKWOOD, 1824

To see unity in the vast conglomeration
of Brother Jonathan *is impossible.*

ALEXANDER COWIE, 1948

The huge manuscript (eventually published in three volumes total-
ling more than 1300 pages) that "Carter Holmes" submitted to
William Blackwood in October of 1824 was Neal's most ambitious
effort.[1] With all its excesses and flaws *Brother Jonathan* conveys,
as does no novel before Melville, the rough exuberance that perme-
ates *Moby-Dick*. D. M. Moir's critique of the manuscript novel
deplores—in language that anticipates the responses of Melville's
puzzled contemporaries—the author's prolix "unwillingness to quit
a theme" and his regrettable tendency to sacrifice "ease and gracefulness" to "metaphysical ingenuity." Neal's 1825 production is a
far cry from *Moby-Dick*, but it displays, in Moir's felicitous phrase,
a "gladiatorship of intellect" exceedingly rare in a decade dominated by the infinitely tamer talents and sensibilities of Irving and
Cooper.

An extended passage may serve to illustrate the style Moir
admires and deplores:

> To know a man well, we should see him at *home*. People
> are very much alike in their out-of-door habits; their
> dress and fashion, before all the world: they are not half

1. *Brother Jonathan, or the New Englanders*, 3 vols. (Edinburgh and
London: William Blackwood and T. Cadell, 1825).

so much alike, at home; in their old coats and big slip-
pers; lounging over the tables and chairs; each after a
fashion of his own—more or less dignified or sloppy,
as he is more or less afraid of being caught. Abroad,
people are seen afar off, as it were. . . . Distance in
space, like distance in time, never fails to confound the
minutiae and particularities of all men, however they may
loom through it, like a great ship through a fog.

. . . See him at home, therefore; whoever he may
be; whatever he may be; good or bad; great or little, if
you would know his true value. Is it a pyramid? go
near it, if you would know its real strength;—it may have
been built of pebbles. Is it a ruin? go near to it—nearer:
—it may have been richly sculptured; it may be a treas-
ury of ornament.

A man may be a hypocrite all his life long, before
the publick; but no man ever was, before his own
family. . . .

For this reason it is, that we love to follow men
home to their own fire-sides. The table itself . . . is a
criterion, by which the refinement of a people may be
determined. . . . The rude, barbarian virtues; the coarse
hospitality; and substantial fierce welcome of every people
in a savage state, are all of a piece.

The black broth of the Spartans; the raw frozen
fish, and sea-blubber of the Laplander; the sour crout
of the Germans; the fish-and-potatoes of the Yankee; the
corn bread and homony of an old Virginian; the oatmeal
cakes, bannocks, and crowdy, of a Scotchman; the train
oil of the Esquimaux; the substitutes of a Frenchman; the
horse flesh and mare's milk of a wild Arab; the brave,
coarse meat of the North American—that of a strangled
bear, perhaps; the potatoes and point of an Irish peasant;
the live, quivering steak of an Abyssinian; the buck wheat
cakes of a New Yorker; the lion's meat of some people;
the broken glass, brick bats, and old iron of the ostrich;
or, worse than all, perhaps, the abominable plum pudding
of an Englishman; that which, if he were not "brought
up" on it, the ostrich himself could not manage; what are
all these things, but so many infallible measures of refinement and character. They are always detestable to
strangers, and always agreeable to the "natives." Those

who are "brought up" on them, love them: those who are not, bring them up—with a curse. They work upon us, nevertheless—all of them—like our mother's milk; and keep us yearning toward our home, even to the last (1: 73–76).

All this and more are preliminary to "half a dozen sweeps of our brush" depicting a Yankee supper in a Connecticut village shortly before the outbreak of the Revolution. The idea is commonplace enough: only when he is at home, unmasked and unguarded, can we learn the truth about a man. The simple thought is expanded and dramatized by a flood of language and a word- and rhythm-intoxicated style suggestive of Biblical splendor and backwoods sermon oratory. The home as a mirror of truth is celebrated in a series of sentences marked by parallelism and antiphony ("Is it a pyramid? go near it . . .") to which is appended a remarkable Old Testament catalog of foods and peoples—an impressive introduction to a Yankee supper. The truth of the heart and hearth thus ranges out to ancient times and savage climes—until we are brought up short by the astounding ostrich, capable of digesting anything and everything except the Englishman's plum pudding. Poetry slides momentarily into parody; the passage closes with a lyricism teetering on the brink ("They work upon us . . . even to the last").

Behind this virtuoso performance is a playful narrator quite capable of interrupting a flood of eloquence to defend (in a passage omitted above) his dwelling at such length on what "everybody knows" because books that introduce new truths "put people to the trouble of thinking." Moir was not to be put off by such mock-serious interpolations. After paying tribute to the novel's acuteness and power, he adds a cautionary note for Blackwood's benefit: these are qualities "alas! not much in request by novel readers"; nine out of ten want to be amused without fatigue and interested "with the least possible expenditure of thought." That we truly learn about a person only when he is at home may be an old idea but the cataract of Biblical cadences intermingled with Yankee vernacular makes it new. Moir was concerned (justifiably, as its disappointing sale was later to confirm) about a novel that demands of its readers so dynamic and unconventional an involvement.

Neal obediently cut away large portions of the novel regarded by Blackwood and his advisers to be excessively digressive or indecent.[2] But a great mass of such matter—including the long passage quoted above—was retained in the published version. Paradoxically it is these passionate and wide-ranging prose-poetic excursions that provide *Brother Jonathan* with some unity of effect despite its chaotic structure. Loosely enveloping all is a narrator whose viewpoint reflects an unflagging (if frequently incoherent) exuberance, a shrewd satiric angle of vision, a quirky search for truth, an unquenchable passion for that which is grand in nature and man.

To the extent that the narrator focuses on the fortunes of "our hero," young Walter Harwood, there is also a semblance of structural unity. In the course of about a year, the time span of the novel, we follow young Harwood through a succession of adventures—amatory, military, farcical, pathetic. An enraptured innocent, atremble with animal vitality and dangerously susceptible to women, our hero is "an overgrown lout of a boy, brought up in the Back Woods of America—with a stoop in his shoulders, a swing in his gait, hob-nailed shoes upon his feet, a smock-frock upon his back, a nasal twang in his speech, and almost every phrase he utters regular Yankee."[3]

After a fashion, a plot emerges dealing with our hero's rite of passage to manhood as celebrated in a series of anecdotal set pieces. His heart belongs to Edith Cummin—a lifelong companion and, like himself, a child of nature. The idyllic life and love of Walter and Edith, and the tranquility of the village, are shattered

2. One such lengthy digression was published as the article, "Character of the Real Yankees . . ."; another later appeared in altered form as a story, "Otter-Bag, the Oneida Chief," in *The Token* for 1829, pp. 221–84.

3. This description is from a review of the novel in Patmore, ed., *Rejected Articles*, pp. 273–74.

by the arrival of a portentous and mysterious stranger, Jonathan Peters. It soon becomes apparent that Peters has an unexplained influence over Walter's father, Abraham Harwood, the village preacher; worse, he seems attracted to Edith, and she shows signs of responding to his interest.

Young Walter undergoes great emotional travail as he seeks to purge himself of jealousy. It is his habit to sleep under the stars accompanied by his great dog Panther. One night, troubled about Edith and Peters, he reclines on a steep mountainside unaware of a threatening flash flood. The peaceful grandeur of his surroundings calms him, and he falls asleep. He is awakened by his dog's growls. The storm is approaching. The great flash flood and its nearly fatal aftermath are depicted in a vivid prose poetry emblematic of Walter's inner turbulence (1, chap. 11). Other episodes similarly illustrate Neal's deployment of incident to signal the stages of our hero's painful progress toward an understanding of the world as it is: Walter's stage coach trip to join General Washington's forces in New York; his experience in a cheap New York hotel; his encounter with the seductive "Mrs. P."

When a meddling Yankee in the stage coach makes a sly remark about the girl he has just left behind, Walter savagely rebuffs him—the boy's "first essay in outbraving 'real imperdence.'" Incongruously dressed in "go-to-meetin' finery" and jammed between two country bumpkins in the jolting coach, Walter feels his spirits lift as he looks out to see the clouds rise from the mountains: "Instantly, as it were, the clouds of his heart were gone over; the new sunshine played upon it—the wind blew over it—and he felt as if, the very waters, that he saw, were rippling through it." Then the horses break loose; the careening coach finally comes to a halt at the edge of a precipice. The wild journey has been enlivened by fire ignited earlier by some careless pipe smokers and a large keg that "skipped an' bobbed about, among our toes," dribbling its powdery contents into the smoldering straw. At the edge of the precipice the driver examines the keg and straw with great care. "'Gold dust, I should think,' said Walter, who had often read of it in story books and poetry." When he learns that the gold dust is gunpowder, he meditates silently for several hours. And the narrator, who never holds back his opinions, reflects thus on the state of the republic:

> America—as every body knows, *there*—is the land of liberty and equality; "the land of the brave; and the home of the FREE." Wherefore, it would be no easy matter for a person travelling, to persuade a full-blooded republican "driver," that a keg of gunpowder—and a live pig—with warming pans—cod fish, broad axes, and hollow ware,—paid for inside, were not fit company for half a score of human beings, paid for, inside—with lighted pipes. (2:67–68)

In a New York hotel, Walter witnesses with disbelief the morning activities of guests artfully rearranging their worn and dirty cravats and collars; "combing their long hair with their fingers, and thumbs; sopping their faces, one after another—it made him sick— . . . with one and the same towel." But when they are finished and he finds himself surrounded by well-dressed, polished young men, poor Walter forgets their filth and subterfuge and is ashamed of his own clean, countrified look. At breakfast he observes a crowd of boarders hurrying to table in their coats and hats, carrying their saddlebags. "He knew not how cautious your 'country trader' is, when he first gets into a large tavern. He never moves, but with all his property, except his horse about him." On settling his bill he finds to his horror that it comes to a dollar and a quarter; to the amusement of all, he counts out 250 half coppers— almost two-thirds of the fortune he has been accumulating since childhood. Depressed and confused, he goes out into the whirl and press of the city streets in search of a benefactor to whom he carries a letter of introduction. He finds himself caught up in a funeral procession, follows it to a graveyard, and when the clods of earth begin to fall on the coffin—a child's—he feels "as if the moisture of his heart were dried up, with a frightful suddenness" as he envisions the dead face of his mother and the funeral of his younger brother. But by the time he leaves he has caught a glimpse of a beautiful girl—a girl he would like to see again (2:137–52).

He does meet the girl, Olive Montgomery, at a party, and she like several other women in the novel—falls in love with him. He is attracted to her; but shapely, seductive Mrs. P. (whose husband is away in the war) lures our susceptible hero from his tête-à-tête with Olive, and before long Walter finds himself (almost involuntarily) escorting her home to the accompaniment of giddy prattle and playful attempts to match his long stride ("step to what musick she might, where was the man—the young man, we would say, who would not have stepped, with her—to the self same air?"). They are walking alongside the North River and see mysterious lights blinking over the water. What seems to be a large shrouded vessel floats silently by. They hear challenges and muffled commands. "The poor lady caught her breath; our hero put his arm about her waist—how could he do less?—took her two, dear little hands, with great fervour, into his—how could he do more? —and held her so closely to him, that every jump of his heart was answered by a jump of hers." A battery of guns lets go. They are curtly warned away from the river by a stranger, apparently a general, who then turns from them to consult with his aides about battle strategy. Walter, in a rage, refuses Mrs. P.'s invitation to stop in at her house; he is piqued by the general's rebuff, perhaps sensitive to the fact that he has been playing at love instead of fighting in the war. A few days later he meets General Washington and joins his forces (3:2–25).

At the Battle of Brooklyn Heights he comes through his baptism of fire after a terrible internal struggle. ("His heart shook. . . . He knew not whether to run, or stay.") When Washington appears riding slowly across the field at the head of a troop of young officers, a great cheer goes up—"a long, loud roar of religious joy." The cowardly New Yorkers and Pennsylvanians who have fled the battle are forgotten, and Walter experiences a convulsive rapture that leaves him "instantly relieved, assured, happy—steadfast—without a single fear" (3:91–93).

Arthur Hobson Quinn has suggested that, in *Brother Jonathan*, "the sordid side of the Revolution is brought in with a realism that is early." [4] One example of this aspect of the novel is the full-scale drunken brawl that breaks out between Buckskins (Virginians) and Yankees while all are celebrating the Declaration of Independence (2:380–401). Neal's handling of the execution of Nathan Hale illustrates, in another way, his substitution of graphic detail for idealized heroics. Young Walter, disguised as a rustic civilian behind enemy lines, witnesses the approach of an execution party escorting Hale to his death. He involuntarily cries out his recognition and is himself captured. He manages to break loose and hears a joyous shout from Hale as he flees. He looks back to see the prisoner run up on the gallows. "Two or three struggles—a snap—a swing, or two—and all was over." Paralyzed by the spectacle, Walter is recaptured. He is spared Captain Hale's fate when a family friend (a Quaker loyalist) intercedes. The episode closes with an indignant comment on the oblivion into which Nathan Hale has fallen: "History is full of the young British martyr [André];—while the name of the American, is only to be found up, to this hour, in a single book of his own country, that country, for which he died so cruel a death" (3:148–59). The reference is to Hannah Adams' *A Summary History of New England* (1799) in which Hale's story and dying speech were first published.[5] That famous speech is omitted from *Brother Jonathan* where it would have clashed with the dramatic recognition scene, Walter's escape, and the grim abruptness of the execution.

What makes it increasingly difficult to respond to—or even follow—the fortunes of Walter Harwood is the gratuitous introduction of an enormous quantity of Gothic mystification. Preacher Harwood, Walter's presumed father, turns out to be the murderer of the twin brother of Walter's real father, Robert Evans—who has previously appeared alternately disguised as Jonathan Peters and Warwick Savage. To these complications are added Bald Eagle, an

4. Quinn, *American Fiction*, p. 49.
5. See G. D. Seymour, *Documentary Life of Nathan Hale* (New Haven, 1941), pp. 550–51. Hannah Adams's account is quoted in James Thacher, *Military Journal* (Boston, 1823), pp. 275–76, and in Jedidiah Morse, *Annals of the American Revolution* (Hartford, 1824), pp. 259–61.

ancient Indian who helps Walter in several crises; and two other shadowy figures, a prophet and a witch, Penobscot Indians who portend salvation and disaster at irregular intervals. (Walter, it later develops, is a remote descendant of the tribe.)

Walter himself undergoes a bewildering transformation in the course of his adventures. William Blackwood had complained —about the version first submitted—that his "libertinism" is unexplained, that there are not sufficient causes given "for so wholly changing the character of a romantic virtuous high minded young man." Blackwood was troubled by details like these that survive in the published novel: Goaded by unfounded jealousy, "our boy" joins a madcap friend in a drunken spree and a visit to a prostitute named Emma who has long admired him from afar. Walter flees before succumbing, but on another occasion—his jealousy over Edith newly revived—he revisits Emma and stays with her. He proposes marriage (Neal may have injected this and the complications that follow to mollify Blackwood), but the shameless girl argues a code of morality that rules it out: "If a man love, he is faithful . . . without law. But, if there be no love in his heart, of what use, pray, is the law?" He leaves her and her "wretched fallacies" as one "infatuated, with some evil spirit." (When she bears his child, they are reunited in their love for the infant. It dies and they part—with a chaste and a chastened love for one another.)

Blackwood's long letter about the original version suggests that the publisher himself persuaded Neal to delete from the novel details that would have helped explain Walter's sudden libertinism. The manuscript Neal first submitted called for the seduction of Edith Cummin by Jonathan Peters (Walter's true father) and her subsequent death, circumstances that would greatly clarify Walter's agonized gyrations. "Look again at the terrible end of poor Edith," urged Blackwood. "Her story however powerfully wrought out is out of nature. Such a being should never have been seduced even by Jonathan Evans [later Peters] endow him as you please —she ought to have been the good angel of Walter—there is a purity in such a creature, which while it must have saved herself even from the evil one, must also have received and restored her lover." [6] Neal did look again and removed a central motivation for Walter's jealousy and guilt by obediently deleting Edith's seduction and death. The original emphasis in the novel on the sexual susceptibility of both hero and heroine is also weakened by the revision.

It must be added, however, that Neal might not have yielded to Blackwood if not for his own confusion and uncertainty about Walter's function in the novel. "Deuse take Brother Jonathan," he wrote the publisher after its disastrous reception. "Peters would have made a capital hero; but—but—I did not think of him, in that shape, till it was too late, and I was weary of the work." [7] The notion that Peters should have been the hero seems a weary afterthought, for it is this shadowy figure and the tortuous mystification surrounding him that dissipate the force of Walter's story.

Whatever was lost in plot and characterization through revision, the extraordinary colloquialism of *Brother Jonathan* seems to have survived intact—a colloquialism far in advance of his earlier works. Neal is in love with live talk in this book, and his characters produce it in prodigious quantities and with astonishing verisimilitude. He celebrates the color and vigor of Yankee family conversation (1:34 ff.), Virginia hill-country dialect (2:388 ff.), mid-Atlantic states rustic talk (3:87); and intermittently, through Bald Eagle and other Indians, we are given what seem to be authentic transcriptions of Penobscot pidgin. [8]

Neal's innovations in colloquialism reach for more than authentic transcriptions of regional dialects. To intensify the immediacy of the dialogue in *Seventy-Six*, he had dropped conventional identifying tags:

6. Blackwood to "Holmes," November 8, 1824, Blackwood Letter Books.

7. Neal to Blackwood, September 1, 1825, NLS.

8. In this and the paragraph following I have made use of (while taking exception to some of its conclusions) Harold Martin's "The Colloquial Tradition in the Novel: John Neal," *New England Quarterly* 32 (1959):455–75.

'You had better keep out of the way awhile'—said Archibald, with some emotion—'will you?'
['No.']
'But what will you do?'
'Exactly what I have always done.'
'But they will insult you.'
'I expect it.'
'Challenge you.'
'Undoubtedly.'
'Cut your throat.'
'I don't believe it.'
'Shoot you.'
'Probably.'
'And yet, dear Copley,' said Archibald. . . .'[9] (2:244)

In *Brother Jonathan* Neal seeks to heighten immediacy even more by running the dialogue together without paragraph indentation:

"Only three ways left!" quoth he; muttering to himself—"only three ways, I tell ye, boy. Swear 'em out—or lie 'em out—or face 'em out. Here they come, sure enough! Don't be alarmed—I'll bring you off." "Bring me off!"—"Certainly—never fear—take the blame on myself!"—"The deuse you will!"—"Don't swear."—"Who, I!—I—Hush! the Philistines are up: I'm asleep, you know; dead asleep;—dreaming o' fire. . . . (2:225)

(In his later novels, Neal was to go still further by dispensing with quotation marks.) During the same decade in which Cooper said of a nursing foal that it "exacted the maternal contribution," Neal's adventurous experiments contributed significantly to our colloquial tradition.

Live talk was, for Neal, not necessarily low talk. The narrator's voice ranges from racy vernacular to Biblical-prophetic. His lofty style is not—as is Cooper's—pompously Latinic, but instead echoes the poetic grandeur of the Old Testament in its development

9. Copley's rejoinder ('No.') is omitted in the British edition, the only one available to me; it appears in the American edition, as quoted by Martin, "The Colloquial Tradition," pp. 470–71.

of a thesis through "catalogue and allusion, proverb and allegory." [10]
In this passage the narrator offers up an extraordinary picture of a
prophet (Walter's good angel) in language and intonation appropriate to its subject:

> He had seen a little white-haired old man, before,
> whose tresses were like those of a battle charger—a
> prophet, perhaps. Wherefore, he gazed upon him now,
> with amazement. He was a sort of miniature king. His
> firm tread—his erect—severe carriage—they were abso-
> lutely regal. Nay—his look, altogether, was that of one
> who had grown old, not so much in the revolution of
> seasons—as of empire; not so much, in the adventures
> of common life, as in the biography of nations—the
> afflictions of the sky—the changing of what appears un-
> changeable. He stood and spoke, in short—not so much
> like one, to whom old age is a heavy incumbrance; as like
> one, to whom it is the sign of wisdom and power—
> dominion—authority—prerogative: the urim and thum-
> mim of survivorship—the lawful inheritance—the badge
> of him, who has outlived all the priesthood of his race;
> and concentrated for a time, all their endowments—all
> their miraculous potency upon himself. (2:192–93)

The aura of "miraculous potency" that surrounds Neal's ancient
Indian adumbrates Melville's magical evocations: the lumbering
tortoises of "The Encantadas" ("Yea, they seemed the identical
tortoises whereon the Hindoo plants this total sphere"); the tat-
tooed chest of a renegade sailor in *Omoo* ("a sort of Urim and
Thummim engraven . . . the seal of his initiation").[11] Both writers are indebted to the ancient colloquialism of the Hebrew story-
tellers.

Although the narrator in *Brother Jonathan* does not come
close to matching the spectacular flexibility of Melville's style, he occasionally strikes a prose-poetic note suggestive of neither Old

10. I have borrowed an observation applied to Melville's style by
Nathalia Wright, *Melville's Use of the Bible* (Durham, N.C., 1949), p. 168.

11. *The Piazza Tales, The Works of Herman Melville* (London, 1923),
10:190; *The Writings of Herman Melville*, ed. Harrison Hayford et al.
(Evanston and Chicago, 1968–), vol. 2, *Omoo* (1968), p. 32.

Testament grandeur nor high-spirited rusticity, as in the following distinctively Nealian fusion of cadenced colloquialism and inspired metaphor:

> He felt as he stood looking at all the unseemly rubbish, that lay about him, very much as a fat crab might, if he were driven to a choice of the worn out shells, which he had thrown off, a twelve-month before; nevertheless, he undertook the process of re-investiture; working his way, inch by inch, into his old clothes, like a smooth, shiny overgrown rattlesnake, into last year's coat; left, in a warm day, underneath a rock heap—or a pile of rotten wood. (3:143)

The plethora of commas is distracting and the abrupt shift from crab to snake disturbing; but the passage unmistakably signals, in 1825, an emerging national literature.

That promise would never be fulfilled by John Neal. The British critic who found *Brother Jonathan* "the most extraordinary work of its kind which this age of extraordinary works has put forth" shrewdly suggests that its author has a great future if this is a first novel—but "we almost despair of his ever writing a better" if he has already written in this vein.[12] Neal himself displayed a clear understanding of his dilemma as a creative artist in a letter to Blackwood written after the failure of his most ambitious book. He admits to the error of "straining after effect"; but it is, he claims, a response to a more pernicious tendency among American writers—imitation:

> I, wishing to avoid what is common, am apt to run off into what is not only uncommon, but unnatural, and even absurd. I am aware of this, and would have corrected it, long before this, were I not afraid of uprooting some valuable characterstick of my own, while tearing up the roots of that which I acknowledge to be vicious.

He promises to correct these exaggerations as much as he can "without endangering the vitality of my individual character, the very source of my fertility & power."[13]

12. Patmore, ed., *Rejected Articles*, pp. 265, 312.
13. Neal to Blackwood, September 28, 1825, NLS.

Out of this determination came a story accepted for publication by Blackwood but never printed. Shortly after his return to Portland, Neal revised and expanded the story into the short novel *Rachel Dyer*, a work that comes closest to fulfilling the promise of *Brother Jonathan*—and avoiding its absurdities.

III
homecoming

11 The Long Visit
Poe and Other Discoveries

The wild eagle had alighted again
on his own peak.
JAMES BROOKS, 1833
As you gave me the first jog
in my literary career,
you are in a measure bound to protect me,
and keep me rolling.

EDGAR ALLAN POE TO JOHN NEAL, JUNE 4, 1840

Neal arrived in New York from Havre in June of 1827 with the expectation of setting aside his literary career to return to the practice of law. He sent for his law library, stored in Baltimore, and prepared to open an office. But first he went up to Portland to see his mother and sister "and such of my friends and relations as might be willing to acknowledge me." [1] When certain townspeople made it emphatically clear that he was not welcome in his native town, he prolonged his visit for forty-nine years—until his death in 1876.

His "American Writers" series had aroused a strong feeling of outrage. A Boston reviewer saw in the publication of these "abusive" essays a convincing indication of the degeneration of *Blackwood's*. A New York critic sneered that the magazine had "sadly fallen off when a man who could not find a reader in America, goes to England, and ranks first quill." A former friend, Joseph T. Buckingham, deplored the "gross and vulgar caricatures of New-England customs and language" in *Brother Jonathan*, to say nothing of the "unnatural" and "unprincipled" warfare Neal had waged on his countrymen.[2] In Portland the semi-autobiographical

1. *Wandering Recollections*, p. 324.
2. "Blackwood's Edinburgh Magazine for February and March, 1825," *United States Literary Gazette* 2 (1825):113; "Blackwood's Edin-

123

Errata—with its corrosive treatment of prominent citizens like Stephen Patten and the Willis family—was by no means forgotten. On hearing of his visit, his sister's closest friend called to offer her condolences; with tears in her eyes, she urged Rachel and her mother to be comforted and to put their trust in God.

While sauntering down Middle Street several days after his return, Neal heard the shout "Keep Cool! Keep Cool!" coming from a group of young toughs standing outside a tavern. He walked over, bloodied the nose of their leader, and routed the others. After several such incidents he was pleased to receive a supper invitation from some Bowdoin College students eager to meet a literary lion. But on arrival in Brunswick he was greeted by printed placards prominently displayed in town and at the college. Headed "Bulletin Extra," they announced in bold black letters:

> *ARRIVED*, at Portland, on Saturday evening last, in the Steam-Boat in a short passage from London, via New-York, the celebrated author of "Keep Cool," "Randolph," "Errata," &c., &c., in a state of great bodily and mental exhaustion, owing to his excessive labors in furnishing matter for Blackwood's Edinburgh Monthly Magazine. It is said much of the elevation of the American character is owing to this distinguished author. Since his arrival in his native town, it has been recommended to put himself under the care of the Hon. STEPHEN JONES, M.D. an eminent Southern Physician. This has been done, and the Doctor reports favorably. On Wednesday afternoon he was walking with his Physician apparently much better. Dr. JONES, however, recommends his immediate removal to Baltimore, or some other Southern Climate, for his complete restoration.

A second "Bulletin Extra," less subtle in its abusiveness, calls the author "infamous" instead of "celebrated," a "renegado" who "basely traduced his native town and country for hire." "Dr. Jones" was an elderly Negro of feeble mentality hired by Neal's enemies

burgh Magazine. Number XCII. September," *Atlantic Magazine* 2 (1824–25):158; Buckingham's commentary is in "Neal—Brother Jonathan," *New-England Galaxy*, September 2, 1825.

to follow him about. Neal promptly turned the tables by warning the old man about intruding when others were present, but otherwise warmly welcoming his company. Before long "the confederates, finding the laugh was against them, began to count the cost, and left me in peace for the next following forty years." [3]

In response to this and similar unpleasantnesses, Neal had his library and furniture shunted from New York to Portland, rented spacious offices on Exchange Street, and settled down to the practice of law in his native town. It did not flourish. His fellow Down Easters were a litigious folk, but he had little patience for interminable pettifogging over disputed boot jacks and tin dippers, and there was a surplus of lawyers in town. He soon turned his abundant energies to other matters: civic affairs, gymnastics, love, and literature.

At a town meeting Neal was accused by his uncle James of being an aristocrat who had been too long abroad; others took the position that he had not been abroad long enough. Neal pressed for a drastic reorganization of municipal government to make possible some badly needed improvements. Portland had no sidewalks, "and if you saw an aged man poking about in the mud, with a cane, you were tempted to ask if anybody was missing." Before long— thanks in part to Neal's strenuous efforts—there were brick walks, slate crossings, and a five-mile road traversing the peninsula, with parks and promenades at either end "where the population could get a mouthful of fresh air, and look out upon panoramas of unequalled beauty and vastness." [4]

While in London Neal had taken a course in gymnastics with Carl Völker, a giant of six feet four who "nearly wrenched me limb from limb, with the assurance that it 'doot me goot.'" He became so enthused about the value of bodily exercise for people of studious habits that he wrote Thomas Jefferson urging him to make "a gymnastick school, quite an indispensable part" of the

3. *Wandering Recollections*, pp. 323–35. Copies of the "Bulletin Extra" (in both versions) were salvaged by Neal and are preserved among his papers, HL.

4. *Wandering Recollections*, pp. 345–46.

newly established University of Virginia, and offering Völker's help in recruiting an instructor.[5] Shortly after his return to Portland Neal organized a gymnasium and soon had about fifteen classes under his charge, at first in the upper story of the old town hall and later at the old fort on top of Munjoy's Hill. At the invitation of Bowdoin College, Neal established its first gymnasium in 1828; another was initiated in nearby Saco. His enthusiasm was somewhat dampened, however, when he attempted to integrate his Portland classes. Most of the gymnasts were ardent abolitionists, but when a group of Negroes petitioned for admission, they were rejected by an overwhelming majority. "This, I acknowledge, went far to dishearten me; for what was bodily training? what a system of gymnastics, weighed against humanity and consistency?"[6]

In the midst of these strenuous civic and gymnastic activities Neal found time for courtship and marriage. He had been waiting for "ten or a dozen years . . . till I should be rich enough to marry." He was still far from ready, but with a semiremunerative law practice and a lively new literary weekly under way (*The Yankee*), Neal felt emboldened to put an end to "the dreariness, the loneliness, the utter hopelessness of a bachelor's life." The ob-

5. *Wandering Recollections*, p. 116; Neal to Jefferson, August 5, 1825, Jefferson Collection, Library of Congress.

6. *Wandering Recollections*, pp. 333–35. It must be added, however, that Neal was extremely hostile to abolitionist sentiment and became an active participant in the colonizationist movement. His long-standing feud with William Lloyd Garrison began about this time and did not end until Neal admitted his error about colonization and abolition in 1865. See *The Letters of William Lloyd Garrison*, vol. 1, *I Will be Heard!, 1822–1835*, ed. Walter M. Merrill (Cambridge, Mass., 1971), pp. 63 and passim. Leonard L. Richards accuses Neal of involvement in mob action against an 1833 abolitionist meeting, but offers only suspicious speculation as evidence (*"Gentlemen of Property and Standing": Anti-Abolition Mobs in Jacksonian America* [New York and London, 1970], pp. 26–29). Neal's version of the affair is that he prevailed against the Southerners disposed to violence and was consistently for fair play and open discussion. See letter from Neal to R. R. Gurley, October 2, 1833 (the day after the near-riot), quoted in L. Richards, *"Gentlemen of Property and Standing,"* p. 27, and *Wandering Recollections*, pp. 401–2.

ject of his affection was his second cousin Eleanor Hall, nineteen-year-old daughter of a well-to-do Portland merchant who, like Neal, was a descendant of the prolific Hate-Evil Hall. His courtship was unorthodox—or, perhaps, unusually old-fashioned. "I had always been in love from my earliest boyhood; and I knew . . . something of what women might be persuaded to do, without ever troubling either mama or papa, after the affections were once engaged." Before Eleanor knew of his serious interest, Neal made approaches to Mr. and Mrs. Hall. They gave their blessing, and on August 7, 1828, he wrote to his old friend John Pierpont, in an offhand postscript: "I have got in love and hope to be married in the fall." The wedding took place on October 12.[7]

In early 1826, three years after their bitter break, Neal had sent a friend to Pierpont with a note of introduction. The minister had responded with cautious warmth. He had forgiven and would willingly forget forever "the evil which I have thought you have intended to do to others, near me." Neal, snappish about such magnanimity, asked for an end to talk of forgiveness, claiming that he had more to forgive than anyone; but he warmed to the offer of a reconciliation: "We should never quarrell with each other—we of all men alive—and why. Because, like Peachum and his colleague in the Beggars Opera (is it?) we know too much of one another."[8] Neal's marriage seems to have removed any lingering animosity in Mrs. Pierpont; the two families exchanged news and visits at frequent intervals over many years. Conspicuously absent from Neal's letters are the passionate confidings of his correspondence from Baltimore; the stormy years are over. But decades later, after the untimely death of his son James, Neal was to turn again to his old friend as he had in the desperate reachings of his youth.

Neal's hopes for financial security in his marriage rested rather precariously on law, lecturing, and his editorship of *The Yankee*, a rambunctious literary weekly that started publication on

7. *Wandering Recollections*, pp. 356–57; Neal to Pierpont, PML.
8. Pierpont to Neal, February 2, 1826, HL; Neal to Pierpont, March 22, 1826, PML.

January 1, 1828, and lasted for exactly two years.[9] For five hundred dollars a year (payable largely in law books and stationery), Neal edited this journal that, in his words, "burst like a northern meteor upon our people." [10]

A college student who visited editor Neal during the brief heyday of *The Yankee* has left a vivid picture of the man in motion:

> my attention was attracted by a man about five feet, eight or nine inches high, with a fine head, light-coloured silky hair, robust, athletic, iron-built; in short, the man to make a statue of, every limb was so well developed, and there was so much manhood in the whole figure. He was in a strange-shaped jacket, with a vest after his own form and fashion, for he has all things made according to his notions, dictating to tailors, furniture-makers, house-builders, book-binders. . . . He was over careful and very neat in his person, but not a fop nor a dandy, for *they* follow fashions, and he sets all at defiance. Neal was then alternately talking with a lot of men who were boxing and fencing, for he was a boxing-master, and fencing-master too, and as the printer's devil came in crying "copy, more copy," he would race with a huge swan's quill, full gallop, over sheets of paper as with a steam-pen, and off went one page, and off went another, and then a lesson in boxing, the thump of glove to glove, then the mask, and the stamp of the sandal, and the ringing of the foils.[11]

The journal was ostensibly devoted to the dissemination of Utilitarian doctrine and carried as its masthead motto "The greatest happiness of the greatest number—Bentham." The less than

9. Beginning with the number dated August 20, 1828, a merger changed the name of the journal to *The Yankee and Boston Literary Gazette*. During its last six months, from July through December 1829, *The Yankee and Boston Literary Gazette* was issued in a new series as a monthly journal.

10. *Wandering Recollections*, p. 336.

11. James Brooks, "Letters from the East—John Neal," *New-York Mirror* 11 (1833–34) :69.

cordial atmosphere that surrounded Neal's hasty departure from the Bentham household had not dampened his enthusiasm for the cause. In March 1830, shortly after the birth of his first child, Neal wrote the philosopher of the event and promised that his infant daughter, "being born a utilitarian, shall, if I can so manage it, become the mother of nations in the faith." His involvement, however, seems to have been largely emotional and, suggests Peter J. King, was hardly "an asset to the Benthamite cause; too many of his pages were devoted to self-praise and never enough to explaining or even understanding Bentham." But Neal's caricatures of the old philosopher (curious amalgams of ridicule and affection) and witty attacks on his critics enliven the pages of *The Yankee*—and occasionally strike a note distinctively and outrageously American. Though published elsewhere, this portrait is characteristic: "I can see [Bentham] now, it is the fourteenth of June, thermometer at 76°; there he goes with a pair of thick leather gloves on, woolen stockings rolled up over his knees outside, his coat-tail shaved away like a sailor's round-about, and stooping, with his reverend rump, pushed out like that of a young chicken." [12]

Benthamism—such as it is—shared space in *The Yankee* with Neal's slapdash but far more successful campaign to encourage native literature. During its short life the journal provided the first substantial sponsorship or praise of the fledgling efforts of Poe, Whittier, Hawthorne, and Longfellow and earned the approval of veteran literary nationalist Mathew Carey for its "fearless independence." [13]

In September 1829 Neal inserted a literary notice of far reaching consequences: "If E. A. P. of Baltimore—whose lines about *Heaven* . . . are, though nonsense, rather exquisite nonsense—would but do himself justice, he might make a beautiful and perhaps magnificent poem." In a long letter to Neal published in

12. Peter J. King, John Neal as Benthamite," pp. 64–65; Neal's letter to Bentham is dated March 11, 1830, British Museum; the description of Bentham, written shortly after the demise of *The Yankee*, is in Neal's Introduction to *Principles of Legislation*, p. 82.
13. Carey to Neal, December 21, 1828, HL.

The Yankee three months later, young Poe calls these words "the very first words of encouragement I ever remember to have heard." Poe's letter prefaces extracts from "Al Aaraaf" and "Tamerlane" —the latter dedicated to Neal in the volume of poetry published in Baltimore soon after.[14] (Neal later notified a friend that Poe was only prevented from dedicating the entire volume of poems to him by "my assurances that such a dedication would be a positive injury to him [Poe] and to his book.")[15] It was an appropriate dedication for a poem haunted by Byron's *Giaour* and *Childe Harold*—for the production of a youth who cries out to his mentor: "I am young—not yet twenty—*am* a poet. . . . I appeal to you as a man that loves the same beauty which I adore. . . . It cannot . . . be said that

> 'I left a calling for this idle trade,
> A duty broke—a father disobeyed'—

for I have no father—nor mother." Neal introduced Poe's letter— and the extracts from his poems—with a comment the young poet would never forget:

> He is entirely a stranger to us; but with all their faults,
> if the remainder of Al Aaraaf and Tamerlane is as good,
> as the body of the extracts here given—to say nothing of
> the more extraordinary parts, he will deserve to stand

14. *The Yankee*, n.s. 1 (September and December, 1829) :168, 295–98. The "lines about *Heaven*" are from a poem retitled "Fairyland." *Al Aaraaf, Tamerlane, and Minor Poems* (Baltimore, 1829), was published shortly after Neal printed extracts from it. Arthur Hobson Quinn, *Edgar Allan Poe: A Critical Biography* (New York, 1941), p. 153, suggests that Poe probably sent advance sheets of the volume to Neal. In *The Yankee*, n.s. 1(1829) :295, Neal refers to Poe's "manuscript-works . . . about to be published in Baltimore."

15. Neal to Mary Gove Nichols, November 30, 1846, quoted in Irving T. Richards, "Mary Gove Nichols and John Neal," *New England Quarterly* 7 (1934) :338. Neal must have been referring to *Al Aaraaf, Tamerlane, and Minor Poems* (Baltimore, 1829), though he erroneously describes it as Poe's "first volume of poems"; the first, *Tamerlane and Other Poems* (Boston, 1827), was published before the two men became acquainted.

high—very high—in the estimation of the shining brotherhood.

In the same numbers of *The Yankee* in which Poe received his first encouragement and expressed his gratitude (September and December 1829) are two installments of Neal's five-part series of essays on drama—an elaboration of Schlegel's and *Blackwood's* doctrine of effect. Young Poe almost certainly took note—in the number calling attention to "E. A. P. of Baltimore"—of Neal's exploration of "certain movements of the human heart" that must take place before a man is capable of committing a murder. And he probably read (in the October number) this explanation of the way the heart of the reader is aroused by an artistic manipulation of his relationship to the characters in a story:

> A tale of suffering will always go more directly to the heart, when it is calculated to excite the same kind of emotions in the reader which it represents the characters to be excited with. Hence it is, that . . . we are so unwilling to be told what the conclusion of a story is, before we have read it through.[16]

Poe's theory of the tale of effect and some of the stories embodying that theory may have been influenced by these articles. He was to insist, for example, that "it is an obvious rule of Art that effects should be made to spring as directly as possible from their causes"—causes rooted in three faculties of the reader: "the intellect," "the heart," and "the soul." Having selected a single effect, the skilful artist "then invents such incidents, he then combines such events, and discusses them in such tone as may best aid him in establishing this preconceived effect."[17] Paralleling Neal's observations on reader psychology in a "tale of suffering" are Poe's

16. *The Yankee*, n.s. 1 (1829). Neal's notices of Poe are on pp. 168 and 295–98; his articles on "The Drama" are on pp. 57–68, 134–45, 195–209, 249–58, 303–17; the passages quoted are on pp. 207, 143.

17. "The Poetic Principle" [1850], in *Works*, 14: 275; "Tale-Writing—Nathaniel Hawthorne . . . ," [1847], *Works*, 13:141. For a valuable discussion of Poe's psychological concept of effect, see Blair, "Poe's Conception of Incident and Tone in the Tale," 228–40.

later formulations of "means whereby the author may stir . . .
the heart of the reader." [18]

Poe's thorough familiarity with *The Yankee* and with Neal's
critical views is documented by an approach he made to the publishers of *The Atlantic Souvenir* several months before his encour-
aging reception by Neal. Poe informs Carey and Lea that he would
be proud to see his work in their annual "notwithstanding the assertions of Mr J^no Neal to the contrary." Neal's contrary assertions
are incorporated into his caustic review of *The Atlantic Souvenir*
for 1829.[19] Poe must have been following Neal's journal very closely
to have noticed it, and to remember it seven months later. In his
letter to the *Souvenir*, Poe refers slightingly to Neal's "now and
then hitting, thro sheer impudence, upon a correct judgement in
matters of authorship." But the desperate fledgling is obviously
seeking to ingratiate a prospective publisher and was soon to respond with fervor to the critic he had disparaged.[20]

Two years later, reviewing the *Poems* (1831), Neal calls
Poe "a fellow of fine genius" capable of "Pure poetry in one page
—pure absurdity in another." "To Helen" is quoted as an example of pure poetry, by one who "has the *gift,* and betrays the
presence . . . that cannot be mistaken." Neal concludes his essay
with the (for him) familiar plaint that he is "sick of poetry" and
"would not have meddled with this volume" if not for the genius
and promise of its young author. Young Poe, sick of writing poetry
that did not pay, submitted his first tale later that year. The critic
who gave him "the first jog in [his] literary career" (as Poe puts
it in an 1840 letter to Neal) may have contributed to his decision
to try a new career as a writer of tales.[21]

18. These formulations are fully discussed in Blair's article (see
preceding note), from which the passage last quoted is drawn (p. 230).

19. Review of *The Atlantic Souvenir* for 1829, *The Yankee* 1 (1828):
378.

20. Poe to Carey, Lea and Carey, July 28, 1829, *Letters,* 1:27.

21. "Poems by Edgar A. Poe," *Morning Courier and New-York
Enquirer,* July 8, 1831. For Poe's debut as a writer of tales, see Quinn,
Edgar Allan Poe, pp. 191–92. Poe credits Neal for launching him in his
literary career in a letter dated June 4, [1840], *Letters,* 1:137.

Another young writer fired by Byronic melancholy had turned to and received comfort from Neal. In October of 1828 John Greenleaf Whittier let loose his despair to a man he felt would understand:

> I have just written something ["The Vestal"] for your consideration. You dislike—I believe you do, at least— the blank verse of our modern poets. . . . Nevertheless, I send you a long string of it. If you don't like it, say so privately; *and I will quit poetry, and every thing else of a literary nature,* for I am sick at heart of the business. . . . Insult has maddened me. The friendless boy has been mocked at; and, years ago, he vowed to triumph over the scorners of his boyish endeavors. With the unescapable sense of wrong burning like a volcano in the recesses of his spirit, he has striven to accomplish this vow, until his heart has grown weary of the struggle.

To an earlier outcry (now missing) Neal had responded with a long letter of praise and encouragement; now he lifted young Whittier's spirits with another friendly letter and, more important, published "The Vestal" and several other poems in *The Yankee*.[22]

Two aspiring young writers who had admired Neal's wild novels as undergraduates at Bowdoin College received significant critical mention in *The Yankee*. In what may be the first review of Hawthorne's first novel, James W. Miller (Neal's coeditor) observes that, though it bears marks of "haste or inexperience," many parts of *Fanshawe* are "powerful and pathetic" and its author "should be encouraged to persevering efforts by a fair prospect of future success." It is unfortunate that this first effort—"full," says Norman Holmes Pearson, "of Neal's damned rant and Scott's 'racing and chasing o'er Cannobie Lee' "—should have just missed being commented on by the writer who, in Hawthorne's

22. Whittier's letter is quoted in *Wandering Recollections*, p. 337; Neal's reply, dated September 4, 1829, is quoted in John A. Pollard, *John Greenleaf Whittier: Friend of Man* (Boston, 1949), p. 72. "The Vestal" was published in the November number; "Judith at the Tent of Holofernes" and "The Minstrel-Girl" are in the October and December numbers.

own words, "almost turned my boyish brain with his romances."
Earlier that year Neal had praised Longfellow's "The Spirit of
Poetry" for passages of exquisite beauty in "the language of a
close and feeling observer of nature." But the poem is on the
whole far too derivative for Neal, "too Barry-Cornwallish, or . . .
Milman-ish, or Bryant-ish, or Percival-ish." Mr. Longfellow has "a
fine genius and a pure and safe taste" and is only lacking "a little
more energy, and a little more stoutness." [23]

Young Longfellow may have read Neal's comment on his
poem, for he enthusiastically pored over several numbers of *The
Yankee* in far off Göttingen while visiting a former Bowdoin College classmate studying there. The two Portland youths talked with
delight about (among other things) John Neal and the stir he
was making back home. Longfellow's trip abroad had aroused dormant feelings about his native land; shortly before his stopover in
Göttingen, he had written to Carey and Lea to propose a "Sketch
Book of New England, in the stile of Irving's Sketch Book of Old
England and from the variety of topics which naturally present
themselves to the mind of an American, when in a foreign land, he
recalls the blessings and endearments of home." The publishers
rejected the proposal, reminding the young author that the absence
of copyright protection made it hard for original books—"so
much so, that it appears to us there is less inducement for writing
now than ten years since." Several of Longfellow's sketches came
out in *The Token* and other periodicals; his collection was eventually published as *Outre-Mer*, an Irvingesque sketch book with
little native flavor. He sent a copy to Neal, who acknowledged it
with a friendly admonition: "But why not be yourself—and yourself only." [24]

23. Neal's critique of Longfellow is in "More Portland Poetry," *The
Yankee* 1 (1828):32; Miller's review of *Fanshawe* is at ibid., p. 358. The
quoted extract linking *Fanshawe* to Neal and Scott is from Norman Holmes
Pearson's Introduction to *The Complete Novels and Selected Tales of
Nathaniel Hawthorne* (New York, 1937), p. 8.

24. See Lawrance Thompson, *Young Longfellow, 1807–1843* (New
York, 1938), pp. 132–36, 190–91.

Literary celebrities like Irving and Cooper come off far less favorably in *The Yankee* than do struggling unknowns with a promise of individuality. Neal announces in the opening issue that he has done more for America than "the author of the Sketch Book" and "the author of the most popular novels of our country," for they neither tell nor try to tell "the plain truth of our institutions or our people." Cooper's incongruous fusion of pretentious imagery and artificial diction is ridiculed when Neal encounters a passage in a pseudonymous story that sounds "Cooperish": "a cloud of canvass dropped from her spars—and solicited the breeze." The first part, says Neal, is Cooper—

> no matter who wrote it for the Souvenir; and the latter part—*solicited the breeze,* I'd swear to for his; nobody but the Walter Scott of America ever thought of such finery, in such a place. The moment after you have rounded to a glorious thought, like this of a *cloud of canvass—dropping* from the spars of a great ship, you are to be affronted with a touch of the lackadaisical or a flourish of the Della Cruscan.[25]

There was nothing lackadaisical or della-cruscan to affront the readers of *The Yankee,* subjected as they were to a continuing colloquial barrage of controversy and miscellany ranging from Bentham to blackberrying. According to James Brooks, it was one of the strangest journals ever heard of in which "Men, women and children there thought *out loud* . . . to gain that self-confidence which has helped, and will help them through life." A typical breezy exchange between reader and editor will convey something of the lively rapport that Brooks admires: "I resolved years ago," writes a subscriber, "to talk to you in some way or other before I died, and when we met . . . your word-mill was in such tremendous and continual operation, that it was impossible for me to manufacture a whole piece myself." Neal's comment: "immaterial —too common a charge to excite remark." The wide appeal of

25. Review of *The Atlantic Souvenir* for 1829, in *The Yankee* 1 (1828):378. The story under discussion is "Esmeralda" by Godfrey Wallace (pseudonym of J. H. B. Latrobe).

The Yankee could not, however, save it from collapse. Brooks attributed its failure to its being "a thousand miles too far 'down East.' . . . It was like throwing a great rock off the shores of Lake Superior to agitate the whole surface, instead of throwing it into the centre." [26]

Neal was not daunted ("So much the worse for the public," he wrote Pierpont), but the fate of *The Yankee* was a portent. John D. Seelye has suggested that a provincial environment was a disastrous influence "on a brilliant but erratic mind." During the years immediately after his return, Neal's literary production and performance are impressive: three novels, a number of extraordinary tales, a vigorous Yankee farce. In the long run, however, Portland proved to be a dead end. Neal, Lowell was to proclaim twenty years after the prodigal's return, "wasted in Maine/The sinews and cords of his pugilist brain." [27]

26. Brooks, "Letters from the East—John Neal," p. 69; "Natural Writing," *The Yankee* 1 (1828) :380.

27. Seelye's Introduction to a facsimile edition of *Rachel Dyer* (Gainesville, Fla.: Scholars' Facsimiles and Reprints, 1964), p. vii; James Russell Lowell, "A Fable for Critics," in *Complete Writings of James Russell Lowell* (New York, 1966), 12:55.

12 Salem Witchcraft
Rachel Dyer

Read John Neal's Rachel Dyer,
a tale of Witchcraft.
Some parts very powerful.

LONGFELLOW, 1868

Writing in 1884 of the terrible events in Salem two centuries before, S. A. Drake asserts that prior to the appearance of Longfellow's *New England Tragedies* (1868) "there had been no serious attempt to make use of this sinister chapter for any other purpose than that of impartial history." But Longfellow's journal reveals that he had turned to Neal's novel of witchcraft while working on his verse drama and had found "Some parts very powerful." In his survey of early fictional treatments of witchcraft unnoticed by Drake, G. Harrison Orians finds *Rachel Dyer* (1828) important as "the sole unrelieved tragedy" among them. Hawthorne's enthusiasm for Neal probably extended beyond Bowdoin to 1828, a year in which he was busily seeking out native material back home in Salem. *Rachel Dyer* "could well have been the inspiration for the quest which resulted in *The Scarlet Letter*," says John D. Seelye.[1]

While it is still not the book he would have written if he had had more leisure, nor the book he hoped to write before he died, Neal proclaimed *Rachel Dyer* to be "some sort of atonement for

1. See G. Harrison Orians, "New England Witchcraft in Fiction," *American Literature* 2 (1930) :54, 58. Longfellow's journal entry is quoted in Samuel Longfellow, *Final Memorials of Henry Wadsworth Longfellow* (London, 1887), p. 104. Seelye, Introduction to *Rachel Dyer*, facsimile ed., p. xii.

the folly and extravagance of my earlier writing."[2] His description of the manner in which the novel was conceived and written underscores his determination to conform to his own requirements for effective authorship of a work designed to arouse the heart. "I will correct my redundancies," he wrote Blackwood about the original short story version, "so fast as I can without endangering the vitality of my individual character, the very source of my fertility and power." Soon after, he informed Blackwood that the tale was almost finished, that "It abounds with historical truth; and I might make of it, either a tragedy or a novel, without any great labour." What Neal finally made of his unpublished tale is a tragic novel far more concentrated in effect than any of his earlier works. His success in adhering to *Blackwood's* doctrine of effect in *Rachel Dyer* may be explained by the fact that he fleshed out a skeleton prepared for *Maga* with (for him) unusual care.[3]

Neal's "historical truth," largely gleaned from the 1823 edition of Robert Calef's *More Wonders of the Invisible World,* is invested with an aura of the supernatural. The novel opens with an impassioned plea for a tolerant attitude toward the "witch-hunters" of earlier times. A belief in witchcraft was rooted not in the ignorant but in the learned; and a fear of the supernatural has persisted among wise men from ancient times to the present. In the face of such authority,

> What right have we to say that witches and witchcraft are no more, that sorcery is done with forever, that miracles are never to be wrought again, or that Prophecy shall never be heard again by the people of God, uplifting her voice like a thousand echoes from the everlasting solitudes of the sea, or like uninterrupted thunder breaking over the terrible and haughty nations of our earth. (p. 24)

After sketching the history of man's universal fear of the supernatural, the narrator turns to another basic trait, one illus-

2. Preface to *Rachel Dyer: A North American Story* (Portland: Shirley and Hyde, 1828), p. iv (all references to the novel are to this edition).

3. Neal to Blackwood, September 28 and October [?], 1825, NLS.

trated by the history of our founding fathers. Having fled the old world to escape religious persecution, the pilgrims, as soon as they were safe and secure, fell upon the Quakers, who had followed them with the same hope. "Such is the nature of man! The persecuted of to-day become the persecutors of to-morrow." When an aged woman of the Quakers, Mary Dyer, is put to death, Elizabeth Hutchinson—later herself exiled—prophesies disaster for the persecutors. "And lo! after a few years, the daughter of the chief judge, before whom the prophecy had been uttered with such awful power, was tried for witchcraft and put to death on the very spot (so says the tradition of the people) where she stayed to scoff at Mary Dyer, who was on her way to the scaffold at the time." There follows a time of trouble and terror: earthquake, fire, storm, showers of stars, war, and strife in the church. A "wo without a shape" was upon the land. For a time the bloody struggle known as King Philip's War was thought to be the fulfillment of the prophecy. But that over, the ominous atmosphere continues until it culminates in the terrible events in Salem: "lo! the Destroyer himself appeared! The shadow of death gave way for the visage of death—filling every heart with terror, and every house with lamentation." The opening chapter of *Rachel Dyer* thus establishes the witchcraft excitement of 1692 as a prophetic retribution for the sins of the fathers—a retribution suggestive of supernatural intervention, but also involving mortal weakness. The stage has been set for a spectacle in which the heart of the reader is to be aroused to pity and sympathy.

The scene shifts to the household of Matthew Paris, preacher of Salem village. He is an "aged, poor and solitary man," sick with unsupportable sorrow over the untimely death of his young wife. This man of sorrow centers his life on his daughter Abigail ("the live miniature of [her] mother") and his niece Bridget Pope. Suddenly, the lovely and innocent children are transformed into snarling, spiteful creatures of the devil. They accuse an Indian couple, servants in the household, who in turn implicate an old and harmless woman, Sarah Good. A tragic chain reaction has been initiated.

It is during the trial of Sarah Good that the Reverend George

Burroughs makes his dramatic first appearance. For his hero, Neal builds on the sketchy records that have survived concerning the most prominent victim of the Salem hysteria. He must have been struck by the fact that Burroughs had lived in Falmouth (Portland) and had been driven from his pastorate in nearby Casco when that town was destroyed by Indians in 1690. At the time of his arrest he had settled in the comparative safety of Wells. Neal must also have relished the tradition that the minister, though small of stature like himself, was possessed of extraordinary strength and agility and acquired a reputation as one of Harvard's first athletes. But perhaps most impressive to lawyer Neal would have been Calef's vivid report of the minister's eloquence on the scaffold—a speech "uttered with such . . . fervency of spirit, as was very affecting, and drew tears from many." [4]

Out of these materials Neal fashioned a fiery, tender, courageous protagonist much akin to the Byronic heroes of his earlier novels. The ancestry of the real George Burroughs is obscure, that of Neal's preacher much more so. His mother, captured by Indians as a child, grew up among them and married a warrior descended from a white man. She bears him a son but, on being converted to Christianity, leaves her family to begin a new life among believers. When his father falls in battle, young George seeks out his white mother and adopts her faith. George Burroughs becomes so fervent a Christian "that he came to be regarded, while yet a youth, as a new hope for the church that had sprung up from the blood of the martyrs."

It is this fiery advocate who strides into the courtroom where Sarah Good faces death and cries his defiance of Governor Phips, Doctor Mather, and the assembled magistrates. He succeeds brilliantly in exposing the error of a witness who claims he was stabbed by "the shape of Sarah Good"; but his success merely pro-

4. "More Wonders of the Invisible World," in Samuel P. Fowler, ed., *Salem Witchcraft* (Boston, 1865), p. 278; Calef's account of Burroughs' gallows speech is on p. 254. Neal reprints these accounts (from the Salem edition of 1823) in an appendix to *Rachel Dyer* entitled "Historical Facts," pp. 272–73.

vides the judges with new evidence of the devil's power to overthrow the righteous and aid those in his service. Burroughs
vainly protests that this line of reasoning leaves no possible escape
to the innocent, "for whatever should happen, you would believe it
a trick of the father of lies." Puritan legalism triumphs over justice;
Sarah Good is condemned; and from that day on, George Burroughs
is regarded with "unspeakable terror."

On the gallows the old woman protests her innocence and
prophesies death for other innocents who are watching her die.
Among the spectators is one who echoes her words:

> Yea of a truth! cried a woman who stood apart from the
> people with her hands locked and her eyes fixed upon
> the chief-judge. It was Rachel Dyer, the grand-child of
> Mary Dyer. Yea of a truth! for the Lord will not hold him
> guiltless that spilleth his brother's blood, or taketh his
> sister's life by the law—and her speech was followed by
> a shriek from every hill-top and every house-top, and
> from every tree and every rock within sight of the place,
> and the cart moved away, and the body of the poor old
> creature swung to and fro in the convulsions of death.
> (p. 64)

Rachel Dyer is the hunchbacked, redheaded sister of the lovely
Elizabeth; both these pious Quaker girls come to love Burroughs
during his unavailing struggle with the magistrates. (Neal's
preacher is unmarried—a widower twice-over; the historical Burroughs was married to his third wife at the time of his arrest.)
Rachel's fate is to die with the man she loves; the condemned
Elizabeth, too ill to be executed, is spared when the hysteria lifts,
almost as suddenly as it had descended.

George Burroughs seals his fate in a vain attempt to save
Martha Cory, another old woman accused of witchcraft. By now the
accusations have multiplied, and the hearts of the people are
numbed by fear: "The judges were in array against the people, and
the people against each other; and the number of the afflicted in-
creased every day and every hour." Burroughs inveighs against a
legal procedure which makes false confession and accusation the
only avenue of escape for those under suspicion. He attacks the

court's assumption of guilt until innocence is proved, its failure to provide counsel for the accused or to insure the presence of defense witnesses. Underlying all these criticisms is the fact that, just as the hearts of the accusers have been numbed by fear, so have the hearts of the judges been hardened through a subjugation of their individuality to a perverted legalism.

The execution of Martha Cory arouses Burroughs to more determined efforts. He has come to think of himself as "a messenger of the Most High, with every faculty and every power of his mind at work to baffle and expose" those who, either through fear or malice, are bringing death to so many innocents. But it is only through martyrdom that he finally triumphs. His own trial, comparatively brief, is climaxed by the malicious testimony of a jealous girl who resents his friendship with Elizabeth Dyer. The shapes of Burroughs' dead wives have appeared before her and told her that he murdered them. Crushed by this testimony, the preacher is sustained in his agony by the comforting presence of Rachel Dyer. When he cries out to the spirits of his dead wives to appear and accuse him to his face, there is a terrible commotion; his accusers point to the shapes that *have* come. He knows he is doomed and begins "to give way himself now, with a convulsion of the heart, before the tremendous array of testimony and weight of delusion." Justice has been defeated by fear; the jury finds him guilty and his execution is ordered for the following day.

But his fighting spirit now revives, and he persuades the magistrates to allow him to remain in the courtroom to witness the trial and condemnation of Rachel Dyer. There is a farewell meeting during which the two courageous hearts come to a new and full understanding. He goes to his death with simple heroism. (The gruesome details in Calef's account of the execution are omitted.[5]) Rachel escapes the ordeal of a public death; when the

5. Neal deletes this passage from his transcription (in "Historical Facts") of Calef's account: "When he was cut down, he was dragged by the halter to a hole, or grave, between the rocks, about two feet deep, his shirt and breeches being pulled off, and an old pair of trowsers of one executed

high sheriff comes for her, she is dead—with "a smile about her mouth" and her Bible at her side. They do not die in vain; their martyrdom breaks the spell. The sentence of death is never carried out upon Elizabeth, or anyone else: "the terrible infatuation was over, the people had waked up, the judges and the preachers of the Lord; and the chief-judge, Sewall, had publicly read a recantation for the part he played in the terrible drama."

By placing these terrible events in ordinary settings—countryside, cottage, village courtroom—Neal imparts immediacy to the historically remote. Old Salem is described with loving (occasionally portentous) particularity: the schoolhouse, "a log-hut plastered with blue clay in stripes and patches . . . , a meeting-house with a short wooden spire, and a figure of death on the top for a weather-cock." Light and dark are deployed throughout to reinforce the emotional atmosphere. Before their "visitation," we see the Paris children "searching for sun-baked apples in the short thick grass, or feeding the fish in the smooth clear sea." After their affliction they are constantly "hiding away . . . in holes and corners" until "pursued and plucked forth to the light." The jury that dooms Martha Cory does so in a gloomy dusk ("there was but just light to see their faces"). Burroughs is brought to trial in the midst of a great thunderstorm, and his defiant pronouncements are punctuated by the heavens. The dead Rachel is lifted up from the bed in her dark cell "and carried out into the cool morning air."

In *Errata* Neal had argued that as writing comes closer to living speech "the more powerful is [its] operation upon the heart of man." In his "Unpublished Preface" to *Rachel Dyer* (the preface for the series of North American stories projected for *Blackwood's*, the first of which was the witchcraft tale), he sounds again the familiar call for authentic Yankee character and speech and repeats his intention never to write "what is now worshipped under the name of *classical* English . . . the deadest language I

---

put on his lower parts; he was so put in, together with Willard and Carrier, that one of his hands and his chin, and a foot of one of them, were left uncovered." Fowler, *Salem Witchcraft*, pp. 254–55. Such grim details would have nullified the pathos of the death scene as Neal presents it.

ever met with." Neal's novel displays an unprecedented flexibility in ranging from Burroughs' impassioned courtroom rhetoric to the broken stammerings of his last meeting with Rachel. From the time of Burroughs' leavetaking to her very last breath, the doomed Martha Cory can only say over and over again "the words of a child in the voice of a child, Ah me—ah me—." A breathless down-east youngster testifies thus in court:

> an' so he stopped me an' axed me where the plague I was running to; an' so I up an' tells him all I know about the knife, an' so, an' so, an so, that air feller, what dooze he do, but he jounces me up on that air plaguy crupper and fetches me back here full split, you see, and rides over everything, and makes everybody get out o' the way, an' *will* make me tell the story whether or no. (pp. 79–80)

Much of the novel consists of dialogue stripped of quotation marks and interrupted by a minimal amount of narration.[6] The narrator's style, in turn, is also varied to reinforce a mood or emotion. Matthew Paris' terror at the transformation of his afflicted children is rendered in the cadence and diction of the Old Testament:

> A new fear fell upon him, and his knees smote together, and the hair of his flesh rose, and he saw a spirit, and the spirit said to him look! And he looked, and lo! the truth appeared to him; for he saw neighbour after neighbour flying from his path, and all the heads of the church keeping aloof and whispering together in a low voice. Then knew he that Bridget Pope and Abigail Paris were bewitched. (p. 58)

Rachel Dyer represents a significant development in Neal's career as a novelist. While he does not hesitate to depart freely from the historical record whenever it serves his fictional purpose, he is shaping his novel from events that have their own compelling sweep and form. The trial and execution of a George Burroughs in Salem is a more clearly defined subject than the adventures of a

6. Dialogue is predominant in sixteen of the twenty-one chapters; in several chapters there is virtually no narration.

Jonathan Oadley or Walter Harwood in the Revolutionary War. The tendency to sprawl, so characteristic in all Neal's works, is at last under some control here. The essayistic opening chapters, in which the narrator establishes his sympathy for the delusions of the persecutors, have a relevance absent from some of the more spectacular digressions in other works. It is significant that Whittier found "magnificent poetry" in them, a poetry that could only spring from deep conviction. (Neal's defense of a belief in the supernatural was to give way toward the end of his life to an almost desperate faith in spiritualism.) More important, as Alexander Cowie has observed, Neal's opening chapters enable him to focus "upon the victims of the delusion and on their heroic, pitiful efforts to oppose it." But Neal's control, even in *Rachel Dyer,* is fitful. With all its honesty and power, the novel does wander off into excessive polemics, especially in the courtroom scenes, where the lawyer in Neal gets somewhat the better of the novelist. The excessively elaborate exposures of unjust trial procedure overshadow the intriguing jealousies that swirl about Burroughs and motivate the young women who are his accusers; these are hinted at but not really clarified. There are other weaknesses—lapses here and there into conventional melodrama and bathos. But on the whole, "Constrained, perhaps, by his great theme," says Cowie, "Neal for once abandoned his literary monkeyshines and wrote in simple sincerity of real people." [7] Hawthorne and Melville were to write far mightier novels on similar themes. In 1828, *Rachel Dyer* stands alone.

7. For Whittier's appreciation of the poetic opening section of *Rachel Dyer* see his review of *Authorship,* in *Whittier on Writers and Writing,* ed. E. H. Cady and H. H. Clark (Syracuse, N.Y., 1950), p. 42. The view that the novel wanders off into polemics is expressed by Tremaine McDowell, "In New England," in *Literary History of the United States,* ed. Robert E. Spiller et al., 3d ed. rev. (New York, 1963), p. 291. Cowie, *Rise of the American Novel,* pp. 174–75.

13 Divertimento and Disaster
Authorship and *The Down-Easters*

And now the author repeats
to the people of America, one and all,
farewell;
assuring them that there is
little probability of his ever appearing
before them again as a novel-writer.
"UNPUBLISHED PREFACE" TO RACHEL DYER

Neal was too fond of the grand gesture for us to take too seriously his public farewell as novelist in his "Unpublished Preface"
included in *Rachel Dyer*. But *Authorship* (1830) is a short, casual
affair, and there are indications that it was written before he
expanded his *Blackwood's* witchcraft tale into a novel, while he
was still living in the Bentham household.[1] *The Down-Easters*
(1833) is a patchwork of steamboat sketches, published separately
in 1830, and then clumsily attached to an outrageously Gothic
melodrama written, like *Authorship*, in the Bentham household.
Neal did not publish another novel for twenty-six years. In a sense,
therefore, *Rachel Dyer* is indeed a farewell to the genre.

Both the farewell and the novel went virtually unnoticed. Five
months after publication, a reviewer noted that Neal's style in
Rachel Dyer "has fewer of the peculiarities of its peculiar author"
than any earlier work of his. A British critic, three years later,
found George Burroughs, "the wild preacher of the woods, . . . a

1. *Authorship: A Tale* (Boston: Gray and Bowen, 1830). In *Wandering Recollections*, p. 260, Neal states that he wrote *Authorship* while
writing for *Blackwood's*. Internal evidence in the novel suggests that it was
written after his break with Blackwood and during his stay in the Bentham
household.

146

personage worthy of the dramatic era of Elizabeth." Whittier, about the same time, also praised the novel. The rest, except for two notices of the work (one of them by himself) in *The Yankee*, was almost total silence.[2] Neal now directed his talents to journalism and to the short story.

The slender novel titled *Authorship: A Tale* was published in Boston in July 1830. Its author was identified only as "a New Englander Over-Sea." Perhaps in reaction to the somber story of witchcraft that preceded it, Neal tossed off this improvisation that alternates between high farce and tongue-in-cheek seriousness. The narrator, an American author visiting England under the fictitious name of Carter Holmes, encounters a beautiful woman in Westminster Abbey. Despite her heavy veil, he falls precipitously in love with her ("I saw that with a superb figure and the walk of a Spanish woman, she knew how to love") and persuades himself that her male escort is not her husband. For three years he is haunted by the encounter and looks for her in every social gathering, all the while rebuking himself for behaving like a "great green boy" or a "youthful poet crazy with such love as they retail in the toy-shops and circulating-libraries." Then, while touring the Isle of Wight, he sees the couple again. He follows them to a mountainous area, the Needles, and is both alarmed for the woman's safety as she walks carelessly amidst danger and charmed by her feet ("the prettiest feet in the world—they were enough by themselves to give a sculptor the heart-ache"). Holmes intervenes to save her escort from a fatal fall and is flabbergasted when this man who is a stranger to him addresses him familiarly as Carter Holmes and mockingly identifies himself as Edward Molton, Echo, Randolph, and a string of other characters from Neal's novels. He finally lets it be known that his name is Edwards and invites the bewildered author to stay with him and his wife Mary. Holmes

2. Review of *Rachel Dyer* in *The Atlas* 1 (1829) :261; "England and the United States," *The Englishman's Magazine* 1 (1831) :68; *Whittier on Writers and Writing*, p. 42; "Neal's New Novel" and "Rachel Dyer," *The Yankee* 2 (1829) :37–38, 39.

accepts and spends the happiest week of his life with the mysterious couple, though he feels in their company "very much as a man would feel, if he were thrown with his face uncovered, among a party of masked people."

What adds zest to the novel thus far is the artful balance (never managed quite so expertly in any of the earlier works) between the comic and serious. The narrator hits out at things around him (the sham splendor of historic England, tourists, the world of authorship) and at himself—his own foibles and follies as he muddles through his bewildered and bewildering infatuation. At one point, an Englishman describes his response to Carter Holmes in terms that apply almost equally well to Holmes himself and to the reader: "I never could make out whether he was laughing at me, or I at him."

The delicate balance is carried through to the very end. The wife pleads with Holmes to save her husband. He is in the clutches of dangerous men, apparently gamblers (though even more lurid activities are hinted at). Edwards' relationship with the narrator is curiously ambiguous: He informs Holmes that they are "wonderfully" alike (he too was once an author) and "if any thing should happen to me, I bequeath [my wife] to you." He urges Holmes to kiss her as a token of friendship and throws them together by themselves on several occasions.

At one such meeting Mary tells Holmes her life story: "My mother did not love me—I could see that—she would neither caress me, nor let me caress her, and I could not live without being caressed by somebody." She grew up a stunningly beautiful woman with a basic aversion to all other women and an extraordinary responsiveness to kindness in men—so powerful that she feels ready to fall upon the neck of a stranger as if he were her own father if he seems a good man touched with sorrow. She and Carter Holmes have met before: After a disastrous love affair with a married man, she had encountered Holmes in a coach en route to Birmingham; he had given her comfort and advice that brought her through a difficult time. Soon after, she met and married Edwards who, she tells Holmes, "reminded me of you forty times in

Illustrations

1. John Pierpont in 1821

From a pencil sketch by Rembrandt Peale
Collection of the Pierpont Morgan Library

THE undersigned, (1) having entered into some correspondence with the reputed author of "Randolph;" who is, or is not, (2) sufficiently described as JOHN NEAL, a gentleman by indulgent courtesy;—informs honourable men, that he has found him unpossessed (3) of courage to make satisfaction for the insolence of his folly. (4)

Stating thus much, the undersigned commits this Craven (5) to his infamy. (6)

- EDWARD C. PINKNEY.
Baltimore, Oct. 11, 1823.

1) The *undersigned*—quite *diplomatick*. (2) That is—I have challenged John Neal, who *is*, or is the author of Randolph—because he *is*. (3) Beautifully expressed. How much *more* beautiful, and ious, than to say—I found him *without* courage, or *destitute* of courage. (4) To be read either —"insolence of his folly"—or "folly of his insolence." (5) Craven—Blackstone— The young tleman has read law, to great advantage. (6) Awful, to be sure—what will become of poor Mr. , after that dooming; or *consignment*, rather.—ED.

2. Neal posted as a coward, 1823

Facsimile of the printed card posted
in the streets of Baltimore, as reproduced,
with Neal's annotations, in *Errata*

3. "Carter Holmes" writes to the House of Blackwood

The opening page of Neal's first letter, April 7, 1824
National Library of Scotland

My dear Sir,

I send the manuscript, of which I spoke, herewith. It is in three volumes; and, so far as historical facts, *or national peculiarities*, are concerned, is faithful. — You must judge of the rest.

I have tried, by bestowing *here* more time upon it, ten times over, than I *have* ever upon anything else, to make it precisely, what I believe to be now required by the publick appetite. — No matter what may be the merit of the novel writers, now in vogue — the publick have grown too familiar with all their peculiarities — excellencies, — styles and subjects. — They want something new, though it be worse. — These are my notions: you will judge for yourself.

I think very well of McCadell's book, on many accounts: and am now preparing to take it up, for an article, which I hope to make both entertaining and solidly instructive.

Sincerely yours

Carter Holmes

N.B.
Oct. 7 1824
7 Warwick St. Pall Mall

4. "Carter Holmes" submits a novel (*Brother Jonathan*)

Neal to William Blackwood, October 7, 1824
National Library of Scotland

5. William Blackwood

From a portrait by William Allan
Collection of William Blackwood and Sons Ltd.
Photo Tom Scott, Edinburgh

BULLETIN EXTRA.

ARRIVED, at Portland, on Saturday evening last, in the Steam-Boat, in a short passage from London, via New-York, the celebrated author of "Keep Cool," "Randolph," "Errata," &c., &c., in a state of great bodily and mental exhaustion, owing to his excessive labors in furnishing matter for Blackwood's Edinburgh Monthly Magazine. It is said much of the elevation of the American character is owing to this distinguished author. Since his arrival in his native town, it has been recommended to put himself under the care of the Hon. STEPHEN JONES, M. D. an eminent Southern Physician. This has been done, and the Doctor reports favorably. On Wednesday afternoon he was walking with his Physician apparently much better. Dr. JONES, however, recommends his immediate removal to Baltimore, or some more Southern Climate, for his complete restoration.

July 12.

6. Neal posted as a traitor, 1827

Facsimile of the printed placard (first bulletin extra)
posted at the gates of Bowdoin College and
throughout the village of Brunswick
Houghton Library

BULLETIN EXTRA.

ARRIVED at Portland, on Saturday evening last, in the Steam Boat, in a short passage from London, via New-York, the infamous author of *"Keep Cool,"* *"Randolph,"* *"Errata,"* &c. &c. who has basely traduced his native town and country for hire. A renegado, who, unable to obtain an honest living at home, and driven from his native country by the scorn and contempt of honest indignation, picked up a scanty living in Edinburgh and London, by being a pander for scandal against the country that nourished him, in the periodical journals of those cities. How much of the elevation of the American character is owing to this distinguished author, let an enlightened public judge! He has been long laboring under symptons of insanity, and since his arrival in his native town, it has been recommended to put himself under the care of **STEPHEN JONES, M. D.** an eminent African Physician. This has been done, and the Doctor reports favorably. On Wednesday afternoon he was walking with his Physician apparently much better. Dr. **JONES** however, recommends his immediate removal to Baltimore, or some more southern climate, for his complete restoration. *July* 12, 1827.

N. B. It is understood this celebrated author has returned from the East, without much improvement.

7. Neal posted as a traitor, 1827, second version

Facsimile of the revised and expanded printed placard
(second bulletin extra) posted in the streets of Portland
Houghton Library

8. Neal family portrait, around 1843

From a daguerreotype
Collection of Mrs. Sherwood Picking

9. Lecturer on women's rights, the Broadway Tabernacle

From a contemporary sketch of the Broadway Tabernacle

10. John Pierpont in his old age

From a portrait by F. B. Carpenter
Collection of the Union League Club of New York
Photo Frick Art Reference Library

11. John Neal in his old age

Photo the Newberry Library

the course of a day." They were blissfully happy until his failure as
an author led him to his current embroilment with what seems to be
a group of gamblers.

The wife's confession takes place in a house where her
husband and his dangerous friends have gathered to play at high
stakes and discuss their mysterious plans. Holmes joins them
and finds himself the uncomprehending target of cryptic raillery
about authorship and sly digs at the farfetched plots of current
novels. Some of the gamblers claim to be authors, and one insists
that he has written a work based on "the true and faithful history
of a young man who fell desperately in love with his own grand-
mother." (Poe was to write a tale "The Spectacles" of a young
man who falls desperately in love with his own great-great-grand-
mother.) Another suggests that a plot worthy of our day would
have a brother and sister marry each other "in the last page of
a fourth volume; she in the dress of a man, he in the dress of
a woman, each believing the other to be what the dress intimated."
Edwards stamps on the toe of someone ridiculing a novel that
sounds very much like the production of Carter Holmes.

The party is suddenly broken up by a stranger who escorts
Edwards away, apparently under arrest; an offer of bail money
by Fontleroy, the leader of the gamblers, is rejected. Before leaving, Edwards gives his wedding ring to Carter Holmes—to be
delivered to his wife. She faints at the news, and when Holmes
rushes off for a doctor in the middle of the night, he is arrested
as a suspicious character. He is confined in the watch house
until morning, and by the time he is finally able to get back,
Mary Edwards has vanished.

In perplexity and grief Holmes declares that "I would journey
the world over to see her again"; but in a footnote (apparently
added to the manuscript shortly before publication) Neal adds:
"No not now; but I would when this was written." Holmes is
unable to find any trace of the missing Maria (her real name)
and tries to find solace by traveling in the country. Still desperate
five weeks later, he comes to the realization that literary labor
is his only salvation. He takes a post chaise to London and drops

off into a troubled sleep. The tolling of a heavy bell "connected in some way or other with a dream I had" wakens him. The carriage is at a standstill, surrounded by an enormous crowd. Holmes comes to the realization that he is only a few yards from the scaffold outside Newgate. Snatches of conversation from spectators swarming over the coach disclose to him that he is about to be an involuntary witness to a public execution: "I was terror struck—fascinated with fear—and though I withdrew my head and shut my eyes, and stopped my ears before I drew my breath, I had time to see the figure and shape of the man who was about to die. . . . Let me pass over what followed." The execution of Fontleroy as a notorious forger (for it is he) leaves Holmes in a state of shock: "If he was a forger, what were they who appeared so inferior to him? Could this be the authorship they meant?" he asks himself and trembles to think about what has become of the woman he loves and her unfortunate husband.

He returns to his writing desk in London, too fearful to inquire further. Soon after, Holmes learns that Edwards was not arrested but saved from Fontleroy's fate when he was escorted from the gambling house; his rescuer was Maria's former lover and present benefactor. His informant will not tell where the couple is now: "I am afraid she cares a little too much for you. . . . And you a little too much for her!" But Holmes finally manages to draw out the fact that they are on their way to "the United States of North America." "Gracious God!" he cries out as the novel ends, "you don't say so, then I shall see her again!"

A good deal of the humor in *Authorship* is playfully private. In describing the atrocious service at an Isle of Wight inn, Holmes says that the egg he had ordered for breakfast "was not endowed with the faculty of forthcomingness—to borrow a word from Q. S. P." (p. 55). How many readers could possibly recognize the reference (with nothing in the context to provide the slightest help) to Bentham's residence, Queen's Square Place, and to one of the old philosopher's amusing word coinages? There is an allusion to William Blackwood (p. 92), rather cryptic even to those who might know that Carter Holmes was the name Neal used when he was corresponding with the publisher. How many readers could follow the discussions of Neal's Baltimore novels, identified as "W—— A——" (for *Errata, or . . . Will. Adams*) and "R——" (for *Randolph*)? How many could relish the whimsy of the husband in giving himself the names of Neal's fictional characters while withholding his own?

Fact and fancy are so commingled that it is almost impossible to draw the line between them. The Fontleroy of the novel is a real person, Henry Fauntleroy, executed publicly outside Newgate prison on November 30, 1824, just three months after his arrest for forgery.[3] When the mysterious couple balk at giving Holmes their real names because "you'll put us in a book if we do," he exclaims: "In a book—zounds! I'll put you in a book if you don't" (p. 102). The safely married (but anonymous) John Neal inserts a footnote in 1830 vetoing the passionate determination of Carter Holmes to pursue Maria to the ends of the earth. But is the footnote Neal's, or that of a fictitious editor playfully created by Neal?

There is more than playfulness in these bewildering alternations of reality and illusion. The *ménage à trois* that gambols provocatively throughout the novel provides occasions for some provocative glimpses into the anatomy of love. It is understandable that Whittier should find *Authorship* "not a good book," not worthy of the author of *Rachel Dyer*. But he is struck by Neal's "accurate conception of the human heart" and quotes admiringly this passage describing a feeling that "every bosom" must recognize:

> I saw that she could not bear the idea of parting with me; I saw that she would be miserable after I had gone whatever she might say, and so, much as I loved her, I was all the happier for it. Strange! I would have died for that woman—I would, upon my life—and yet I could not

3. See Horace Bleackley, ed., *Trial of Henry Fauntleroy and Other Famous Trials for Forgery* (Edinburgh and London, 1924), Introduction, p. 46: "A more stupendous throng had never gathered around the grim walls of Newgate."

bear the idea of being forgotten by her, though I knew
that if she remembered me, it would make *her* life a
burthen to her. Such is love—such is the very nature of
man! Love as we may, we never love another so much
as we do ourselves, even though we destroy ourselves
to make that other happy—it would kill us to know that
one we care for could be happy without our help.[4]

Rarely in nineteenth-century American fiction has the love of an
unmarried man for a married woman been treated with such
penetrating insight into the role of the ego in affairs of the heart
—and with such cool indifference to the marital status of the
woman in question.

If, as seems likely, Neal wrote *Authorship* while living in
the Bentham household, about four years intervened between
its composition and the magazine publication (in April 1830)
of the steamboat sketches later expanded to comprise the first
and more memorable half of *The Down-Easters*. The almost un-
believable disparity between the farcical realism that opens the
novel and the rampant Gothicism of the last half suggests that
Neal was hard pressed to make a book in 1833. The young firm
of Harper and Brothers was responsive to the mounting popularity
of humor with an emphatic native flavor—humor which, according to Walter Blair, "amusingly displayed localized characters and
characteristics as well as various American social and political
foibles." In the same year as *The Down-Easters*, Harper also
brought out *Sketches and Eccentricities of Colonel David Crockett
of Tennessee* and a book of letters in Down-East vernacular,
purportedly written by Major J. Downing—an imitation of the
widely acclaimed "Jack Downing" letters by Seba Smith of
Maine.[5]

4. *Whittier on Writers and Writing*, pp. 42, 45; the passage quoted
by Whittier is in *Authorship*, p. 155.

5. In a postscript to his Preface, Neal says that the original sketches
were submitted in 1830 to a short-lived New York magazine, not identified;
The Down-Easters, &c. &c. &c., 2 vols. (New York: Harper and Brothers,
1833), vol. 1, p. [viii]. For the emergence of native humor in this period,
see Blair, *Native American Humor*, esp. pp. 38–42; for the contributions

Neal's preoccupation with authentic Yankee character and talk is reflected in earlier criticism and fiction—most notably in his attacks on Cooper and in *Seventy-Six* and *Brother Jonathan*. In *Rachel Dyer* the tragic courtroom scenes are interspersed with countrified high jinks featuring the bailiff; the massacre at Casco Bay is preceded by the crude banter and horseplay of some high spirited and simplehearted Yankees who ignore Burroughs' warning that an attack is imminent. It is uncertain whether the regional wit and realism in the novel was a part of the original North American tale prepared for *Blackwood's* or whether they were added to the expanded version written in Portland.[6] Either way, Neal's continuing and increasing involvement with regional realism is attested to by two series of articles he ran in *The Yankee* ("Live Yankees" and "Sketches from Life")—and by the very conception of the magazine itself. It finds its fullest expression in *The Down-Easters*.

The rapid changes taking place in our country, warns the Preface, will soon leave us with hardly a vestige "of our strongest and sharpest peculiarities." The rough live talk of our forebears is a precious heritage preserved in only a tiny fraction of the hundreds of volumes purporting to represent the New Englander —in a few stories by Timothy Flint and John Neal, an occasional passage of Catharine Sedgwick, some of Paulding's portraits, and Cooper's early efforts. Charles Brockden Brown and Washington Irving are reluctantly excluded: "their books are not American, though they themselves are." This book prepares the way for a change, but the main job of creating a truly American literature he must leave to younger writers.

The novel opens on the crowded deck of a steamboat en route to Baltimore from Philadelphia in May 1814:

---

of Harper and Brothers to this trend, see Eugene Exman, *The Brothers Harper* (New York, 1965), pp. 41–42.

6. See *Rachel Dyer*, pp. 69–71, 158–63. Localized humor is omitted in a short version of the novel (perhaps the original *Blackwood's* story) entitled "New England Witchcraft," *New-York Mirror* 16 (1838–39):337, 345–46, 353–54, 361–62, 369–70.

> The war, chess, politics, flirting, pushpin, tetotum, and jackstraws (cards being prohibited,) newspapers and religious tracts, had all been tried, and all in vain to relieve the insipidity of a pleasant passage, and keep off the drowsiness that weighed upon our spirits like the rich overloaded atmosphere of a spice-island, breathing about a soft summer sea. Even the huge negroes felt and enjoyed the delicious warmth, as they lay stretched out, heads and points, over the piles of split wood, with their fat shiny faces turned up to the sky, and their broad feet stiffening in the shadow. (1:1)

A catalog of diversions, a figure invoking a Spice Island, a word picture of sprawling Negroes—all these evoke, in two sentences worthy of Melville, the sunlit drowsiness that pervades the deck. And the metaphorical flights of Stephen Crane are startlingly foreshadowed in this glimpse of a Yankee, sprawled asleep "with all his legs and arms stretched out here and there over the costly furniture, as if they had been all shipwrecked together" (1:5).

The narrator (a young man named Peter Fox, mainly an observer here but more active later in the book) gives us a series of set pieces to show off an assortment of New Englanders —shrewd, ridiculous, disgusting, heroic. These Yankees talk to one another with infinite indirection and unconcern, always answering a question with a question. Our narrator reproduces with fidelity all the shadings of vernacular—and audacity. When a deck hand is injured in an accident, a Yankee peddler makes an instant appearance with some salve that will "cure ye, if ye'd jammed your leg off—take the bruise right out by the roots." When rudely rebuffed after offering his product to a passenger suffering from chapped lips, he manages to salvage his dignity with considerable artistry:

> Frind!—I meant no offence, an' I'm sorry for it; but if you'll allow me to express my opinion, I should say that a leetle o' that are—a very *leetle*—scooping out as much as he could with his thumb-nail, and holding it up—. . . jess slicked over your lips, *inside an' out*, you'd be a

much easier man for the rest o' the day; an' talk more to
other people's satisfaction. (1:14–17, 57–58)

A Down Easter carries on at length about the Negroes in his
home town in a manner that anticipates Pap Finn's oratorical
flights (in another dialect) a half century later: "if there's a drop
o' nigger-blood in 'em, they'll always show it in their temper,"
he exclaims. "Why taint more'n a month ago t'I heard a great
he-nigger tell a white man that if he struck him with his whip,
hed split his head open with the axe—why, in our part o' the
country they think themselves most as good as white folks, every
bit election days" (1:66–67).

We are provided with a full-scale description of two hundred
passengers at dinner with no holds barred. Elbows jostle, sauces
spill, and the carcass of a chicken bounds off and on the table
—more than once. A Down Easter is filled with wonderment at
a non-native who starts his meal with soup: "Eatin' brawth fust!
when there's duck an' green peas at three dollars a peck right
under your nose" (1:89–100). Soon after, a young woman is
jostled overboard by some rollicking children. A rescue follows,
full of commotion and broad farce. The rescuer is a "great raw-
boned, half-Scotch, half-methodist looking fellow, with his arms
dangling to his knees, the water running in a puddle from the
legs of his trowsers, and his coal-black hair streaming over his
shoulders like the mane of a cart-horse." This brawny Yankee
ignores some fearful injuries sustained in his dive and quietly
but firmly refuses any reward or compensation from a grateful
father ("neighbor, that aint the way I git my livin' ").

From these vivid characters and events the novel shifts
abruptly—and disastrously. Peter Fox goes to New York to
await the arrival of a ship for a voyage to the South Seas.
During his wait, he becomes involved with Mrs. Laura Amory,
a seductive widow whose social hypocrisies are rendered in amusing detail ("while she was giving her hand to A, she was talking
to B, smiling to C, and bowing to D"). In a characteristically
sudden Nealian transformation, Peter Fox stops being the amused
observer to become—instantaneously and unaccountably—the

slavish and extravagantly jealous lover. When the widow's affections are transferred to Gerard Middleton, a fiery young Southerner who had made an earlier appearance on the steamboat, the rejected lover leaves the country to travel through Europe for three years. He comes back to find Laura on her deathbed, betrayed by Middleton. She dies declaring her unworthiness to Peter but exacting a pledge from both (Middleton also turns up in the midst of her lengthy leavetaking) of eternal friendship for one another (chaps. 10–15).

These absurdities are infinitely compounded in the six concluding chapters (17–22),[7] which are given over almost entirely to the life story of Gerard Middleton as told to Peter Fox by the profligate Southerner's closest friend. The tormented Middleton has pursued and been pursued by dozens of beautiful women. Among his victims was the innocent Quaker girl, Elizabeth Hale, the girl who was rescued after falling from the deck of the steamboat. In collusion with another young woman betrayed by Middleton, Elizabeth carries out a grotesque revenge that seems unparalleled in Gothic melodrama or sexual psychopathology.[8] (Hawthorne might have borrowed and tamed it for "Rappaccini's Daughter.") Pretending to be an eager but timid new admirer, she has her friend arrange an assignation in a totally dark house. Prior to Middleton's arrival, Elizabeth takes a slow poison ("the blood of a strange herb") that will put her to death during the act of love: "While you are embracing me dear," she writes in a note he finds the morning after, "death shall be at work through all my arteries. You shall yet live to lavish your endearment, your caresses, your passionate love upon a dead body; you shall yet strain a corpse to your heart in the convulsion of your joy."

7. Because of a printing error, the chapter numbering skips from 15 to 17.

8. Prevalent in folk literature is the "poison damsel"; the tales in which she figures deal with the poisoning of husband or lover through a fatal look or breath or from intercourse, without harm to the poisoner. See Stith Thompson, *Motif-Index of Folk-Literature*, 6 vols. (Bloomington, Ind., 1955–58), 3:173 ff.

She at first planned a more private suicide but is now certain, she adds, that after this night he "will never risk the death of another innocent, by touching the red lips of a live woman with lips that have clung to the white lips of the dead." After Elizabeth's burial, "the very grass about the grave [is] scorched as with fire . . . and all about the roots of the old apple tree, underneath which they had put her, [is seen] a perceptible agitation of the loose earth, as if it were all alive" (2:92 ff.).

The story of Middleton's profligate life and Elizabeth's grotesque death, as told by Middleton's friend, concludes with the dateline "January 26th, 1827." It is likely that Neal completed this Gothic narrative on that date, during his residence in the Bentham household, and arbitrarily tacked it on to his steamboat sketches to make a novel. An afterword, dated October 1, 1833, suggests that the author does not take these horrors very seriously. The publishers, he informs us, have complained (in a letter sealed with black wax) about his omission of a proper "catastrophe." It is in vain for him to tell them "that if a fine girl . . . were to destroy herself, it would be the fault of the narrator, if people were not interested, without knowing *all* the causes, *all* the circumstances, *all* the consequences." But he obliges with a playful disposition of the characters: Elizabeth has not loved and died in vain; Middleton has reformed and is said to be a Methodist preacher. As for the others, they are all alive and well except for those "who have either married outright or died a natural death" (2:109–10).

Neal's parting jest, equating marriage and death, is an unwitting variation on the necrophilic fantasy that precedes it. Both jest and fantasy reflect Neal's characteristic vacillation in his approach to sexuality—from playfulness to fascination to horror. Neither of the novels Neal dredged up from his bachelor days in England is an ideal hymeneal to the young bride of his middle years.

Neal's grand plan to outshine Cooper as a novelist had come to a dead end. *The Down-Easters* seems to have been something of a *succès de scandale;* a first edition of 1500 copies was completely sold in three months.[9] But Elizabeth's revenge was apparently too much for the reviewers; the novel seems to have been totally ignored. Timidity may have also infected the youthful House of Harper, for there was no second edition. Neal waited twenty-six years before writing another novel.

9. E. W. Hoskin to Neal, January 17, 1834, HL. Hoskin, who represented Neal in his dealings with the publisher, writes that "The Harper's tell me they have sold off the whole edition [totaling 1500 copies] & regret there were not 500 more printed."

14 Storytelling
"David Whicher" and
Other Tales

And what is the great business of life,
the chief employment of all mankind?
Storytelling.

JOHN NEAL, "STORY-TELLING," 1835

[Melmoth's] laughter freezes and torments
the bowels of mercy and love.

BAUDELAIRE, 1855

Early in his career Neal had turned from verse to what he regarded as the poetry of the future, the novel. The disastrous
reception of *Brother Jonathan* in 1825 seems to have permanently
dashed his hopes of writing the great American novel. His preface
to *Rachel Dyer* makes it clear that it is a lesser work than he
had hoped to achieve. After his return to Portland, Neal's enthusiasm shifted to the tale—a feeling he had already conveyed to
William Blackwood in his proposal for a series of "genuine"
North American tales. That grand plan also eventually trailed off
into inconsequence. But the best stories of John Neal suffer only
by comparison with the best productions of Irving, Hawthorne,
and Poe. Two of them, "David Whicher" and "Otter-Bag," overshadow the less inspired efforts of his more famous contemporaries
and add a dimension to the art of storytelling not to be found
in Irving and Poe, rarely in Hawthorne, and rarely in American
fiction until Melville and Twain decades later (and Faulkner a
century later) began telling their tales.

Neal's stories are characterized by a spontaneity and
exuberance conspicuously absent in Irving's graceful and witty
elaborations, in Poe's masterfully controlled constructions, in
Hawthorne's delicately shaded profundities. Melville's admiration for Hawthorne and his tales is almost unbounded ("Irving

159

is a grasshopper to him"), but he also finds "something lacking
—a good deal lacking to the plump sphericity of the man. What
is that? He does'nt patronize the butcher—he needs roast-beef,
done rare." [1] The self-educated Melville found lacking in Hawthorne's artful subtlety the "careful disorderliness" and vigor that
characterize his own storytelling. Neal's best stories fall short of
Melville's greatness, but significantly foreshadow it.

Neal did not dedicate himself to the tale as intensively as
Hawthorne or Poe. His contempt for the flourishing literary annuals (he called them "baby house annuals") and his volatile
relationship with Samuel G. Goodrich, who published most of
Hawthorne's early tales, prompted him to bring out his masterful
"David Whicher" anonymously; it has only recently been disinterred and identified as Neal's. The total oblivion into which
"David Whicher" was consigned for 130 years parallels the fate
of other tales that deserve to be read. The massive *Short Story
Index* compiled by Dorothy Cook and Isabel S. Monro (1953,
1956, 1960) fails to list a single story by Neal among the more
than five thousand collections surveyed. It was not until 1962
that "David Whicher" and "Otter-Bag" were reprinted by Hans-
Joachim Lang in Germany. To Lang goes the credit of being the
first critic since Poe to take Neal seriously as a short story
writer. [2] John Neal, that "eager apostle of American literature,"
had to wait for recognition as a storyteller to come from abroad.

Neal's tales range from these tragicomic masterpieces of
heroic travail of settler and Indian to darker, somewhat less suc-

1. Melville to Evert A. Duyckinck, February 12, 1851, *The Letters of
Herman Melville*, ed. Merrell R. Davis and William H. Gilman (New
Haven, 1960), p. 121.
2. For details concerning the publication of "David Whicher" and
Neal's relationship to Goodrich, see Benjamin Lease, "The Authorship of
'David Whicher': The Case for John Neal," *Jahrbuch für Amerikastudien*
12 (1967):124–36; for Lang's discovery of "David Whicher" and recogni-
tion of Neal's importance as a short story writer, see his Introduction to
"Critical Essays and Stories by John Neal," pp. 204–9, and his "The
Authorship of 'David Whicher,'" in the same volume, p. 288.

cessful, explorations of the mind's frontiers. In an age dominated by sentimentality and timid conventionality, Neal cried out for those "faithful representations of native character" that would reveal "what we are most anxious to conceal . . . [about] our own peculiarities and our own faults." [3] The darker regions of the mind are probed in several stories (most notably "The Haunted Man," "The Squatter," and "Idiosyncrasies") that dwell on the hell man creates for himself through compulsive self-destructiveness. Neal's imp of the perverse is linked to Poe's, and it is not surprising that the younger writer should, while complaining about their lack of unity, pay tribute to Neal's stories: "In the higher requisites of composition, John Neal's magazine stories excel—I mean in vigor of thought, picturesque combination of incident, and so forth—but they ramble too much, and invariably break down just before coming to an end." Despite Neal's failure to conform to Poe's rigorous standards for a well-constructed tale (standards that also find Hawthorne wanting and are fully met only by himself), Poe ranks Neal "first, or at all events second, among our men of indisputable *genius*." [4] Such praise goes far beyond the gratitude due to the writer who first recognized and encouraged his youthful literary efforts.

With exuberance and carelessness (Poe praised the one and deplored the other) Neal employs humor and satire in several of his tales to tell the truth about "our own peculiarities and our own faults." Human foibles in love and marriage are his target in "Courtship," "The Utilitarian," and "The Young Phrenologist." Neal's fictional autobiography of a confidence man, "The Adventurer," is a racy hoax on a hoax (John Dunn Hunter's memoirs of his experiences as an Indian captive), a lively contribution to rogue literature. "The Ins and Outs" is a biting satire on the cynical masquerade that constitutes friendship and office-seeking in the nation's capital.

These ten tales, published between 1828 and 1843 along

3. Preface to *The Down-Easters*, 1:iv.
4. Poe, "Tale-Writing—Nathaniel Hawthorne . . ." [1847]; Poe, "Marginalia" [1849], in *Works*, 13:154; and 16:152.

with numerous less successful efforts, establish Neal as a force to
be reckoned with in the development of the American short story.[5]
Lang has reminded us that quantity is not an index of importance:
"Irving is justly famous as a pioneer of the American short story,
but where are his pieces of real excellence, except the two named
['Rip Van Winkle' and 'The Legend of Sleepy Hollow']?" That
Neal should be so completely forgotten in histories of the genre,
he adds, "seems the more pitiable and irrational in view of the
fact that he abounded in the very quality Irving so conspicuously
lacked: moral energy." [6]

1. "DAVID WHICHER"

Several of Neal's stories—and many of Hawthorne's—were published in *The Token*, the most successful of the literary annuals
that flourished in the 1830s and 1840s. Unlike Hawthorne, who
kept to himself his distaste for its promoter and editor, Samuel
G. Goodrich, Neal blew up intermittently at the editorial liberties
Goodrich took with his stories. In April of 1831 the volatile Neal
announced to a rival publisher that he was through with *The
Token*, but two months later he changed his mind and submitted
"David Whicher" to Goodrich.[7] It appeared anonymously, along
with four Hawthorne tales, in *The Token* for 1832. It remained
unnoticed and unrecognized, moreover, until 1962, when its publication in the *Jahrbuch für Amerikastudien* marked the first
critical appreciation of a masterpiece of black comedy that invites

5. These stories include "David Whicher," *The Token* for 1832, pp.
349–72; "Otter-Bag, the Oneida Chief," *The Token* for 1829, pp. 221–84;
"The Haunted Man," *The Atlantic Souvenir* for 1832, pp. 221–46; "The
Squatter," *The New-England Magazine* 8 (1835) :97–104; "Idiosyncrasies,"
Brother Jonathan (the magazine) vol. 5, May 6 and July 8, 1843; "Courtship," *The Yankee*, n.s. 1 (1829) :121–28; "The Utilitarian," *The Token* for
1830, pp. 299–318; "The Young Phrenologist," *The Token* for 1836, pp.
156–69; "The Adventurer," *The Token* for 1831, pp. 189–212; "The Ins
and the Outs," *The Family Companion and Ladies' Mirror* 1 (1841–42):
13–23.
6. Lang, "Critical Essays and Stories," pp. 207–8.
7. See Lease, "The Authorship of 'David Whicher,'" pp. 130–33.

comparison with "My Kinsman, Major Molyneux," "The Town Ho's Story," and the tragicomic tales of Twain and Faulkner.

The story is based on a frontier anecdote recounting the remarkable exploit of Daniel Malcolm, an early settler of Brunswick, Maine, "a man of undaunted courage, and an inveterate enemy of the Indians, who gave him the name of Sungernumby, that is, a very strong man." While alone in the woods, readying a log for splitting with wedges, Malcolm is captured by five Indians, but he persuades them to help him finish the job before leaving as their prisoner. After tricking the Indians into grasping the tree in a way that would serve his purpose, Malcolm "then suddenly struck out his blunt wedge, and the elastick wood instantly closed fast on their fingers, and he secured them." The tree-trap motif apparently fascinated Neal, for he had published in *The Yankee* a harrowing account of a woodsman's accidental self-entrapment in a tree.[8]

For "David Whicher" Neal transformed these folk materials with dramatic effect. He made the strong woodsman a weak one and reduced the number of Indians from five to four. The faceless Malcolm outwitting his captors becomes a vivid portrait of a man of God whose life is founded on nonviolence and unswerving faith in Providence. David Whicher's terrible ordeal, the ultimate test of that faith, is enlarged and intensified by the setting, Merry-Meeting Bay, and by a shadowy action peripheral to the central drama: Shots are heard on the other side of the bay. A fire flashes on a distant hill. Conch shells sound and resound until a stillness prevails "more awful than that of midnight in the depth of a northern winter; for the hot sunshine was

8. J. Farmer and J. B. Moore, eds., *Collections . . . Relating Principally to New Hampshire* (Concord, N. H., 1824), 3:103; reprinted in Benjamin Church, *The History of Philip's War* (Exeter, N. H., 1829), p. 336. Neal may have read Church's *History*, containing the source; he demonstrates a familiarity with its contents in his *Oration . . . July 4, 1838* (Portland, 1838), p. 15. I am indebted to Professor Lang for calling my attention to the anecdote-source. For Neal's anecdote of the woodsman entrapped in a tree, see his "Live Yankees, No. 2: Their Fortitude," *The Yankee* 1 (1828) :135.

over all the earth, and the green leaves and the slant shadows were motionless, and the blue waters of the bay like a steel mirror." These terrible events on the pre-Revolutionary frontier are linked to the present and to an ancient past rapidly receding as "ten thousand villages [burst] into life on every side" but where, in the North, one may still stand "in the everlasting shadow, and hear the solemn, steady, perpetual roar of the very pines, underneath whose branches, . . . battles were fought, ages and ages ago, by armies so numerous that their bones have altered the very nature of the soil."

In this violent time and place, David Whicher has entrusted himself and his children to God's providence.[9] This quiet inoffensive woodsman will not heed the warnings of the other settlers who never travel unarmed and who justify their precautions with quotations from the Old Testament ("to the faithful the heathen should be given for an inheritance"). In answer, he would only smile "and say something about charity, and brotherly love, and the New Testament; as if brotherly love or charity had anything to do with the red heathen, or the New Testament with a North American savage."

Even when he is suddenly surrounded by the four savages and confronted with uplifted tomahawk and glittering knife, his faith does not waver. His courage gains him a reprieve, during which he shares a meal and amuses his captors with some bark wristlets he has woven. He comes close to attempting an escape while playfully handcuffing them, but loses his chance. While buying more time with a demonstration of his extraordinary skill in basketry, he notices scalps—still bleeding—buckled on the chest of one of the warriors. Sick and faint, he recognizes the blue beads of his youngest child and the dark chestnut hair of his only daughter. "Could he be mistaken? Was it for this that he

9. Whicher's attitude toward Indians is strikingly similar to that of the folk hero Johnny Appleseed (John Chapman, 1774–1847), a fellow Yankee and Swedenborgian. See Walter Blair, *Tall Tale America* (New York, 1944), p. 100; and Robert Price, *Johnny Appleseed: Man and Myth* (Bloomington, Ind., 1954), pp. 77–78.

had kept aloof, when all the land was mustering to war; he alone? . . . Could it be, that all his life long he had been shutting his eyes to the truth?"

He controls any visible sign of anguish that will betray him to hatchet or knife, restrains an impulse to spring at the murderer's throat. He will make up for a lifetime of error and take his revenge. But before acting in violation of his lifelong faith, he must be certain of the truth. When his captors are puzzled by the little wedge lying in the grass and turn to him for an answer, "A sudden light flashed through his ruptured and riven heart; a fierce, fervid hope, . . . vague, to be sure, and shadowy, but ending in a tremendous consummation." His own survival is of incidental importance; he must know the fate of his children. Only the tree-trap can provide the answer. He hangs on to his courage and his cunning long enough to carry it through; at the crucial moment, he strikes the fateful blow, crying out as it descends: *"The sword of the Lord and of Gideon!"* The tree springs together with a loud report; the four savages are now "pinioned by their crushed hands, like the strong man of old who strove to tear asunder the gnarled oak, and perished for his presumption." But, like King David who tried to spare his undeserving son Absalom, entrapped in a tree (2 Samuel 18), David Whicher, even after he confirms the fact that the dangling scalps are indeed those of his children, still cannot take the vengeance of the Lord upon himself. "Blind and sick with un-utterable horror and loathing," he stumbles away until his foot strikes his axe. Then thinks he of the Old Testament, of Abraham and the animal entangled in the thicket, and of himself "called to the priesthood, with power to offer up victims." But his inner nature still rebels; he cannot strike the blow. He flings away the axe and weeps. And the entrapped Indians are amused and em-barrassed by this contemptible show of weakness. They listen to Whicher's farewell speech with apparent comprehension as he calls their attention to the lurking wolves and leaves them to God—the same Lord God who takes bloody revenge on the children of Beth-el for mocking the prophet Elisha (2 Kings

2:23–24). His concluding prayer is supremely ironical: "Thy tender mercies are over all thy works!"

"The sublimity of the treatment," suggests Hans-Joachim Lang, "lies in the fact that Whicher, in trying to execute the murderer of his child, feels that he slays only another son, while the Indians, whose lives are so far spared, cannot be grateful for this and mutely reproach him." The irony of noncommunication is complete, Lang adds, when Whicher leaves them to a God who, he persists in believing, will protect the innocent—the same God who "has served him indifferently well." [10]

An even greater irony is generated by the way the story is told. The stark tragedy of David Whicher is enclosed in an elaborate comic framework. It is difficult to take seriously, at the opening of the story, the "little man with spectacles, who had been reading a volume of poetry, through the nose, during a violent shower" and who declaims so poetically and portentously (and interminably) about the vanishing tribes. But we move gradually and totally into the harrowing story of the woodsman. On the anniversary of his terrible bereavement, Whicher returns to the tree—and poignance suddenly dissolves into outrageous anticlimax as the auditor-narrator boggles at the tall-tale account of four skeletons "still striving to tear the tree asunder."

> "What on earth do you mean?" cried I, starting up from my chair when my companion with the green spectacles had come to this part of the story, and looking about me with amazement.
> "Mean, Sir; I mean what I say."
> "Did I understand you rightly—a *twelvemonth* afterwards—four *skeletons*, did you say?—still trying to tear asunder that log?"
> "Precisely. You see by that, Sir, what the North American savage is capable of."

Another member of the audience chimes in to agree that "them are Injuns are tarnal tough" and almost impossible to kill. The narrator takes his leave from the mysterious storyteller, knowing

10. Lang, "Critical Essays and Stories," p. 208.

"in my heart he intended to hoax me." He has been hoaxed and we have been hoaxed; the ridiculous little storyteller was obviously never to be trusted.

Here Neal's little man (and Neal) echo the satanic agonized laughter of Maturin's Melmoth, whose "double and self-contradictory nature" stirs him to a mocking laughter that "freezes and torments the bowels of mercy and love." [11] The enormous skill with which Neal deploys the tragicomic effect is indicated by the fact that Whicher's agony survives the farcical close— is, in fact, intensified by it. Why should this be so? Susanne K. Langer has observed that the writer must not only give his work an "air of reality" but must also be concerned with *"keeping it fiction."* In life, hearsay is scarcely a voucher for truth; but in fiction the frame device (doubled or even tripled) adds "authenticity" through "poetic transformation." [12] His very absurdity contributes to the aura of mystery and authority that envelops the little man. His story is told with such mastery that his sudden exposure throws into greater relief the magic of his performance. E. T. A. Hoffmann, speaking of modern drama, summed up Neal's achievement in "David Whicher": "only in the truly Romantic do the comic and the tragic mix so intimately that both melt together in a total effect, moving the feelings of the spectator in a uniquely strange way." [13]

2. "OTTER-BAG"

Only slightly less impressive than "David Whicher" is "Otter-Bag," a tale of the Revolutionary War that Neal worked up for *The Token* for 1829 from an episode deleted from *Brother Jonathan* during its final revision.[14] In the novel, the intrepid Bald Eagle, pretending to be a deserter in order to spy on the British, "escapes"

11. Charles Baudelaire, *The Essence of Laughter*, ed. Peter Quennel (New York, 1956), p. 117.
12. *Feeling and Form* (London, 1953), pp. 292–93.
13. Quoted in Guthke, *Modern Tragicomedy*, pp. 102–3. Hoffmann's view finds similar expression in pronouncements by A. W. Schlegel; see Guthke, *Modern Tragicomedy*, pp. 103–4.
14. *Wandering Recollections*, p. 255.

from the American lines under what is supposed to be a volley of misdirected fire. "Unluckily for him, the order for pursuit was given too early; and, worse yet—given, to the celebrated Rudolph, who never dreaming of make believe, pursued him so hotly, with his troop, that poor Eagle had a very narrow escape; —with two severe pistol wounds, for a passport" (*Brother Jonathan*, 3:404–5). This brief passage from the novel (and the deleted episode which it summarizes) is transformed in "Otter-Bag" into a tragicomic masterpiece in which the dashing Captain Rudolph makes a desperate, vain attempt to save the life of the heroic Indian from the malicious (not, as in the novel, mistaken) fire of his men.

Like "David Whicher," the story has a narrative framework that contributes much to the peculiar fusion of farce and pathos that distinguishes it. The opening disquisition on the tragic history of the American Indian is charged with rhapsodic flights that swell its poignant theme: "There may be no such ruins in America as are found in Europe, or in Asia, or in Africa; but other ruins there are of a prodigious magnitude—the ruins of a mighty people." In answer to F. L. Pattee's impatience with this lengthy introduction, Hans-Joachim Lang has defined its contribution to the narrative that follows: "The pathetic fate of a whole race is summed up in the story of a single individual." [15]

That story is given over to a garrulous old veteran of the Revolutionary War whose excitement mounts as he warms to his tale ("I saw that we had now come to the marrow of the story; the old man was all alive with it"), but never so much that he neglects to interrupt his narrative at its most suspenseful and poignant moments to remark on the efficacy of the flip he and his rapt auditor are sipping. [16]

15. Lang, "Critical Essays and Stories," p. 208.
16. The harrowing details of "The Town-Ho's Story" (*Moby-Dick*, chap. 54) are similarly accompanied by the free flow of chicha at the Golden Inn of Lima; Ishmael breaks off his narrative now and then to permit his Spanish friends to refill their cups—and his. For another example of a framed tale told by a garrulous, increasingly excited old Revolu-

The old veteran warms to an extraordinary subject: Otter-Bag is a warrior whose strength and daring have made him a legendary menace to the American troops. His physical endowments are established with Twainian gusto:

> ". . . the boy had merely popped out of the lodge to speak to somebody who lived on the other side of a high brick wall . . . when Otter-Bag snapped him up, and ran off with him—"
>
> "What!"
>
> "Poor Jerry Smith! everybody loved him, and everybody pitied his old father, who had six boys in the army, while the British were in that neighborhood—"
>
> "He must have been a very small boy, to be carried off in that way."
>
> "He was a boy of six feet four, and well put together, and con-sider'ble actyve, as we say in the north—lick his weight in wild-cats any day."

The formidable Indian is eventually captured by four very large brothers of poor Jerry Smith and becomes a loyal adherent of the Revolutionary cause. His unflinching courage under deadly fire arouses the admiration of Captain Rudolph who, after a time, "would never undertake a perilous affair without having him at his elbow." But several of the men in Rudolph's company cannot be shaken loose of their hatred and suspicion ("If he fell upon the foe, it was a trap; if he suffered himself to be fired at, or if he dropped a British officer, it was a trick"). Otter-Bag complains once to Rudolph and then keeps a melancholy silence—until the day of his death.

On that day he leads a patrol of Rudolph's men (against his will and on their insistence) into an enemy ambush. Otter-Bag is pinned down in deep snow, riddled with musket and pistol ball—still alive only because of the prodigious intervention of Captain Rudolph. Rudolph discovers to his horror that the dying

tionary veteran to the accompaniment of some enthusiastic imbibing, see "Jack's Grandfather," in Seba Smith, *The Life and Writings of Major Jack Downing* (1834), reprinted in Blair, *Native American Humor,* pp. 203–8.

Indian has been "butchered by [his] own troop, shot to pieces by the men that [he has] been so faithful to, and so ready to die for." But more terrible to Otter-Bag than all the lead showered into his body is the "bad name" one of his persecutors had called him:

> A frightful change took place in his look, when he alluded to the bad name—he drew a long breath, he knitted his brows, he clenched his teeth, a swift paleness overspread his dark visage, and he fell back as if he were shot through the head, and lay upon the pile of blankets and clothes which were already stiff and frozen wherever his body had touched them, and the last words he spoke, the very last were, "No, no, Oodoff, no, no! Otter-Bag no bard man; he good mans. He die now; Otter-Bag muss die now."

This moving denouement, as in "David Whicher," is now deliberately juggled. The narrator flees from what he fears to be an imminent retelling of the tale by the old soldier: "I was not in the humor to hear the whole of the story repeated—with variations." (Twain's narrator in "The Jumping Frog" takes flight from garrulity in a similar fashion.) An enraptured auditor has suddenly become an impatient one, and pathos gives way to what it has been toying with throughout: the ludicrous. But here it is a flight that understates—and underscores—Otter-Bag's tragic fate.

3. "THE HAUNTED MAN" AND OTHER EXPLORATIONS

Though their settings range from metropolis to wilderness, several stories are linked by their explorations of the frontiers of human consciousness, by their probings into the behavior of obsessed, haunted men. Three such tales are "The Haunted Man," "The Squatter," and "Idiosyncrasies."

On a lovely Sunday in the fall of 1824, the narrator (Neal, thinly disguised) visits a church in the south of England where he blunders into a private, conspicuously placed pew. A stranger, strikingly handsome and pale, joins him and kneels in prayer. As members of the congregation gather about the communion

table, there is a smothered cry; the golden cups have been flung
down by the stranger and the red wine now runs over the
marble floor. The stranger confronts the frightened preacher,
utters another cry, and falls senseless at the altar; the congregation
flees in a panic. Fifteen months later the narrator encounters
the mysterious stranger again, this time in a garden at Versailles.
He suspects that he is in the presence of a madman, especially
so when the stranger turns visibly pale as they pass a fountain
and when he insists that they confer in a private room furnished
without mirrors.[17] At long last the pale young man confesses his
secret: "I am a *haunted man!*"

> I stared, and then he burst into another of those
> fits of uncontrollable laughter, which continued until
> the tears ran down his cheeks and fell, drop after drop
> . . . upon the crimson velvet sofa, to which he was
> clinging with all his might, as if to steady himself in his
> paroxysm of mirth.

The trapped narrator feels uneasy and finally angry. But wrath
gives way to pity when it becomes apparent that "some unaccountable sorrow is eating him away at the core; I could see it
in his eyes, I could hear it in his low breathing, and I forgave
him." The haunted man, sensing the sympathy of the narrator,
tells his story.

The great revelation set forth after such suspenseful preparation is that fourteen years ago he was bitten by a dog suspected
of being rabid—Flora, the dog, "sickened and died soon after,
and we had reason to believe that a very decided case of hydrophobia occurred, among the hounds of a neighbour, where Flora
had been visiting." The absurdity of this revelation is made
tolerable by the fact that the victim himself—and the narrator

17. Neal's portrayal of an obsession with fountains and mirrors anticipates and perhaps influences Hawthorne's "The Haunted Mind" (1835)
and numerous other sketches; see Mathiessen, *American Renaissance*, pp.
273–74: "[Hawthorne's] fascinated use of fountains and mirrors often
enabled him to bring his material to artistic concentration, as well as to
endow his scenes with depth and liquidity."

—are keenly aware of it (" 'Did you ever hear any thing so ridiculous?' 'Never,' said I"). It is ridiculous, and he is aware of it; but his irrational fear has brought him to the brink of suicide. His strange behavior in the presence of sacramental wine, fountains, mirrors is now explained. After an unsuccessful attempt at a cure by logical proof that hydrophobia is a physical impossibility, the narrator succeeds by an amusing psychotherapeutic subterfuge. The afflicted man agrees to a regime of regular exercise, a course of gymnastics in the open air, and an avoidance of medical books and cases reported in the newspapers. Above all, he is to follow a medical prescription written in cryptically abbreviated Latin that is translated for the reader as "the very best of old port wine, and a plenty of it."

Ralph Thompson has praised "The Haunted Man" for its "early use, perhaps the first, of the methods of psychotherapy as material for fiction." [18] More significant than the scientific erudition and ratiocinative acumen of the narrator (akin to Dupin's later brilliancies) is the Doppelgänger motif—reinforced by Neal's characteristic alternation between seriousness and farce. The haunted man is split in two by an absurd phobia; but the narrator is himself haunted—by the haunted man. He is moved to compassion by the plight of a hypochondriac whose marriage seems blasted, whose life is in danger; but he also pictures the absurdities of the haunted man's plight unsparingly, and slyly informs us at the end of the story that the poor fellow is, a year later, "the happiest fellow on the face of the earth, perfectly cured of every thing in the world, except his wife."

"The Squatter" is sterner stuff, a grim exercise in frontier horror. The enemy is forest fire, specifically the great conflagrations of 1824 in the District of Maine. "There is no poetry in this," announces the narrator. "I am not exaggerating. Every word I write is simple truth." In one episode a woodsman, Walker, and two other men are at work in the forest "with

18. *American Literary Annuals and Gift Books, 1825–1865* (New York, 1936), p. 32.

nothing to apprise them of their danger . . . but a little haziness in the atmosphere, which they took no notice of at the time, and only remembered afterwards, while they were running for their lives." A large tree suddenly bursts into flame close by them. The three men look up and, without speaking a word, start off at full speed for the closest body of water—the Schoodic River, forty miles away. "Of these three, one died on the shore, another, Walker himself, about six months later. The other is still living."

In another episode a farmer digging potatoes looks up and sees an old stump on fire. He glances at the sky.

> It was all in commotion—over the top of a hill not far off, the flames were pouring with a steady uninterrupted rush, as if they had overswept a barrier, and were tumbl-ing through some vast cavern of the earth, like the waters of Niagara. Heavy black clouds were gathered about the base, . . . and through these, the fire streamed, in thick flashes, with the roar of approaching battle, a sensible vibration of the earth.

The farmer and his family miraculously escape, but his wife is haunted "to this hour" by her memory of the terrible appearance of the sky. "To her, it was the Last Day."

These and other dread examples of suffering are preliminary to the terrible experience of Hayes, "a rough-looking Down-Easter, with a bear-skin cap, powder-horn, a shot-pouch, a wampum-belt, and a glittering axe swung over his shoulder." This frontiersman is thrown into contact with the narrator who suspects that, in spite of his crude exterior, "he had been, if he was not now, . . . a proud father and a happy husband." Hayes finally tells his story. He had left his wife, taking with him "the only child I was sure of; for between ourselves, my good sir, the devil had put it into my head to be jealous . . . —and so I left her all the children with blue and gray eyes, and took with me the only one that resembled me." Three years later his wife writes that she is coming to him; the three children left with her are dead—two of drowning, one of grief over him. On the day of her arrival, Hayes journeys to town to meet her coach. He leaves his son Jerry (who is eager to see his *"new mother,* as he called her") in the care of a hired girl. To make certain the boy will not go astray, the father ties their Newfoundland puppy Carlo to the post of his trundle bed.

"Well Sir—we met once more—and she forgave me; and we were happy . . . notwithstanding the self-reproach and heaviness I felt, on hearing the particulars of what I cannot bear to speak of yet, or even to think of"—the death of the children he had deserted. As they ride down a hill, about halfway in their journey home, the horses snort. "My wife caught my arm, and as I turned toward her, I saw the whole western sky in a preternatural glow." He spurs his horse, at first urging his wife to follow, then turning back to forbid her from coming closer. He finds the hired girl cowering under a fence. She had fled the fire with the boy until they had fallen exhausted along the path by which Hayes was expected. The last she remembered was little Jerry saying something about going back to untie poor Carlo. "My heart died within me," Hayes continues. "I knew that I was childless—*I knew it*—don't talk to me—I *knew* it. And it was so." He finds the house nearly destroyed; a little way off is the dog Carlo, watching over the body of his son. "That is Carlo you see there. My wife is in the mad-house, at Philadelphia—and here am I. God forgive me!"

The power of "The Squatter" is amplified by the glimpse we are given of the self-destructive forces within Hayes—forces matched and overmatched by the blind fury of the fire.

"Idiosyncrasies" is Neal's "Imp of the Perverse," published two years before Poe's. It is a long, rambling tale, told by a madman, combining two stories with clumsy but compelling effectiveness. The narrator encounters a loquacious stranger named Lee who subjects him, much against his will, to a long account of his courtship and marriage. While courting a young and lovely woman, Lee embarks on a philosophical rhapsody on the nature of Woman and Man only to discover that the object of his af-

fections is fast asleep. He is further chagrined by the presence
of an eavesdropper, a little girl (apparently a younger sister)
who has witnessed the proceedings with evident amusement, and
then with a precocious look of sympathy. "God help me—I cannot
go on—I see that child before me now: I hear the delicate
chiming of her low, clear voice! I see her soft eyes changing
color, as I stoop to kiss her forehead—not her lips—but her
forehead, for the first time in all my life." He knows that the
child understands him; a few years later they marry. They have
a daughter, Biddy, who resembles her mother so much "that I
never could bear the thought of her loving anybody on earth
but me." A second child follows, a handsome spirited boy whom
his mother finds difficult to manage; "and therefore, it was that
I . . . used to try him as with fire and water, almost every day
of his life."

While travelling through the countryside in the middle of
winter, Lee and his family stop at an inn near a mountain. The
boy Willy asks his mother for permission to climb the mountain
next morning to see a sunrise. When Lee hears her discourage the
boy because of the danger, he announces that the whole family,
including their dog Pompey, shall go. He is annoyed by his wife's
asking whether he has inquired about the best path to the top.
"The question itself implied a doubt, and a reproach—for I had
never thought of making inquiries. . . . No, my dear, said I—
I have not inquired, nor do I mean to inquire. I am well acquainted with this neighborhood—my father used to live within
a hundred miles of it. I have Greenleaf's Map and the Gazetteer."

Next morning at five they begin their ascent. Lee has slipped
a length of bedcord into his pocket—hardly knowing why and
ashamed to let anyone know "I had thought it worth my while
to make any sort of serious preparation for a thing I spoke so
lightly of." Eventually they reach the top and watch the sunrise.
But during the descent, Lee sees Biddy's cap flying over the
snow, Pompey plunging after it, and Willy trying to overtake the
dog. Then the dog stops in its tracks, motionless, a few feet from
the cap. The snow begins to give way beneath them. Lee calls

to his son to stretch out and keep still. He fumbles in his pocket
for the bedcord

> which I had so providentially brought with me, when
> my wife interfered again—Oh, for the love of God, save
> him! save him! she cried. This frightened the boy and
> vexed me more than anything she ever did in her life.
> Nonsense! I said—and put the line back into my pocket.
> And then to punish her for such untimely interference, I
> called out to Willy to send Pompey for the cap, and
> *make him fetch it.*

The dog refuses to stir. Lee orders his son to retrieve the cap.
The dog whimpers as the boy moves forward step by step. Willy
reaches for the cap, cries out *"father! father!"* and disappears
from view. There follows a nightmarish account of Lee's attempts
to rescue his son, climaxed by his lowering little Biddy to look
for the lost boy. She descends, calls up that she sees him—and
there is a tremendous fall of snow. To his "unspeakable horror
and amazement," Lee finds the rope immovable. Now he has
lost both his children. His desperate efforts finally bring them
both back to the surface alive. The boy, however, "died within
a twelvemonth afterwards, poor fellow!—perhaps of fright, and
perhaps of something else, but however, that may be—I never
could bring myself to forgive his mother." The auditor is as-
tounded:

> To forgive his mother! what had his mother done,
> I should like to know?
> Why, don't you see, that she was the death of the
> boy? But for that confounded scream, just as he had his
> hand on the cap, the boy would have got back safely
> enough.

The horrified auditor rises to leave but is almost forcibly
detained; Lee insists on telling him the aftermath. He could never
make his wife understand that it was she who was responsible
for the boy's death. One day, as they walk near Wentworth Falls,
he tells her that if he had ordered either one of their children to
leap into the whirlpool beneath them he would have been in-

stantly obeyed. "And if you were, what then? said she." Nettled, he tells her he wishes to heaven he could find another creature capable of such obedience. She asks if that would make him happier. When he says it would, she stops, kisses him, "and whispering, *Be happier then!*" springs into the whirlpool.

> Poor Jenny! . . . what business had she to drown herself without my leave! what a fool to do so at the bidding of a husband! and such a husband! I declare to you, my heart bleeds for her. She has been dead a good while now; but . . . I never *shall* forget my poor Jenny.

The narrator finally makes his escape, but not before being subjected to a final revelation: his daughter Biddy, now grown, plans to marry a man old enough to be her father. "It was not enough that she had a father,—a fond, faithful, doating old father, who never could bear her out of his sight! No, no—what are fathers good for when husbands are wanted?" Of course, he will no longer have anything more to do with her.

In his autobiography, Neal tells of several narrow escapes experienced while traveling with his family through the hills and woods of Maine.[19] On one occasion, five years before the publication of "Idiosyncrasies," he sent his eight-year-old son James into the darkness of a rough wood to head off a chaise traveling behind them. His wife, nine-year-old daughter, "and another little thing of no particular age" remained behind with him. Too late, it occurs to him "that, if [James] tried to go over on the bridge, it might be dangerous, if not fatal to him." He runs in pursuit of the boy, finds the bridge collapsed, "and Master James trying to find his way through the darkness, by feeling."

"Idiosyncrasies" is, of course, an imaginative creation— crude by comparison with Poe's studies in perversity and madness, but capable of conveying a poignance and horror (especially in the rescue episode) never communicated in the younger writer's more polished productions. Some of its intensity may stem from its personal immediacy; Neal was sixteen years older than his

19. *Wandering Recollections*, pp. 427–30.

nineteen-year-old bride (and cousin) and knew her when she was a child. It is with considerable gusto and authority that he recreates himself in the role of the innocently incestuous, lovingly murderous husband-father—an extension of earlier re-creations of self-destructive jealousy.

4. "COURTSHIP" AND OTHER DIVERSIONS

Humor and satire are the dominant note in several stories that, with varying effectiveness, tell the truth about "our own peculiarities" and our strategies for self-deception. In "Courtship" (published in *The Yankee* shortly after Neal's marriage) a prosperous old bachelor discourses at length on his lifelong pursuit of a good wife. From the beginning of his monologue to its end he does not falter or sound a single false note as he recounts with total earnestness and reasonableness the story of his vain quest—with no glimmer of a realization that he is an outrageous fool. His expectations have always been modest: "I wanted no beauty, no heiress, no female of birth or accomplishment." But how was he to learn the actual temper and worth of a woman if he approaches her as a lover, a prospective husband? To visit under such circumstances "would never satisfy me. I should be sure to see my dear in a holiday-humour. No, no—I like to catch people in the suds—I like to fall upon them, by surprise, when it is washing-day not only with their hands but with their temper."

He becomes a brother to lovely Bertha—with disastrous results. He makes excellent progress with a beautiful widow until he gives her to understand, "as gently and delicately as I could, that I wanted to come a year or two on trial." After this rebuff he waits a full five years before trying again. "I had almost forgotten how to walk arm-in-arm; and as for keeping the step, I might as well have gone a-tiptoe through the street." He hits on a new plan: to look for a younger girl—"one that I could educate in my own way"—and then to approach not the prospective bride but her parents. The result is that all the young females in the neighborhood avoid him "as if I had avowed myself a purveyor to the grand Turk—perhaps more." His final desperate campaign involves making a list of all the eligible girls in the area and visiting each in turn so regularly "that before the winter was over they not only knew the day of the week, but the hour of the day, by my step, as I drew near." He is now regarded not only as a hopeless old bachelor but as a thoroughly unprincipled man.

Human foibles in courtship are also the central concern of "The Utilitarian," despite a surface emphasis on ideology. Bentham's antisentimentalism triumphs over timorous conventionality; but more important than preachment is the adroitness with which Neal manages the comic confrontation between the wise Abijah (the Utilitarian) and Joseph, the foolish young bachelor who tells the story. A little child is run down by a runaway horse. Joseph, attempting a rescue almost certainly doomed to failure, is himself saved from harm by a young giant, Abijah, who then proceeds to stop the horses and rescue the child's mother, a beautiful widow. When asked why he interfered with Joseph's rescue attempt, Abijah gives a Utilitarian reply: "You are grown up, your life is worth more to society." Joseph is outraged when Abijah, pencil in hand, ciphers away at full speed to prove that "It has cost some thousands" to raise him, Joseph, to the age of twenty-five and that the chances had been fifty to one against his saving the child. With even more elaborate calculations, Abijah justifies risking his own life to save the beautiful widow. The child recovers, and Joseph proposes to the widow, but he withdraws his attentions when she confesses that she is not really a widow—that the child is (as Joseph puts it to Abijah) "a thing . . . for the mother to be ashamed of." The Utilitarian castigates the timid bachelor: "How you have rewarded her candor, how gloriously you have repaid her truth!" Joseph expresses concern over the prejudices of society; Abijah insists that such sentiments must be weighed against what one stands to gain by running counter to them. The timid young man is not persuaded, and the bold Utilitarian, acting in accordance with his principle, "offered himself, and the great steam-engine of a fellow is now the husband of the fair widow."

In a somewhat similar fashion, the elaborate exposition of phrenology in "The Young Phrenologist" is scarcely more than an excuse for comic byplay between a new bride and groom— and some cautious ribaldry. The young bride awakens in the middle of their first night to learn a terrible truth about her husband: he is a phrenologist. She has had no suspicion of this "till she found him feeling her head, and pretending to be asleep." (Neal was outraged when Goodrich altered this in *The Token* for 1836 to read, "till the secret broke suddenly from his lips, while he was asleep.") [20] She waits until his breathing assures her that he is fast asleep, and slips "out of bed" (delicately emended by Goodrich so that she slips "away") to write a letter to her mother. At the writing desk, she accidentally trips open a secret drawer filled with miniature plaster heads, including one of her own, "the hair wiped off, and the bare ivory scull, written all over with unutterably strange characters." In the midst of these dread discoveries, Edward surprises her and gives his lovely Nell a first lesson in the science of bumps. She interrupts the proceedings with a saucy examination of *his* skull ("Obstinacy— unspeakable! . . . Modesty—wanting. Yankeeism—unequalled") and flounces back to bed. Edward, left alone, reflects on the need to "put a stop to these tantrums, or abandon the idea of a YOUNG PHRENOLOGIST." (Goodrich deletes this sly conclusion.)

"Oh but these gentlemen who cater for young ladies are getting to be *so* squeamish," Neal complains in his preface to an unexpurgated reprinting of the story, "we wonder if butter would melt in *their* mouths!—or if they ever allowed a pretty woman, with a neat ancle, to go up stairs before them in all their

20. Neal reprints a "restored" version of the story, with interpolated jibes at Goodrich, as an appendix to his review of *The Token and Atlantic Souvenir* for 1836, *The New-England Galaxy*, October 3, 1835; Neal castigates Goodrich further in "The Bear and His Outriders," in the issue of October 17.

lives." [21] Neal's own version may strike the modern reader as rather arch and self-conscious, but he was being exceedingly bold for his time; a reviewer of *The Token* for 1836 singles out Hawthorne and Neal for special praise but points disapprovingly to the "slightly *inuendoish*" tendency of "The Young Phrenologist" —in its expurgated state! [22]

5. HOAX AND MASQUERADE

Neal's public quarrel with Goodrich over the alleged indecency of "The Young Phrenologist" ended their relationship. It had been a stormy one almost from the beginning. The second story Neal submitted to the publisher, "The Adventurer," resulted in a sharp disagreement over its conclusion.

Goodrich, knowing of Neal's intimacy in London with John Dunn Hunter, had asked for a sketch of the latter's life for *The Token* for 1831; [23] he got rather more than he bargained for. Hunter was notorious for his widely circulated and largely spurious *Memoirs of a Captivity among the Indians of North America* (1823) and was fair game for the rambunctious Yankee who worked up a tall-tale "autobiography" (purportedly written by Hunter) chronicling a New England childhood and young manhood full of the sharp practice personally familiar to Neal. The story takes an imaginative leap when the intrepid hero, touring the West, decides to set himself up as a physician:

> I had no diploma to be sure; nor had I any very clear idea of the difference between the small pox and a slow fever, a parenthesis and a paralysis; but then I physicked the poor for nothing, drew teeth for a shilling apiece, or ten for a dollar, grew devout, and made friends of all the old women I knew.

All goes prosperously until he chances on a newspaper item telling of the trial of "a self-initiated physician for his life, in

21. *The New-England Galaxy*, October 3, 1835.
22. *The New-England Magazine* 9 (1835):298.
23. Letter from Goodrich to the editors of *The Atlas*, reprinted by Neal in *The New-England Galaxy*, October 17, 1835.

consequence of what happens to every thoroughbred practitioner
—the death of a patient." His medical career over, he joins the
army, then deserts and takes refuge among the Indians. On his
return to New York and civilization, he finds his stories in great
demand, though the version created for the press by his editors
has little resemblance to his experience. With the encouragement
of Jefferson, Madison, and other luminaries, he invades England
with even greater success. As a "lion of fashionable society" he
extracts substantial sums of money for a wide variety of paper
projects before taking refuge once again "among the natives that
wear feathers and scalps." Goodrich angered Neal by deleting,
as "absurd," his fantastic conclusion of Hunter's autobiography
—one in which the adventurer gives "an account of his own
death and burial." [24] A hint of this wild close survives in *The
Token*: "Or would you have me relate . . . how we kicked up
a little revolutionary dust, which ended in my being taken
prisoner by the government of Mexico, and put to death?"

Appearance masquerading as reality is also the theme of
"The Ins and Outs," a satire on "the great men" in Washington
—and the ladies who surround them. The story is told by
Peterborough, a diffident office seeker. (Neal was seeking office,
less diffidently, a year before its publication.) [25] He gives an
account of the extraordinary metamorphoses he observes among
the distinguished personages he encounters. One of them, the
Honorable George Fitzhugh, transports a large audience by his
heartfelt sincerity and compelling dignity in the midst of trying
provocation. When Peterborough seeks out the great man to
convey his gratitude and to try to dissuade him from his announced unavailability to all public office, he is startled by the
cryptic behavior of Fitzhugh's lovely wife and sister-in-law:
"happening to turn my head, I caught Miss Laura making signs

24. "The Bear and His Outriders," *The New-England Galaxy*, October 17, 1835.
25. In a letter to Neal dated March 25, 1841, HL, Charles Naylor
tells of his difficulty in getting a hearing in Washington to further Neal's bid
for a government post.

to the wife, and the wife in great pain, holding a handkerchief to her mouth." He meets many highminded office seekers, each offering in strictest confidence and with total sincerity a slanderous revelation about his closest competitor. All meet and publicly embrace in "The Masquerade," the concluding section of the story. The disenchanted Peterborough, out of control, spouts a farewell soliloquy full of poppycock and portentous poetry:

> Hang me if I don't open a battery of sugar plums upon him [the Cabinet officer he has been petitioning] and pelt him with roses after a fashion of my own!—Ah! what is that? Earth and sea are thundering at brief intervals! . . . The sky is darkened with furled banners—the whole country is in travail! . . . "Watchman! what of the night?"

15 A Yankee Farce with Feeling
Our Ephraim

*I dont think such feelings
most effective in a* Yankee dialect
*nor so well relished by the audience
as broad humour.*

JAMES H. HACKETT TO NEAL, 1834

Neal relished highly the stories "I *over*-hear on board a steam-boat or a stage-coach" and peopled many of his novels and tales with authentic Yankees and other representative Americans. But he did not contribute significantly to what Walter Blair has described as a mounting tide, between 1825 and 1833, of "Humor with an emphatic native quality, which amusingly displayed localized characters and characteristics." [1] He occasionally tossed off a comic newspaper piece like "Old Susap" in which an un-consciously ludicrous Down Easter relates—with dead-earnest garrulity—a frontier tall tale about an indestructible Indian: "At last ole Ben gut him down, and beat him to death, over and over agin." [2] More typically, however, Neal mingled pathos, poetry, and humor (as in "David Whicher" and "Otter-Bag") in a manner unsuited to satisfy the popular appetite for broad native comedy.

In his *Blackwood's* series, "American Writers," Neal had expressed a distaste for the native farces then coming into favor, dismissing them as "sober, childish or disagreeable 'entertain-

1. *Native American Humor*, p. 38.
2. *The Morning Courier and New-York Enquirer*, July 25, 1831.

ments.' " Americans, he suggests, "fruitful, as they certainly are, in a sort of stubborn oddity— . . . have nothing outrageous in their nature; little or no raw material, of their own, for generous, broad, rich, caricature." Compounding the difficulty, these farces were worked up and performed, without exception, not by Americans but by Englishmen. He charges the famous British actor Charles Mathews with some "blundering absurdities" in his stage representations of comical New Englanders.[3] Neal seems to have been much more favorably impressed by the impersonations of Yankee characters by the young American actor James H. Hackett; he befriended him shortly after his Covent Garden appearance in 1827, just prior to his own precipitous departure from the Bentham household and England.[4]

In 1831 Hackett scored a smashing success as Nimrod Wildfire, the Kentucky frontier hero of Paulding's *The Lion of the West.* His career was in full swing when, in early 1834, he wrote to his former benefactor urging him to "squat right down & in your ready style in two or three days conjure me together something *'curious nice.'* " What he had in mind was a short dramatic piece based on Major Jack Downing, Seba Smith's popular Down-East creation.[5] When Neal proposed instead a full-scale "three act piece of genuine Yankee," Hackett responded cautiously. He was especially doubtful about Neal's "notion of mingling in your hero's character 'a touch of the pathetic' "; such feelings were not relished by the audience as much as broad humor. He warned that the "dignity" which Neal also planned to inject "would be equally incongruous in the received notions" of Yankee character. In place of such inappropriate touches, Hackett proposed a straightforward New Englander, a retired, weatherbeaten Nantucket sea captain, the widowed father of a pair of "darters" whose lovers stir up

3. *American Writers,* p. 99; "Reply to Mr. Mathews, by a Native Yankee," *The European Magazine and London Review,* n.s. 2 (1826) :184.

4. *Wandering Recollections,* p. 313; Arthur Hobson Quinn, *A History of the American Drama from the Beginning to the Civil War,* 2d ed. (New York and London, 1943), p. 296.

5. Hackett to Neal, March 10, 1834, HL.

trouble and place him in a ridiculous situation. Practical jokes on the stage, he reminded Neal, "always tell well." [6]

Two months later Hackett emphatically rejected *Our Ephraim, or The New Englanders, A What-d'ye-call-it?—in three Acts* as hopelessly unsuitable for production. The characters, he complained, were too much alike; but "were [they] never so well contrasted," it would have been impossible to find actors capable of impersonating the large number of rustic Yankees called for in the play. He cited as a glaring example of Neal's theatrical ineptitude a quilting scene which reads well but could never be staged; it "could only be made effective, were it possible to congregate the audience immediately around the quilting frame." Hackett told his friend he was "a clever man, but a *very bad dramatist.*" [7]

Equally dismaying to the actor must have been Neal's treatment of his hero, Ephraim Jersey. Paulding had set forth his purpose in *The Lion of the West* as embodying "certain peculiar characteristics of the west in one single person, who should thus represent, not an individual, but the species." Hackett played to the hilt the cavorting Kentuckian, "chock full of fun and fight," who brings to a gratifying comeuppance a fake English nobleman and a supercilious Englishwoman, Mrs. Wollope (a none too subtle allusion to Mrs. Trollope).[8] Neal's hero, despite Hackett's objections, combined high spirits with an underlying dignity and, worse, "a touch of pathos." On occasion, Ephraim showed an unmistakable kinship to George Burroughs, the tragic hero of *Rachel*

6. Hackett to Neal, March 16, 1834, HL. Neal was to be paid $50 on receipt of the play, an additional $50 if it was successful enough for three performances, and an additional $100 if it was given six times.

7. Hackett to Neal, May 24, 1834, HL.

8. Paulding's statement about the purpose of his play appeared in *The New-York Mirror* 8 (1830):191; quoted in Blair, *Native American Humor*, p. 30. For a full account of the play—including Hackett's important involvement with it—see Nelson F. Adkins, "James K. Paulding's *Lion of the West*," *American Literature* 3 (1931):249–58. The text of the play, lost for more than a century, has been newly discovered and published; see James Kirke Paulding, *The Lion of the West*, ed. J. N. Tidwell (Stanford, Cal., and London, 1954).

Dyer, though the somber tone of that novel is avoided. In the 1830s such an alternation of mood was rare; not until after the Civil War and the rise of local color would pathos figure largely in the portrayal of humble Americans.

The plot of *Our Ephraim* is perhaps better suited to melodrama than to farce.[9] Five years before the play opens, our hero left his Down-East village and Quaker sweetheart to seek his fortune. He returns from travel in England and Europe to offer his services to the governor of Massachusetts: he will pretend to be a counterfeiter to expose a gang threatening the security of a nation at war (the time is 1814). The gang ringleader, a foppish Englishman, contrives evidence so that Ephraim is accused of robbery after returning, disguised, to his village. In a climactic courtroom scene, our Ephraim reveals his identity, proves his innocence, exposes the villain and his cohorts, and is permanently reunited with his girl.

Neal's eye and ear for authentic setting and language to some extent redeem these melodramatic absurdities. In a stage direction long enough to have been written by George Bernard Shaw (but sounding more like George Washington Harris), our storyteller-dramatist sets the scene for a rustic party:

> *A large number of women sitting round the walls of an unfurnished room, as close together as they can squeeze; some taking their last cup of tea, others gobbling cake, and others sitting with their hands folded in their laps, their feet pulled up under them, and their eyes fixed on the floor. Dead silence. In another part of the room is a group of men—some standing up before the fire, with their coat-tails pulled apart, others tilted back in their chairs, and trying to balance their cups and saucers on their knees, . . .—all spitting on the floor occasionally, and all flourishing their yellow pocket-handkerchiefs. Now and then, they whisper together,*

9. The unplayable play has survived thanks to the fact that Neal served a stint as editor of *The New-England Galaxy* in 1835 and supplied much of the copy. It was published in five installments: I, i–iii (May 16); II, i–ii (May 23); II, iii (May 30); III, i–ii (June 6); III, iii (June 13).

> *and compare watches, or boots, or feel the quality of*
> *one another's clothes—and two or three times in the*
> *course of the following scene, a woman gets up, gathers*
> *her apron or gown before her, walks to the fire-place, and*
> *shakes the crumbs upon the hearth, without opening her*
> *mouth; or takes a pocket-handkerchief, deliberately un-*
> *folds it, wraps a huge piece of cake in it, and resumes her*
> *unspeakableness.*
>
> (act 3, scene 1)

In a manner that must have been maddening to a practical producer like Hackett, the play not only calls for a plentiful supply of
Yankees of both sexes but also for a rapid succession of realistic
settings: a schoolhouse, a tavern, a parlor, a forest, a kitchen, a
village courtroom. Here again Neal's grasp of authentic detail
transcends the melodramatic plot—as in the opening scene set in
the *"Lumber-garret of a large country school-house; a hole in the*
roof and boards ripped off the end; rough broken branches lying
about—a chimney &c.—"

Also notable in *Our Ephraim*—though of limited appeal to a
producer looking for surefire effects—are Neal's experiments in
stage improvisation. Hackett, like all other celebrated actors, im-
provised freely; but it is unlikely that he warmed to these stage
directions, typical of many others, aimed at large numbers of
minor players and designed to create a documentary realism
through verbal and visual group improvisation:

> *N. B. Throughout the following* [quilting] *scene,*
> *the silence is interrupted, first by one person, speaking*
> *in a low voice, then by another, and another, and grow-*
> *ing louder, till they are all screaming and talking to-*
> *gether.—During the bustle, one stops to thread a needle,*
> *another to stretch a chalk line, another to adjust her chair*
> *&c. &c.—but nobody stops talking. Then one drops*
> *off—then another—and another, till you may hear a pin*
> *fall.*
>
> (act 2, scene 1)
>
> *(Certain of the young men go to balancing chairs,*
> *hopping, jumping over one another at leap-frog, &c. &c.*
> *taking care not to interfere with the points of dialogue.)*
>
> (act 3, scene 1)

The stage directions in *The Lion of the West* are, in sharp contrast, few and brief. The most elaborate (six lines long) describes the management of the climactic episode in which Mrs. Wollope, in a coach, is carried across stage screaming, *"the driver in full view, lashing vigorously the horses, which are not seen* [because of a wall]."

Paulding's concern for regional realism is limited to Nimrod Wildfire's colorful, but stereotyped, renditions of Kentucky frontier vernacular. *Our Ephraim* is heavily freighted with Yankee talk designed to add vividness and homely vitality. (So much emphasis on authentic dialogue must have contributed to Hackett's view that the play was unactable and unacceptable as popular theater.) A college graduate gets "a cowhide for a walkin-ticket"; the Shakers lack energy—"there's never no kind o' sprawl to them fellers"; a suitor is described as "sparkin" and, less elegantly, as "a smellin round"; a lovelorn maid is described as "limpsey as a rag"; a partnership involves "diggin clams at the halves." Neal's accurate ear for such talk is attested to by the fact that these and many other Yankeeisms in *Our Ephraim* antedate their earliest citation in the *Dictionary of American English.*[10]

It is in the hero's speech that Neal shows off his linguistic virtuosity most spectacularly. Ephraim is the "illuminated" Yankee whose travel abroad enables him to range, as his disguise demands, from informal, cultivated talk to broadest Yankee. As the educated outsider, he speaks a live language that shows up the pretentious erudition of Lawyer Chew; when he drops his disguise to talk country style, it is with a relish that conveys affection for his native tongue and for the homespun characters around him. Such a performance makes demands that not even a Hackett could meet—even if it were good theater to do so.

Neal's preoccupation in *Our Ephraim* with the re-creation of the ways and talk of live Yankees was scarcely suited to gain him a trial—much less a success—at the Park Theater where Hackett

10. The compilers of the *DAE* consulted and profited from Neal's *Brother Jonathan, Rachel Dyer,* and *The Down-Easters* but understandably overlooked a play that has eluded Arthur Hobson Quinn and all other historians of the American drama.

had acted *The Lion of the West* to great applause. The play nonetheless represents a significant advance in early American theatrical realism. Neal's failure is in some ways as noteworthy as
Paulding's triumph.

16 A Posthumous Literary Life

*Many thanks . . . for the deep interest you take
in my posthumous works—
for since my death, as a literary man,
I have well nigh forgotten them myself.*

JOHN NEAL TO MARY GOVE NICHOLS, 1846

When Fanny Appleton Longfellow visited Portland as a new bride in 1843, she was mightily impressed by the panoramic vistas of the sea on all sides of the town. She was almost equally struck by another elemental phenomenon, John Neal, a fast friend of Longfellow since 1833 when the young author-professor had sent him, from Bowdoin College, a copy of his first book, *Outre-Mer.*[1] After a ball at Judge Preble's, young Mrs. Longfellow recorded in her journal her impression of their first meeting: "John Neal gave me great amusement with his racy, head-over-heels speeches. His mind seems at the boiling-over point always and froths out at every pore of his face and tongue. Introduced a dozen people to me as one would mow grass."[2]

1. "But why not be yourself—and yourself only?" Neal had responded, charging Longfellow with flagrant imitation of Irving. Neal to Longfellow, August 6, 1833, Longfellow Papers, HL.

2. Journal entry of July 27, 1843, in *Mrs. Longfellow: Selected Letters and Journals of Fanny Appleton Longfellow (1817–1861)*, ed. Edward Wagenknecht (London, 1959), pp. 90–91. Fanny Longfellow's vivid account of Neal's liveliness is confirmed by a journal entry in 1854 by Richard Henry Dana, Jr. "Neal is certainly one of the 'curiosities of literature,'" recorded Dana, commenting favorably on his "fine figure, intellectual and spirited countenance" and superb storytelling. Dana also notes Neal's "strong but not offensive egotism" and observes: "He seems to

Neal was fifty years old and very much alive. Shortly before his lively encounter with Fanny Longfellow he had debated on the rights of women at the Broadway Tabernacle in New York. His audience warmed to his "fine manly appearance" and eloquence; according to one observer, he took his listeners by storm and, "if he did not convince them, he certainly carried off the honors." [3] In an earlier Tabernacle address on the same subject, he had compared the status of women with that of Negro slaves and had called for an emancipation that would have included voting rights, going so far as to suggest that a rebellion against the government by American women would be a blow for justice fully in accord with the revolutionary doctrine of the Declaration of Independence. He had first spoken out publicly on women's rights in 1832 after writing about it for more than a decade. He claimed to have converted Bentham to the cause: "while arguing for universal suffrage, [he] seemed willing to overlook woman, for a while, if not for ever. But he had materially changed his views before I left England." [4]

Neal's increasing involvement with feminism and other reforms was accompanied by a progressive disengagement from any further serious efforts to stay alive as a literary figure. In 1840, when Poe asked for support of his projected *Penn Magazine* in "whatever manner your experience shall suggest," Neal, who had just finished a brief editorial stint with the *New World*, informed his former protégé that he could offer no help, for "I have done

---

have a generous nature, is sudden and quick in quarrel, but bears no malice" (*The Journal of Richard Henry Dana, Jr.*, ed. Robert F. Lucid [Cambridge, Mass., 1968], 2:655). Dana spent a social evening with Neal during a brief visit to Portland.

3. *Selections from the Autobiography of Elizabeth Oakes Smith*, ed. Mary Alice Wyman (Lewiston, Me., 1924), pp. 68–69.

4. For an account of Neal's feminist activities see Augusta Genevieve Violette, *Economic Feminism in American Literature prior to 1848* (Orono, Me., 1925), pp. 57–60. The text of Neal's Broadway Tabernacle lecture is reprinted from *Brother Jonathan* (the magazine) in Daggett, *A Down-East Yankee*, pp. 41–51. Neal tells of his activities on behalf of women's rights and his conversion of Bentham—in *Wandering Recollections*, pp. 410–20.

with the newspapers—have abandoned the journals." [5] It was true for the moment; but he was an incurable journalist, and in the next few years was again, briefly, editing *Brother Jonathan* and contributing to W. G. Simms' *The Magnolia* and other magazines. Young James Russell Lowell and Robert Carter fared better than Poe when they solicited his help for their new journal, *The Pioneer*; Neal sent two essays, "Aaron Burr" and "Newspapers." (Poe, Hawthorne, Whittier, and Jones Very submitted stories and poems.) "I think the paper on Burr will make a noise," Neal wrote Lowell; it well may have, for it charged Burr with, among other things, offering up his daughter Theodosia as mistress to Jeremy Bentham. His essay on newspapers asks, in Whitmanesque periods: "What are armies and treasuries, navies and forts, and magazines and foundries, or senate-chambers and *laws*, in comparison with newspapers—where newspapers are *free?*" Newspapers, he informs Lowell, will soon take the place of novels.[6]

Lowell regarded Neal as an important contributor to be treated with respect; when *The Pioneer* ran into financial trouble, he wrote his partner: "We must get some money soon." Uppermost in his mind was their debt to Hawthorne, Neal, and Poe. On March 29, 1843, Robert Carter, fearing that the time remaining to Neal was limited, urged the literary veteran to devote a small portion of that time "to one carefully planned and carefully written romance." He and Lowell had been enjoying the spirited colloquialism and naturalness of *Randolph*, but felt that it was "terribly unartistical." Why not, Carter pleaded with Neal, leave one work behind "on which your name and fame may rest and to which your friends may point when they speak of you as one worthy to be loved and admired." [7]

5. Poe to Neal, June 4, [1840], *Letters*, 1:137. Neal to Poe, June 8, 1840, quoted in Hervey Allen, *Israfel: The Life and Times of Edgar Allan Poe* (New York, 1934), pp. 719–20.

6. Neal to Lowell, November 20, 1842, Lowell Papers, HL; "Aaron Burr," *The Pioneer*, January, 1843, pp. 6–11; "Newspapers," ibid., February, 1843, pp. 61–65.

7. Lowell to Carter, January 19, 1843, Berg Collection, New York

By 1845 Hawthorne was speculating in print about the slow growth of American literature and the untimely ends of most American writers of promise, singling out for illustration "that wild fellow, John Neal, who almost turned my boyish brain with his romances." [8] Toward the end of his life, Poe reflected in a similar way about Neal and America. Despite the great structural flaws in Neal's tales, Poe was "inclined to rank John Neal first, or at all events second, among our men of indisputable *genius.*" "Is it, or is it not a fact," Poe asks, "that the air of a Democracy agrees better with mere Talent than with Genius?" As late as 1848, Poe still believed that "the philosophical and self-dependent spirit" which contributed to the slipshod excesses of Neal's early novels would "even yet lead him, if I am not greatly mistaken in the man, to do something for the literature of the country which the country 'will not willingly,' and cannot possibly 'let die.' " [9]

Poe's prophecy was not fulfilled. Instead, it was Neal who rallied to keep Poe's reputation alive when it was subjected to a vicious posthumous attack by his literary executor, Rufus Wilmot Griswold. Poe, responded Neal, "saw farther, and looked more steadily, and more inquisitively into the elements of darkness—into the shadowy, the shifting and the mysterious—than did most of the shining brotherhood about him." Griswold is dismissed with scorn as "a Rhadamanthus, who is not to be bilked of his fee, a thimble-full of newspaper notoriety." Neal's counterattack drew blood; in a prefatory note to his edition of Poe's *The Literati*, Griswold struck back at John Neal "who had never had even the slightest personal acquaintance with Poe in his life, [yet] rushes from a

---

Public Library; Carter to Neal, March 29, 1843, HL. Carter's letter is reproduced in Lease, "Robert Carter, James Russell Lowell, and John Neal," pp. 247–48.

8. "P.'s Correspondence" [1845], in *Mosses from an Old Manse* (London, 1846), 2:130; Hawthorne is being jocular most of the time but seems quite straightforward when reflecting on the fate of Neal and Halleck.

9. Poe, "Marginalia" [1849], in *Works*, 16:152; Poe, "Marginalia," *Graham's Magazine* 32 (1848) : 130.

sleep which the public had trusted was eternal, to declare that my characterization of Poe . . . is false and malicious." [10]

Griswold's sneer about Neal's long sleep must also have stung, for there was truth in it. It was echoed in a kindlier way by friendlier critics. Elizabeth Oakes Smith was convinced that Neal's plunge into literary oblivion could have been prevented if he had settled in New York instead of Portland. "Our Nazareths are not the best places for us," she observed.[11] Another talented woman who was much impressed by Neal's "energy . . . animated by genius" commented on his isolation more wittily—and more tellingly. The usually reserved Margaret Fuller was so much drawn into his spell during a social evening in Providence that she uncoiled her hair to submit "her haughty head to his sentient fingers" for phrenological analysis.[12] She wrote him soon after, certain that the "great man of a little town" would be at leisure "except [for] such trifling divertisements, such as attending Portland sidewalks, chastising inhuman teamsters, prosecuting the study of Phrenology, Magnetism. . . ." [13]

Coupled with the physical isolation that set him apart from the literary ferment of Boston and New York were the responsibilities and burdens of a growing family. In 1845 his fourth child died in infancy; his fifth, John Pierpont Neal, was born in 1847. His first-born son, James, proved to be his greatest trial; but his father may have been an even greater one to young James. Neal seems to have been both affectionate and overpoweringly authoritarian. In February of 1831, when James was just one month old,

10. Neal, "Edgar A. Poe," *Portland Advertiser Weekly*, April 30, 1850; Rufus Wilmot Griswold, ed., *The Literati . . .* , by Edgar A. Poe (New York, 1850), Preface to "Memoirs of the Author," p. v.

11. *Selections from the Autobiography of Elizabeth Oakes Smith*, p. 67.

12. Sarah Helen Whitman recalls the phrenological encounter in an obituary tribute forty years later; see "John Neal, of Portland," *Providence (R.I.) Journal*, July 24, 1876. Margaret Fuller records her impressions of Neal in *Memoirs of Margaret Fuller Ossoli* (Boston, 1852), 1:181–82.

13. Margaret Fuller to Neal, January 10, 1838, HL.

Neal wrote to Pierpont at great length about their problem: his son was born with a harelip and would need an operation. It was not enough to ask for the name of a Boston surgeon who could be relied on; Neal had been doing extensive research and provided his friend with detailed descriptions of alternative surgical procedures. Although he stopped short of performing the operation himself, he undoubtedly gave gratuitous counsel to the Bowdoin College Medical School surgeon who later did.[14] That same year Neal wrote a longer and even more extraordinary letter to his friend shortly after Pierpont's fifteen-year-old daughter Juliet had visited his household for several weeks. In twelve crowded pages, Neal supplies details about the girl's slovenliness, obstinacy, and dangerous coquettishness; she "will be *spoiled,*" he warns the Pierponts, "if you do not consult together and agree upon a system of education far different from that you have hitherto supposed."[15]

Seventeen years later, Neal wrote Pierpont in a different vein. He was deeply troubled about his son James and asked whether it would be agreeable to the Pierpont family to take the boy in as a boarder "so long as you may be satisfied with his behavior, and no longer." James "has taken the pledge for one year," Neal wrote, "and will be likely to renew it."[16] The arrangement—and James' temperance pledge—proved to be temporary.

In March of 1851 Neal confided to Elizabeth Oakes Smith that a great change had occurred in his religious life. He had been greatly concerned about the misconduct of "my dear Jamey—that noble boy." After a long struggle *"trusting to my own strength wholly, . . . the influence of Gods holy spirit . . . revealed me to myself."* He now saw for the first time how unworthy and base he had been toward his Heavenly Father and how unfaithful "in the very thing on which I had most prided myself—in the stewardship of a father." His worldliness and self-sufficiency had robbed his

14. Neal to Pierpont, August 21, 1831, PML; see Lease, "The Authorship of 'David Whicher,' " p. 133.

15. Neal to Pierpont, August 21, 1831, PML.

16. Neal to Pierpont, February 20, 1848, PML.

children of a religious education; but he had now come to his senses and saw "the Past, the Present & the Future in a new light, & hear new voices issuing from their midst." Mrs. Smith, an old friend who had always thought of Neal as an unshakable force, scribbled a troubled comment on the back of his letter: "Can it be another friend is to sink under the calamities of life! This seems like the breaking up of a great mind, the first touch of insanity." [17]

Neal's trials were not over. The following year a local newspaper story by his cousin (and bitter enemy) Neal Dow, without mentioning names but unmistakably identifying Neal and his house, called attention to "a skeleton in that house": a young man residing there "has been ruined by an appetite generated and strengthened by the wine which he has habitually taken at his father's table." Neal had long been a champion of temperance reform, and Dow's "wicked, shameless" article was a bitter blow.[18] There was worse to come.

Elizabeth Oakes Smith's son Appleton volunteered to serve with General William Walker in one of his Nicaraguan adventures and, in 1856, arranged for young James Neal to join him. Neal gave his consent in the hope that military discipline and "a new field of labor" might straighten the lad out. But James' craving for drink soon entangled him in further difficulties. On September 3 Neal wrote Mrs. Smith: "I am glad the general has taken a prompt and severe course with him." It was far better for the boy to be in the ranks where he could not find liquor, his father observed, than in a position of trust where he might again be tempted. Even as he the father wrote, however, James Neal was beyond all temptation: he had died two weeks earlier of a fever in Granada. "I have a hope," Neal wrote after learning the tragic news, "that our dear son is not far off—that he reads my heart—& sees my tears—& is waiting to comfort us all." If God would spare young Pierpont (now

17. Neal to Elizabeth Oakes Smith, March 12, 1851, Elizabeth Oakes Smith Papers, Maine Historical Society.
18. Neal quotes Dow's "infamous libel" in *Wandering Recollections*, pp. 385–86.

nine years old), Neal will leave his upbringing "mainly to his mother—perhaps altogether." [19]

The tragic life and death of his son reawakened in Neal a long-standing interest in spiritualism and clairvoyance. Through a clairvoyant named Mansfield he received (he was led to believe) several messages from James, including one directed to John Pierpont: "Say to dear Mr Pierpont work work while the day lasts —his usefulness has but just commenced—he has a host of Angels oreabout [sic] him always." [20] A more tangible legacy of Neal's spiritual travail are two books: the religious tract *One Word More* (1854) and *True Womanhood* (1859), his first novel since 1833.

One Word More, dedicated "with earnest prayer; unfaltering hope; and a trembling faith" to his children, rambles passionately for two hundred pages and closes with breathless metaphor (suggestive of the Epilogue to Melville's *White-Jacket*):

> Farewell! Bright messengers are hurrying between Earth and Heaven, . . . —and like the great ships of ocean— . . . it may be that they are only for a season, and that if we mistake a message, or a signal, or turn away from the swift messenger in his upward flight—we lose our passage——forever! [21]

When Neal yielded, five years later, to the urging of Longfellow and others to write "one more story," it turned out to be a novel that the staid *North American Review* could recommend to pious readers who "generally eschew novels." The author of *True Womanhood*, says the reviewer, shows a warm sympathy for the religious excitement that swept New York in 1857–58 "by bring-

19. Neal to Elizabeth Oakes Smith, [undated, 1856]; August 28, September 3, September 9, October 27, 1856; Mary Neal Sherwood to Elizabeth Oakes Smith, October 3, [1856], Elizabeth Oakes Smith Papers, Maine Historical Society.

20. Neal to Pierpont, September 24, 1860, PML; several subsequent letters also deal with spiritualism and the spirit of his dead son.

21. *One Word More: Intended for the Reasoning and Thoughtful among Unbelievers* (Boston: Crooke and Brewster, 1854), pp. 205–6.

ing nearly all of his *dramatis personae* under its influence." [22] Unfortunately, the authentic fervor that moved Neal is swallowed up by interminable talk and a claptrap plot centering on a grand trial scene in which benevolent Uncle George is exonerated of forgery after Charles Parry, his long-lost nephew, makes a melodramatic appearance with the crucial evidence. Young Charles, a dashing Byronic figure, has been on a mysterious journey to South America (Nicaragua?) and has found God. Before leaving on the journey, he informed his sister Julia that he was going "where I can build up a character for myself without the help of others; where I shall not be checked, and watched, and thwarted, and waylaid at every turn, by my best friends." [23] Transformed from a melancholy malcontent to a cheerful religious enthusiast, Charles not only saves his uncle from unjust imprisonment but wins saintly Edith Archibald, who has rebuffed him until convinced, finally, that he has truly found God. In the meanwhile Julia, who has rejected several suitors because they were not truly Christian, turns down someone she truly loves, her cousin Arthur Maynor, because she is determined "never to marry" and, "certainly, *never to marry with a cousin!*" They thereupon embrace in a transport of Christian joy as it is revealed to both of them that they are now, in a spiritual sense, truly "brother and sister, linked hand in hand forever, and journeying toward the rest appointed for the loving and faithful." [24] (What Neal's wife—and cousin—thought of this denouement is not revealed.)

Neal's career as a writer of fiction finally ground to a permanent halt in the 1860s with three dime novels written out of a desperate need for money. The chief rival of Cooper in the 1820s and the lifelong scourge of editors who dared trifle with his work complained mildly to O. J. Victor, of the House of Beadle, that he had followed Victor's plan for *Little Moccasin* chapter by chapter, had "written the whole 'to order' as it were," and should not now

22. Review of *True Womanhood, The North American Review* 90 (1860):260–61.

23. *True Womanhood: A Tale* (Boston, 1859), p. 57.

24. Ibid., pp. 480–81.

be blamed for its defects.[25] The Beadle Westerns, as Henry Nash Smith brilliantly demonstrates, built their success on a fictional formula borrowed from the Leatherstocking series; Victor himself testified that the dime novels "followed right after 'Cooper's Tales,' which suggested them." [26] It is supremely ironic that Neal should end his career as a novelist as it had begun—struggling vainly against Cooper's pervasive influence. But it is also fitting that the contrived heroics and mystification of *Little Moccasin* and the two Beadle "novels" that preceded it (*The White-Faced Pacer* and *The Moose-Hunter*) should be enlivened by some engaging touches of colloquialism and rustic realism. "Wal, mother, what's to pay now?" asks a homespun Yankee on Thanksgiving Day. "What's to pay! Why, don't you see that ar' stranger a ploughin' through the orchard there?" The stranger is invited to a dinner consisting of a large goose dished up in a huge wooden tray, "along with the baked beans, the Indian puddings, the apple pies, the flapjacks, the generous brown bread, the apple dowdy, the dough-nuts, the apple-sauce, the brown mugs of cider." [27] Such Twainian catalogs are not standard fare in the dime novel.

Longfellow, who helped arrange the publication of *True Womanhood,* had for a long time urged Neal to write his auto-biography. Neal began it in 1859, but the great Portland fire of 1866 destroyed much of the town, including his law office containing a fifty-year accumulation of papers, among them the third draft of his life story. He started anew and produced in 1869 what Tremaine McDowell has called "his most distinctly American and, as a result, his most memorable book," *Wandering Recollections of a Some-what Busy Life.*[28] Longfellow praised the book while complaining mildly about Neal's failure to "follow the usual chronological way;

25. Neal to O. J. Victor, August 1, 1865, John Neal Miscellaneous Papers, Manuscript Division, New York Public Library.

26. See Henry Nash Smith, *Virgin Land: The American West as Symbol and Myth* (New York, 1950), pp. 101 ff.

27. Quoted from Albert Johannsen, "The White-Faced Pacer," in *The House of Beadle and Adams* (Norman, Okla., 1950), 2:215.

28. *Wandering Recollections,* pp. 1–3; McDowell's observation is in *Literary History of the United States,* p. 291.

notwithstanding the reasons you give for taking another course."
Neal's plan is professedly topical rather than sequential, but the
book does move with a rough chronology shot through with free
association. Matters are further complicated by a central "narrative" consisting of journal entries describing events at the time
each portion of the book was being written—also wildly digressive.
The reader's attention must alternate between John Neal present
and John Neal past until digressions from each track merge in an
inextricable tangle. Three-fourths of the autobiography deals
with Neal's early life in Portland, Baltimore, and London. His
forty years in Portland after his return are skimmed over in fewer
than a hundred pages.

Brashness and garrulity are the main ingredients of *Wandering Recollections*. But there is also breathtaking virtuosity in Neal's
colorful colloquialism and in his effortless ability to reach back
forty and more years to tell, for instance, of a Sunday stroll in
London with Solicitor Joseph Parkes of Birmingham, author of
several weighty law treatises. When they reach the New River
they find it covered with skaters rushing in all directions, often
half-leg deep in water as the rotten ice undulates beneath them.
Several have gone under; some have been fished up; others are
drowned or missing. Neal turns to his friend to express horror and
astonishment at such recklessness and folly only to find "my gentleman, this 'potent, grave, and reverend signior' of the law, down on
one knee, and eagerly strapping on a pair of skates that he had
brought with him, under his coat-tail; and before I had time to
remonstrate with him, as he deserved, he was off and away among
the dead men, and about as mad as the maddest." [29]

"I like the book," Longfellow wrote Neal, "because it is like
you: frank and fearless, and full of vigor"; but in his journal he
expressed puzzlement about this "curious book, interesting to me
from personal recollections." [30] Mountains of egotistical trivia tend

29. *Wandering Recollections*, pp. 261–62.

30. Longfellow to Neal, October 26, 1869, Longfellow Papers, HL;
journal entry of October 17, 1869, quoted in Samuel Longfellow, *Final
Memorials of Henry Wadsworth Longfellow*, p. 125.

to overshadow the lively anecdotes and flashes of poetry. But it is a fitting farewell, and with all of its sprawl and incoherency, we can say of it what Whitman says of his *Leaves*: "this is no book,/Who touches this touches a man."

Raking over the past for his autobiography stirred Neal to write several striking articles of reminiscence for *The Atlantic*. Their titles attest to his lifelong preoccupation with his British adventure in the 1820s: "Jeremy Bentham," "William Blackwood," and "London Forty Years Ago." He was further moved to communicate once more with the House of Blackwood, calling attention to his contributions of 1824–25 and indicating his readiness "to give you another series upon the growth, character and prospects of my country"; but *Maga* was not interested. Pierpont's death in August of 1866 occasioned an obituary essay in December, an affectionate tribute reviewing their lifelong friendship.[31]

When he was seventy-nine, he was still vigorous and fierce enough to pitch a rude young man out of a horse car.[32] Four years later, in February 1876, he reminded Longfellow of the poet's suggestion that he republish *Seventy-Six* during the hundredth anniversary of the birth of the republic. "The more I think of it, the more satisfied I feel that it would be a success, being in fact an epitome, with sketches of character . . . & incidents perfectly true which have been overlooked by our writers & historians." But the end was now in sight; Neal was suffering from acute neuralgia, and his letter is written in a tortured scrawl. "God bless you! I 'can no moe,' " it closes. On March 26 Neal wrote his last letter to the friend who had remained loyal and affectionate despite some rather outrageous expressions of playful ferocity. ("You really ought to be hanged—drawn and quartered— . . . to say nothing of your bowels—thrown into the fire before your face," Neal once

31. The articles mentioned are in *Atlantic Monthly* 16 (1865):575–83, 660–72; 18 (1866):224–36, 649–65. Neal to *Blackwood's*, September 15, 1865, NLS.

32. John M. Todd, *A Sketch of the Life of John M. Todd* (*Sixty-Two Years in a Barber Shop*) (Portland, Me., 1906), p. 68.

suggested in response to the sing-song meter of *Evangeline.*) Long-fellow had suggested a neuralgia remedy—a half glass of whiskey before retiring—and Neal reports (almost illegibly) that he has been trying the cure with "considerable advantage." In May Long-fellow expressed concern to Neal's daughter about his friend's worsening condition and proposed a new remedy. He was sorry, too, to learn of J. R. Osgood's rejection of *Seventy-Six* and thought the Harpers might be "the persons now to apply to." The Harpers had published *The Down-Easters* forty-three years earlier, and it was doubtful that they would now be interested in another Neal novel—one disinterred from an even more remote era. The prospect of republishing *Seventy-Six* died with John Neal on June 20, 1876.[33]

In his obituary tribute to John Neal, Llewellyn Deane pre-dicted that "when the history of fiction in this country shall be written, truly he will be assigned an excellent place; when the history of American literature shall be written, justly he will have a foremost position." Deane's prophecy has not come true, but history has also played one of its wry tricks on Harold C. Martin's recent assertion that "the power of the man is not sufficient to warrant literary exhumation." [34] Just three years after Martin's confident pronouncement, Hans-Joachim Lang exhumed two powerful stories and a lively sampling of criticism; in 1964 *Rachel Dyer* was exhumed, the first republication of a Neal novel since 1840.[35] An anthology of Neal's writings is in preparation, and it now seems safe to predict that more fiction and criticism will be made available in the decades immediately ahead.

These works will be of most value to the literary historian sifting the soil from which have sprung the permanent masterpieces

33. Neal to Longfellow, February 21, March 26, 1876; Longfellow to Neal, March 22, May 9 [to Neal's daughter], 1876; Neal's playful re-sponse to *Evangeline* is dated November 27, 1847, HL.

34. Deane, "John Neal," *The Congregationalist*, November 22, 1876; Martin, "The Colloquial Tradition in the Novel: John Neal," p. 459.

35. This must be slightly qualified: Neal's dime novel *Little Moccasin* (New York: Beadle and Co., 1866) was reprinted in London.

of nineteenth-century American literature. What F. L. Pattee said a half century ago about Mark Twain and his works more accurately applies to Neal: "They are not artistic books. The author had little skill in construction. He excelled in brilliant dashes, not in long-continued effort." [36] A few stories survive in their own right as consummate wholes. For the rest, "his greatness must be perceived in passages, or not at all." [37]

Faulkner rated Thomas Wolfe higher than Hemingway "on the gallantry of the failure, not on the success or the validity of the work." [38] By such a standard Neal rates high. Driven by personal demons that haunted and marred his works, Neal evolved a freewheeling poetics that pulled him simultaneously in several opposing directions: toward Schlegelian intensity of effect and epic sweep, toward authentic colloquialism and poetic sublimity, toward comic high jinks and the dark regions of the mind and heart. The gallant failures that resulted from these conflicting impulses augured well for the emergence of a new, authentically native literature. "Mark Twain is all of our grandfather," says Faulkner of himself and his contemporaries. Though he never heard of him, Mark Twain could have said the same about John Neal.

36. *A History of American Literature Since 1870* (New York, 1917), pp. 59–60.

37. I have here borrowed a comment on Mark Twain by Walter Blair, *Native American Humor*, p. 160.

38. F. L. Gwynn and J. L. Blotner, eds., *Faulkner in the University* (New York, 1965), p. 143; the following quotation, p. 281.

Works Cited

For a comprehensive bibliography (compiled in 1933) see Irving T. Richards, "John Neal: A Bibliography," *Jahrbuch für Amerikastudien,* 7(1962):296–319.

LONGER WORKS BY NEAL

Keep Cool: A Novel. Written in Hot Weather, by Somebody, M. D. C. &c. &c. 2 vols. Baltimore: Joseph Cushing, 1817.

Battle of Niagara: A Poem, without Notes; and Goldau, or the Maniac Harper. . . . By Jehu O'Cataract. . . . Baltimore: N. G. Maxwell, 1818.

The Battle of Niagara: Second Edition, Enlarged, with Other Poems. . . . By John Neal. Baltimore: N. G. Maxwell, 1819.

Otho: A Tragedy, in Five Acts. By John Neal. Boston: West, Richardson and Lord, 1819.

Logan: A Family History. 2 vols. Philadelphia: H. C. Carey and I. Lea, 1822.

Logan: A Family History. 4 vols. London: A. K. Newman and Co., 1823.

Logan, the Mingo Chief: A Family History. By the Author of "Seventy-Six." London: J. Cunningham, 1840.

Seventy-Six. By the Author of Logan. 2 vols. Baltimore: Joseph Robinson, 1823.

———. 3 vols. London: Whittaker and Co., 1823.

Randolph: A Novel. . . . By the Author of Logan and Seventy-Six. . . . Published for Whom It May Concern. 2 vols. [Philadelphia], 1823.

Errata, or the Works of Will. Adams. A Tale by the Author of Logan, Seventy-six, and Randolph. 2 vols. New York, 1823.

American Writers: A Series of Papers Contributed to Blackwood's Magazine (1824–1825) by John Neal. Edited by F. L. Pattee. Durham, N.C.: Duke University Press, 1937.

Brother Jonathan, or the New Englanders. 3 vols. Edinburgh and London: William Blackwood and T. Cadell, 1825.

Rachel Dyer: A North American Story. By John Neal. Portland: Shirley and Hyde, 1828.

————. A Facsimile Reproduction with an Introduction by John D. Seelye. Gainesville, Fla.: Scholars' Facsimiles and Reprints, 1964.

Authorship: A Tale. By a New Englander Over-Sea. Boston: Gray and Bowen, 1830.

Principles of Legislation: From the MS. of Jeremy Bentham. . . . By M. Dumont, . . . Translated from the Second Corrected and Enlarged Edition, with Notes and a Biographical Notice of Jeremy Bentham and of M. Dumont. By John Neal. Boston: Wells and Lilly, 1830.

The Down-Easters, &c. &c. &c. By John Neal. 2 vols. New York: Harper and Brothers, 1833.

One Word More: Intended for the Reasoning and Thoughtful among Unbelievers. . . . By John Neal. Portland, Me., 1854.

————. Boston: Crooke and Brewster, 1854.

Oration . . . July 4, 1838. Portland, Me.: Arthur Shirley, 1838.

Our Ephraim, or The New Englanders, A What-d'ye-call-it?—in Three Acts, in *New England Galaxy,* May 16, 23, 30, June 6, 13, 1835.

True Womanhood: A Tale. By John Neal. Boston: Ticknor and Fields, 1859.

The White-Faced Pacer, or Before and After the Battle. By John Neal. New York: Beadle and Co., 1863.

The Moose-Hunter, or Life in the Maine Woods. By John Neal. New York: Beadle and Co., 1864.

Little Moccasin, or Along the Madawaska: A Story of Life and Love in the Lumber Region. By John Neal. New York: Beadle and Co., 1866.

————. London: George Routledge and Sons, 1866.

Wandering Recollections of a Somewhat Busy Life: An Autobiography.
. . . By John Neal. Boston: Roberts Brothers, 1869.
Observations on American Art: Selections from the Writings of John Neal (1793–1876). Edited by Harold E. Dickson. State College, Pa.: Pennsylvania State University Press, 1943.

ARTICLES AND STORIES BY NEAL

Atlantic Monthly.
  "Jeremy Bentham," 16(1865):575–83.
  "William Blackwood," 16(1865):660–72.
  "London Forty Years Ago," 18(1866):224–36.
  "John Pierpont," 18(1866):649–65.
The Atlantic Souvenir for 1832.
  "The Haunted Man," pp. 221–46.
Blackwood's Edinburgh Magazine.
  "Sketches of the Five American Presidents, and of the Five Presidential Candidates, from the Memoranda of a Traveller," 15(1824):508–13.
  "American Writers," nos. 1–3, 16(1824):304–11, 415–28, 560–71.
  "A Summary View of America," 16(1824):617–52.
  "American Writers," nos. 4–5, 17(1825):48–69, 186–207.
  "Late American Books: (1) Peep at the Pilgrims; (2) Lionel Lincoln; (3) Memoirs of Charles Brockden Brown; (4) John Bull in America; (5) The Refugee; (6) North American Review, no. XLVII," 18(1825):316–34.
Brother Jonathan (Journal).
  "Idiosyncrasies," vol. 5, May 6 and July 8, 1843.
The European Magazine and London Review.
  "Observations on the Present State of Literature in the North American Republick," n.s. 1(1825):49–63, 179–89.
  "Sketches of American Character . . . ," 373–80.
  "Reply to Mr. Mathews, by a Native Yankee," n.s. 2(1826):179–87.
The Family Companion and Ladies' Mirror.
  "The Ins and the Outs, or the Last of the Bamboozled, by a Disappointed Man," 1(1841–42):13–23.
Federal Republican and Baltimore Telegraph.
  "The Moralist," March 20, 1819.

Review of Pierpont's "Airs of Palestine," March 25, 1819.
The London Magazine.
　　"Yankee Notions," n.s. 4(1826) :437–50.
　　"Yankee Notions," nos. 2 and 3, n.s. 5(1826) :71–89, 181–97.
Morning Courier and New-York Enquirer.
　　"Poems by Edgar A. Poe," July 8, 1831.
　　"Old Susap," July 25, 1831.
New-England Galaxy.
　　Review of *The Token and Atlantic Souvenir* for 1836, October 3,
　　　　1835.
　　"The Young Phrenologist," October 3, 1835.
　　"The Bear and His Outriders," October 17, 1835.
　　Review of "Paulding's Works," vols. 5 and 6, October 31, 1835.
The New-England Magazine.
　　"Story-Telling," 8(1835) :1–12.
　　"The Squatter," 8(1835) :97–104.
The New Monthly Magazine and Literary Journal.
　　"The Character of the Real Yankees: What They are Supposed to
　　　　Be, and What They Are," 17(1826) :247–56.
The New-York Mirror.
　　"New-England Witchcraft," 16(1838–39) :337, 345–46, 353–54,
　　　　361–62, 369–70.
The Pioneer.
　　"Aaron Burr," January, 1843, pp. 6–11.
　　"Newspapers," February, 1843, pp. 61–65.
The Port Folio.
　　"Airs of Palestine: A Poem, by John Pierpont, Esq. . . . ." 5th
　　　　s. 2(1816) :518–28.
The Portico.
　　"Criticism: Lord Byron," 2(1816) :304–15, 386–98, 476–85.
　　"Criticism: Lord Byron," 3(1817) :53–62.
　　"Fragment in Imitation of Byron," 3(1817) :160–61.
　　"Childe Harold's Pilgrimage, Canto third . . . ," 3(1817) :173–
　　　　84.
　　" 'Bertram: A Tragedy' and 'Manuel: A Tragedy' by the Rev.
　　　　R. C. Maturin," 3(1817) :421–29.
　　"To Byron," 4(1817) :149–50.
　　"Criticism: Manfred, A Dramatick Poem, by Lord Byron,"
　　　　4(1817) :260–74.

"What Is the Chief Excellence of Shakespeare?" 5(1818):410–19.

"Childe Harold's Pilgrimage. Canto IV . . . ," 5(1818):420–38.

Portland Advertiser Weekly.

"Edgar A. Poe," April 30, 1850.

The Token.

1829. "Otter-Bag, the Oneida Chief," pp. 221–84.

1830. "The Utilitarian," pp. 299–318.

1831. "The Adventurer," pp. 189–212.

1832. "David Whicher," pp. 349–72.

1836. "The Young Phrenologist," pp. 156–69.

The Westminster Review.

"United States," 5(1826):173–201.

The Yankee and Boston Literary Gazette.

"More Portland Poetry," 1(1828):32.

"Live Yankees, No. 2," 1(1828):135.

Review of *The Atlantic Souvenir* for 1829, 1 (1828): 377–79.

"Natural Writing," 1(1828):380.

"Rachel Dyer," 2(1829):39.

Review of Bulwer's *The Disowned*, 2(1829):86–87.

"The Drama," parts 1–5, n. s. 1(1829):57–68, 134–45, 195–209, 249–58, 303–17.

"Courtship," n. s. 1(1829):121–28.

"English Scenery—Villages: Leamington, Warwick Castle, Kenilworth," n. s. 1(1829):128–33.

"Trip to Paris," n. s. 1(1829):157–62.

"If E. A. P. of Baltimore . . . ," n. s. 1(1829):168.

"Unpublished Poetry," n. s. 1(1829):295–98.

BOOKS AND ARTICLES ON NEAL AND THE BACKGROUND

Adkins, Nelson F. *Fitz-Greene Halleck: An Early Knickerbocker Wit and Poet.* New Haven, 1930.

———. "James K. Paulding's *Lion of the West*," *American Literature* 3(1931):249–58.

Allen, Hervey. *Israfel: The Life and Times of Edgar Allan Poe.* New York, 1934.

Allen, Michael. *Poe and the British Magazine Tradition.* New York, 1969.

Alterton, Margaret. *The Origins of Poe's Critical Theory.* Iowa City, 1925.

"American Literature." *Boston Commercial Gazette,* October 4, 1822.

"American Novels." *The British Critic* 2(1826):406–39.

"Battle of Niagara," review. *Baltimore Patriot and Mercantile Advertiser,* August 6, 1819.

"Battle of Niagara," review. *New-England Galaxy,* August 3, 1819.

Baudelaire, Charles. *The Essence of Laughter.* Edited by Peter Quennel. New York, 1956.

"Blackwood's Edinburgh Magazine, Number XCII, September." *Atlantic Magazine* 2(1824–25):158.

"Blackwood's Edinburgh Magazine for February and March, 1825." *United States Literary Gazette* 2(1825):113.

Blair, Walter. *Native American Humor (1800–1900).* San Francisco, 1960.

———. "Poe's Conception of Incident and Tone in the Tale." *Modern Philology* 41(1944):228–40.

———. *Tall Tale America.* New York, 1944.

Bleackley, Horace, ed. *Trial of Henry Fauntleroy and Other Famous Trials for Forgery.* Edinburgh and London, 1924.

Bowring, John, ed. *The Works of Jeremy Bentham.* Vol. 10, *Memoirs and Correspondence,* pp. 55–56. Edinburgh, 1843.

Bradsher, Earl L. *Mathew Carey: Editor, Author and Publisher.* New York, 1912.

Brooks, James. "Letters from the East—John Neal." *New-York Mirror* 11(1833–34):69–70, 76–77, 84–85, 92–93, 100–101, 109, 117–18.

"Brother Jonathan . . . Rejected from the Edinburgh Review." In *Rejected Articles,* ed. P. G. Patmore, pp. 263–312. London, 1826.

Buckingham, Joseph T. "Neal—Brother Jonathan." *New-England Galaxy,* September 2, 1825.

Cairns, William B. *British Criticisms of American Writing, 1815–1833.* Madison, Wis., 1922.

Charvat, William. *The Origins of American Critical Thought, 1810–1835.* New York, 1961.

Church, Benjamin. *The History of Philip's War.* Exeter, N.H., 1829.

Clavel, Marcel. *Fenimore Cooper and His Critics.* Aix-en-Provence, 1938.

Clemens, Samuel L. "Fenimore Cooper's Literary Offenses." *The North American Review* 161(1895):1–12.

Cowie, Alexander. *The Rise of the American Novel.* New York, 1948.

Daggett, Windsor P. *A Down-East Yankee from the District of Maine.* Portland, Me., 1920.

Dana, Richard Henry, Jr. *The Journals of Richard Henry Dana, Jr.* Edited by Robert F. Lucid. 3 vols. Cambridge, Mass., 1968.

Deane, Llewellyn. "John Neal." *The Congregationalist* (Boston), November 22, 1876.

Edinburgh Literary Journal 1(1828–29):386. A footnote on *Brother Jonathan.*

Edwards, George Thornton. *The Youthful Haunts of Longfellow.* Portland, Me., 1907.

Elwell, Edward H. *Portland and Vicinity.* Portland, Me., 1876.

"England and the United States." *The Englishman's Magazine* 1(1831): 65–68.

Exman, Eugene. *The Brothers Harper.* New York, 1965.

Farmer, J., and Moore, J. B., eds. *Collections . . . Relating Principally to New Hampshire*, 3:103. Concord, N.H., 1824.

Flanagan, John T. *James Hall: Literary Pioneer of the Ohio Valley.* Minneapolis, 1941.

Fowler, Samuel P., ed. *Salem Witchcraft.* Boston, 1865.

Garrison, William Lloyd. *The Letters of William Lloyd Garrison.* Vol. 1, *I Will be Heard!, 1822–1835*, ed. Walter M. Merrill. Cambridge, Mass., 1971.

Goold, William. *Portland in the Past.* Portland, Me., 1886.

Griswold, Rufus Wilmot, ed. *The Literati . . . ,* by Edgar A. Poe. Preface to "Memoirs of the Author," p. v. New York, 1850.

Guthke, Karl S. *Modern Tragicomedy.* New York, 1966.

Gwynn, Frederick L., and Blotner, Joseph L., eds. *Faulkner in the University.* New York, 1965.

Hawthorne, Julian. *Nathaniel Hawthorne and His Wife.* 2 vols. Boston, 1885.

Hawthorne, Nathaniel. *The Complete Novels and Selected Tales of Nathaniel Hawthorne.* Edited by Norman Holmes Pearson. New York, 1937.

———. "P's Correspondence." In *Mosses from an Old Manse*, 2:113–32. London, 1846.

Johannsen, Albert. *The House of Beadle and Adams.* 2 vols. Norman, Okla., 1950.

Kaser, David. *Messrs. Carey and Lea of Philadelphia: A Study in the History of the Booktrade.* Philadelphia, 1957.

"Keep Cool," review. *The Portico* 4(1817):161–69.

King, Peter J. "John Neal as Benthamite." *New England Quarterly* 39 (1966):47–65.

Klain, Zora. *Educational Activities of New England Quakers. A Source Book.* Philadelphia, 1928.

Lang, Hans-Joachim. "The Authorship of 'David Whicher.'" *Jahrbuch für Amerikastudien* 7(1962):288–93.

————, ed. "Critical Essays and Stories by John Neal." *Jahrbuch für Amerikastudien* 7(1962):204–88.

Langer, Susanne K. *Feeling and Form.* London, 1953.

Lease, Benjamin. "The Authorship of 'David Whicher': The Case for John Neal." *Jahrbuch für Amerikastudien* 12(1967):124–36.

————. "Hawthorne and *Blackwood's* in 1849: Two Unpublished Letters." *Jahrbuch für Amerikastudien* 14(1969):152–54.

————. "*John Bull* versus Washington Irving: More on the Shakespeare Committee Controversy." *English Language Notes,* vol. 9(1972), in press.

————. "John Neal's Quarrel with the *Westminster Review*." *American Literature* 26(1954):86–88.

————. "Robert Carter, James Russell Lowell, and John Neal: A Document." *Jahrbuch für Amerikastudien* 13(1968):246–48.

————. "Sidney Lanier and *Blackwood's Magazine*: An Unpublished Letter." *Georgia Historical Quarterly* 53(1969):521–23.

————. "Yankee Poetics: John Neal's Theory of Poetry and Fiction." *American Literature* 24(1953):505–19.

Leonard, William Ellery. *Byron and Byronism in America.* Boston, 1905.

[Lockhart, John Gibson.] "Letters of Timothy Tickler." *Blackwood's Edinburgh Magazine* 16(1824):219–304.

"Logan, a Family History," review. *Columbian Observer.* Undated clipping, Neal's scrapbook.

Longfellow, Fanny Appleton. *Mrs. Longfellow: Selected Letters and Journals of Fanny Appleton Longfellow (1817–1861).* Edited by Edward Wagenknecht. London, 1959.

Longfellow, Samuel. *Final Memorials of Henry Wadsworth Longfellow.* London, 1887.

Lowell, James Russell. "A Fable for Critics." In *The Complete Writings of James Russell Lowell,* 12:1–87. New York, 1966.

Lubbell, Albert J. "Poe and A. W. Schlegel." *Journal of English and Germanic Philology* 52(1953):1–12.

Mabbott, Thomas O., and Pleadwell, Frank L. *The Life and Works of Edward Coote Pinkney.* New York, 1926.

McCloskey, John C. "The Campaign of Periodicals after the War of 1812 for a National American Literature." *PMLA* 50(1935):262–73.

———. "A Note on the *Portico*." *American Literature* 8(1936):300–304.

McDowell, Tremaine. "In New England." In *Literary History of the United States*, ed. Robert E. Spiller et al., pp. 284–305. 3d ed. rev. New York, 1963.

Martin, Harold C. "The Colloquial Tradition in the Novel: John Neal." *New England Quarterly* 32(1959):455–75.

———. "The Development of Style in Nineteenth-Century American Fiction." In *Style in Prose Fiction: English Institute Essays, 1958,* ed. Harold C. Martin, pp. 114–41. New York, 1959.

Matthiessen, F. O. *American Renaissance: Art and Expression in the Age of Emerson and Whitman.* New York, 1941.

Melville, Herman. *The Works of Herman Melville.* 16 vols. London, 1922–24.

———. *The Writings of Herman Melville.* Edited by Harrison Hayford et al. 7 vols. to date. Evanston and Chicago, 1968–.

———. *The Letters of Herman Melville.* Edited by Merrell R. Davis and William H. Gilman. New Haven, 1960.

Morse, Jedidiah. *Annals of the American Revolution.* Hartford, 1824.

Mott, Frank Luther. *A History of American Magazines, 1741–1850.* New York, 1930.

Oakes Smith, Elizabeth. *Selections from the Autobiography of Elizabeth Oakes Smith.* Edited by Mary Alice Wyman. Lewiston, Me., 1924.

Orians, G. Harrison. "New England Witchcraft in Fiction." *American Literature* 2(1930):54–71.

Ossoli, Margaret Fuller. *Memoirs of Margaret Fuller Ossoli.* 2 vols. Boston, 1852.

Pattee, Fred Lewis. *The First Century of American Literature, 1770–1870.* New York, 1935.

Paulding, James Kirke. *Letters from the South.* New York, 1817.

———. *The Lion of the West.* Edited by J. N. Tidwell. Stanford, Cal., and London, 1954.

Pierpont, John. Preface to *Airs of Palestine and Other Poems.* Boston, 1840.

Poe, Edgar Allan. *The Complete Works of Edgar Allan Poe.* Edited by James A. Harrison. 17 vols. New York, 1902.

———. *Al Aaraaf, Tamerlane, and Minor Poems.* Baltimore, 1829.

Poe, Edgar Allan. *The Letters of Edgar Allan Poe.* Edited by John
    Ward Ostrom. 2 vols. Cambridge, Mass., 1948.
————. Review of Neal's works, in "Literati of New York." *Godey's
    Lady's Book* 32 (January–June, 1846) :271.
————. "Marginalia." *Graham's Magazine* 32 (January–June, 1848) :
    130.
Pollard, John A. *John Greenleaf Whittier: Friend of Man.* Boston, 1949.
Price, Robert. *Johnny Appleseed: Man and Myth.* Bloomington, Ind.,
    1954.
Quinn, Arthur Hobson. *American Fiction: An Historical and Critical
    Survey.* New York, 1936.
————. *Edgar Allan Poe: A Critical Biography.* New York, 1941.
————. *A History of the American Drama from the Beginning to the
    Civil War.* 2d ed. New York and London, 1943.
Rachel Dyer, review. *Atlas* 1 (1829) :261.
"Rachel Dyer," review. *The Yankee and Boston Literary Gazette* 2
    (1829) :37–38.
Researches on America . . . , review. *The Portico* 2(1816) :103–11.
Richards, Irving T. "John Neal's Gleaning in Irvingiana." *American
    Literature* 8(1936) :170–79.
————. "Mary Gove Nichols and John Neal." *New England Quarterly*
    7(1934) :335–55.
Richards, Leonard L. *"Gentlemen of Property and Standing": Anti-
    Abolition Mobs in Jacksonian America.* New York and London,
    1970.
Rubin, J. J. "John Neal's Poetics as an Influence on Whitman and Poe."
    New England Quarterly 14(1941) :359–62.
Schilling, Hanna-Beate. "The Role of the Brothers Schlegel in American
    Literary Criticism as Found in Selected Periodicals, 1812–1833:
    A Critical Bibliography." *American Literature* 43(1972) :563–79.
Schlegel, A. W. von. *Lectures on Dramatic Art and Literature.* Trans-
    lated by John Black, 2d ed. London, 1886.
Seymour, G. D. *Documentary Life of Nathan Hale.* New Haven, 1941.
Smith, Henry Nash. *Virgin Land: The American West as Symbol and
    Myth.* New York, 1950.
Spencer, Benjamin T. *The Quest for Nationality: An American Literary
    Campaign.* Syracuse, N.Y., 1957.
Spiller, Robert E. "The Verdict of Sydney Smith." In *The Third Dimen-
    sion: Studies in Literary History,* pp. 39–51. New York, 1965.

Spiller, Robert E., and Blackburn, P. C. *A Descriptive Bibliography of the Writings of James Fenimore Cooper.* New York, 1934.

Streeter, Robert E. "Association Psychology and Literary Nationalism in the *North American Review,* 1815–1825." *American Literature* 17(1945):243–54.

Strout, A. L. *A Bibliography of Articles in Blackwood's Magazine, Volumes I through XVIII, 1817–1825.* Lubbock, Texas, 1959.

Thacher, James. *Military Journal.* Boston, 1823.

Thompson, Lawrance. *Young Longfellow, 1807–1843.* New York, 1938.

Thompson, Ralph. *American Literary Annuals and Gift Books, 1825–1865.* New York, 1936.

Thompson, Stith. *Motif-Index of Folk-Literature.* 6 vols. Bloomington, Ind., 1955–58.

Todd, John M. *A Sketch of the Life of John M. Todd (Sixty-Two Years in a Barber Shop) and Reminiscenses of His Customers, Written by Himself.* Portland, Me., 1906.

The Token and Atlantic Souvenir for 1836, review. *New-England Magazine* 9(1835):294–98.

Tredrey, Frank D. *The House of Blackwood, 1804–1954.* Edinburgh, 1954.

True Womanhood, review. *The North American Review* 90(1860):260–61.

Uhler, John Earle. "The Delphian Club." *Maryland Historical Magazine* 20(1925):305–46.

Violette, Augusta Genevieve. *Economic Feminism in American Literature prior to 1848.* Orono, Me., 1925.

Whitman, Sarah Helen. "John Neal, of Portland." *Providence* (R.I.) *Journal,* July 24, 1876.

Whittier on Writers and Writing: The Uncollected Critical Writings of John Greenleaf Whittier. Edited by E. H. Cady and H. H. Clark. Syracuse, N.Y., 1950.

Williams, Stanley, and McDowell, Tremaine, eds. *Diedrich Knickerbocker's A History of New York,* by Washington Irving, Introducton. New York, 1927.

Willis, William. *The History of Portland, from 1632 to 1864.* Portland, Me., 1865.

———. "Memoir of the Rev. Thomas Smith." In *Journals of the Rev. Thomas Smith and the Rev. Samuel Deane,* pp. 7–34. Portland, Me., 1849.

Winterich, John T. "Savanarola of Hollis Street." *Colophon,* Part 20 (1935), n.p.

Wright, Nathalia. *Melville's Use of the Bible.* Durham, N.C., 1949.

MANUSCRIPT SOURCES

Baltimore. Maryland Historical Society. Delphian Club Records.

Boston. The Houghton Library, Harvard University. John Neal Papers, including letter books and scrapbooks. Henry Wadsworth Longfellow Papers. James Russell Lowell Papers.

Charlottesville. The Clifton Waller Barrett Library of the University of Virginia Library. Letter from Neal to his son James, June 6, 1848.

Edinburgh. William Blackwood and Sons Limited. Letter books containing copies of letters from William Blackwood to John Neal and to other correspondents (with reference to Neal).

———. National Library of Scotland. Blackwood Papers, letters from Neal to William Blackwood.

London. British Museum. Letter from Neal to Jeremy Bentham, March 11, 1830.

New Haven. Yale University Library. Cooper Collection, letter from Neal to James Fenimore Cooper, October 18, 1822; autobiographical letter from Neal to Elizabeth Oakes Smith, August 21, 1856.

New York. New York Public Library. Berg Collection, James Russell Lowell–Robert Carter Correspondence. Manuscript Division, John Neal Miscellaneous Papers.

———. The Pierpont Morgan Library. Pierpont Papers, letters from Neal to John Pierpont and from Pierpont to Neal.

Philadelphia. The Historical Society of Pennsylvania. Letters from Neal to Carey and Lea and from Carey and Lea to Neal.

———. University of Pennsylvania Library. Letter from Neal to Mathew Carey, November 15, 1823.

Portland. Maine Historical Society. Elizabeth Oakes Smith Papers, letters from Neal to Elizabeth Oakes Smith.

Washington, D.C. Library of Congress. Jefferson Collection, letter from Neal to Thomas Jefferson, August 5, 1825.

Index

217

DATE DUE